Answer Book for Student Workbooks

Celebration Series

PERSPECTIVES®

A Comprehensive **Answer Book** for
Student Workbooks Preparatory to Level 8

Contents

FREDERICK
HARRIS
MUSIC

18 17 16 15 14 13 12 11 10 09 08   1 2 3 4 5 6 7 8 9 10

Preparatory Student Workbook Answers

The Tired Turtle Express

Christine Donkin (b. 1976)
Preparatory Student Workbook, p. 4

The word "tired" makes you think of "slow" and the word "express" makes you think of <u>fast</u>.

When you send a parcel by express mail, you hope it arrives quickly. When you catch the express train, you hope it moves along quickly to your destination.

What tempo words does Christine Donkin use to guide your playing?
<u>slowly and deliberately; rit. poco a poco; exhausted</u>

In measure <u>14</u>, the turtle is so tired that he doesn't move at all!

Fill in the blank spaces above the counters with rests.

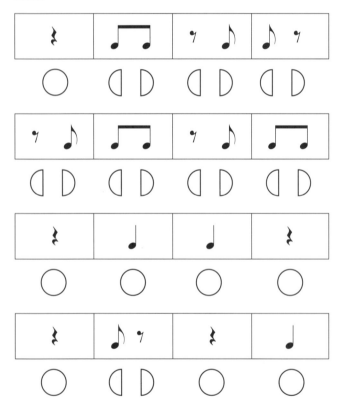

Put a "yawn" on the face beside the words or symbols that show that the turtle is tired. The first one is done for you.

rit.	(· ö)
a tempo	(· ·)
rit. poco a poco	(· ö)
𝄐	(· ö)
♩.	(· ·)
exhausted	(· ö)

Halloween Pranks

Boris Berlin (1907–2001)
Preparatory Student Workbook, p. 6

Circle all the black keys that you play in this composition.

Match the words to the rhythms and count how many times you see each of them in your music.

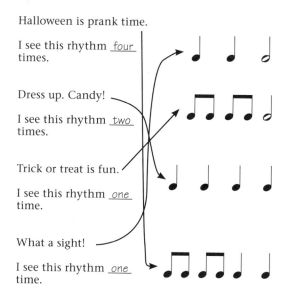

Halloween is prank time.
I see this rhythm _four_ times.

Dress up. Candy!
I see this rhythm _two_ times.

Trick or treat is fun.
I see this rhythm _one_ time.

What a sight!
I see this rhythm _one_ time.

There are two things that tell you *Halloween Pranks* is getting spooky.

One thing is the changing dynamics in the last two lines. Starting in measure 9, the dynamics change from **mp** to _mf_ , then from **mf** to _f_ , and finally from **f** to _ff_ .

The second thing that helps you feel the scariness is that in line 3 you are playing one note at a time, in line 4 you are sometimes playing _two_ notes at a time, and when it gets *really* scary right at the end you are playing _five_ notes all at once! Yikes!

Youthful Happiness

Daniel Gottlob Türk (1750–1813)
Preparatory Student Workbook, p. 7

The energetic *staccatos,* marked with ▾ will make you want to jump up and start clapping. Those signs are found in measures _2_ and _10_.

Circle all the *hap-pi-ness* words that have three parts. (One has been done for you as an example.)

Draw ♪♪♪ after the words with three parts.

but-ter-fly ♪♪♪ mer-ri-ly ♪♪♪ danc-ing
smil-ing pat-ty-cake ♪♪♪ slid-ing

If ♪ = 1, then ♪♪♪ = _3_

If ♪ = 1, then ♩ = _2_

If ♪ = 1, then ❼ = _1_

If ♪ = 1, then ♩. = _2_

Using a different colored pencil or marker for each note or rest, shade in the boxes to show how many beats each would be held. You can use these colors or choose your favorites!

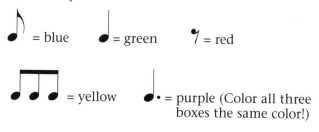

♪ = blue ♩ = green ❼ = red

♪♪♪ = yellow ♩. = purple (Color all three boxes the same color!)

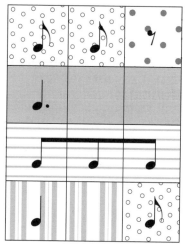

4

An Argument

Joan Last (1908–2002)
Preparatory Student Workbook, p. 9

It takes more than one person to participate in an argument. How many people do you think are arguing in this composition? <u>two</u> How can you tell when each person is arguing? <u>contrasting dynamics</u>

Mark all the dynamic signs and symbols that you find in your music in the measures below:

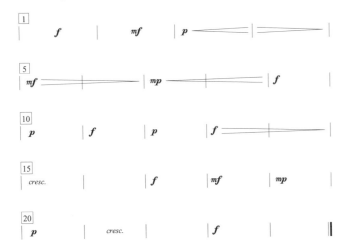

There are other signs or symbols that tell us that this argument was "heated"!

How many times can you find an accent (>) ?
<u>three</u>

Singin' the Blues

Elvina Pearce
Preparatory Student Workbook, p. 10

The following chart shows the structure of *Singin' the Blues,* including the repeats of the first section (mm. 1–8). How many times do you play the first section? <u>three</u>

Each measure in the chart has a Roman numeral to show the chord that Elvina Pearce uses in *Singin' the Blues.* You can make a beautiful color-by-number picture by using a different color for each number (chord) that you see:

I   =   red
IV =   yellow
V   =   green

When there is a "blue note" in the chord, mix a little blue into your color to make it sound a little extra bluesy!
CLUE: A♭ is one of the "blue notes" in this piece.

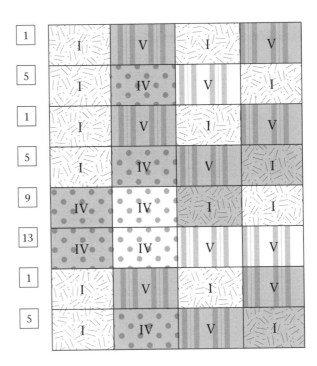

Jumping Jacks

Andrew Markow (b. 1942)
Preparatory Student Workbook, p. 11

The rhythm that you see throughout *Jumping Jacks* could be said:

harp - si-chord jacks

Find this rhythm in the piece *Jumping Jacks.* It appears in every measure except measure <u>8</u>.

Aeolian Lullaby

Joan Hansen (b. 1941)
Preparatory Student Workbook, p. 13

Scale Search
Circle the scales that you find in the puzzle below.
You might find some scales more than once!

Circle a C MAJOR SCALE in red.

Circle a C MAJOR PENTASCALE in blue.

Circle a A MINOR NATURAL SCALE in pink.

Circle a A MINOR PENTASCALE in black.
(This one is done for you.)

Circle a G MAJOR SCALE in yellow.

Circle a E MAJOR PENTASCALE in orange.

Circle a E MINOR PENTASCALE in brown.

Circle a F MAJOR PENTASCALE in purple.

Circle a D MINOR PENTASCALE in green.

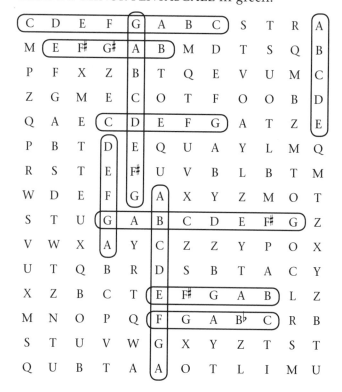

Birthday Morning

Jean Coulthard (1908–2000)
Preparatory Student Workbook, p. 14

Here are some words that fit the rhythms in *Birthday Morning*.

I'm hap-py

birth-day par-ty pres-ents

birth-day par-ty cake

birth-day par-ty

Print the words in the same order as you see the rhythms in this piece.

It's my birthday!	I'm happy I'm happy	Birthday party cake	I'm happy birthday party
birthday party presents	I'm happy I'm happy	birthday party cake	birthday party cake
Birthday party cake	Now hold the cake	Happy birthday	to you!

Where do the hugging notes change to 𝄢? measure _8_

Bouncing on My Bed

Anne Crosby (b. 1968)
Preparatory Student Workbook, p. 15

Here is a two-note slur found in *Bouncing on My Bed*.
Play it with your RH.

How many times do you
see this slur? _eight_

Here is another two-note slur found in this piece.
Play it with your LH.

How many times do you
see this slur? _three_

Here are *staccato* notes found in *Bouncing on My Bed*.
Play them with your LH.

How many times do you
see these *staccato* notes?
five

Minuetto, op. 37, lesson 2

James Hook (1746–1827)
Preparatory Student Workbook, p. 16

This *Minuetto* is made up of little musical ideas that
are each two measures long. On the map of the
music on the next page, put a shape in each box to
represent each two-measure idea.

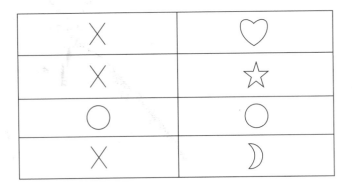

Broken Music Box

Stephen Chatman (b. 1950)
Preparatory Student Workbook, p. 18

Music boxes have a high, tinkling sound. What
symbol in *Broken Music Box* helps you make a high
sound on your piano? _8va_

Lady Moon

Lynn Freeman Olson (1938–1987)
Preparatory Student Workbook, p. 19

Circle the black keys and color the white keys that
you see in each line of your music for both the RH
and LH.

Did you find two lines that begin with the same
pattern? _yes, lines 1 and 4_

The Path of the Ping-Pong Ball

Christine Donkin (b. 1976)
Preparatory Student Workbook, p. 20

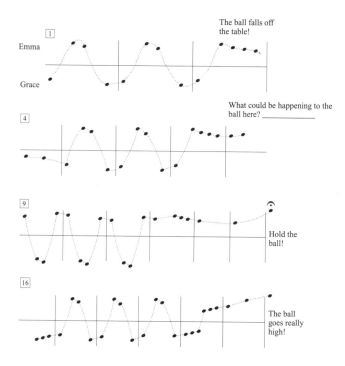

Arietta in C Major, op. 42, no. 5

Muzio Clementi (1752–1832)
Preparatory Student Workbook, p. 21

An arietta is a short aria. An aria is an elaborate song for solo voice. How does *Arietta in C Major* announce prominently that it is in C major? (HINT: Which RH triad do you see in the first measure of four out of the five lines of music? C major)

Here is a fun crossword puzzle for you. All of the words have something to do with *Arietta in C Major*.

			¹S	H	A	²R	P					
						E						
						S						
³S	I	X	⁴T	E	E	N	T	H				
			I									
⁵C	L	E	M	E	N	T	I					
			E									
⁶C	R	E	S	C	E	N	D	O				
			I			⁷D			⁸P			
			G	⁹A		¹⁰E	I	G	H	T	H	
			N	L		M			R			
¹¹F	L	A	T	L		¹²Q	U	I	E	T		
		T		E		N			A			
¹³S	L	U	R	G		¹⁴Q	U	A	R	T	E	R
		R		R		E			E			
	¹⁵D	E	C	R	E	S	C	E	N	D	O	
		T		T		N		D				
¹⁶A	R	I	E	T	T	A		O				
				O								

Birding

Stephen Chatman (b. 1950)
Preparatory Student Workbook, p. 22

The lines below represent the telephone wires on which the chickadees are performing. Draw the chickadees to show where they perform in the first line of your music. Write the rhythms by your pictures.

Chickadees begin the next scene. One chickadee begins; another chickadee enters two beats later, copying the first chickadee with the same words and rhythm. The first chickadee starts to sing again, but this time is answered by crows. Draw the chickadees and crows. Write the rhythms by your picture.

The chickadees and crows continue to have a chatty performance—it seems that the chickadees have more to say than the crows. Draw the next scene here.

Struttin'

Christopher Norton (b. 1953)
Preparatory Student Workbook, p. 23

How many times do you see this exact same rhythm in the RH of this composition? __four__

How many LH phrases do you see with a 𝅝? __seven__

Find all the stepping patterns in the bass clef.

How many times is  repeated? __three__

How many times is repeated? __two__

How many times is repeated? __two__

Write the final steps of the piece here:

Old MacDonald Had a Farm

Traditional, arr. Boris Berlin
Preparatory Student Workbook, p. 24

Old MacDonald had many different animals on his farm.

You will need to look at your music closely to find out how many of each animal was on the farm:

Anteaters: __ten (including A#)__
Bullfrogs: __twelve__
Chickens: __three__
Dogs: __eleven__
Elk: __six__
Foxes: __three__
Goats: __forty (including G#)__

Count the "sharp" animals on the farm. Count the ones with accidentals and the ones that are sharp because of the key signature. How many "sharp" animals are there? __seven (F#, G#, A#)__

Which animal appears most often? __goats__

Sakura

Japanese koto song, arr. Pierre Gallant
Preparatory Student Workbook, p. 25

The RH melody of *Sakura* is based on a pentatonic (five-note) scale.
Count how many different note names there are in the treble staff in this piece. Write them here:

__A__   __B__   __C__   __E__   __F__

Now write these five notes on the staff as a pentatonic scale beginning on A.

The LH of this piece uses six different note names. Write their names here:

__A__   __B__   __C__   __D__   __E__   __F__

How many times can you find the rhythm for

♩ ♩ 𝅗𝅥 ? __four__
Sa - ku - ra

and for ♩ ♩ ♩ ♩ | ♩ ♫ 𝅗𝅥 | ? __three__
cher - ry blos - soms they smell so sweet

What signs or words remind you to play this composition as beautifully as the cherry blossoms look?

Circle your answer:

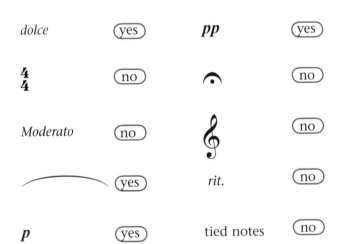

dolce	(yes)	*pp*	(yes)
4/4	(no)	𝄐	(no)
Moderato	(no)	𝄞	(no)
slur	(yes)	*rit.*	(no)
p	(yes)	tied notes	(no)

Chimes

Paul Sheftel (b. 1933)
Preparatory Student Workbook, p. 26

In *Chimes,* Paul Shefel has used two sets of chimes that are all tuned to the C major scale: a little set and a big set. How many times is the four-note stepping pattern repeated in the little chimes (RH)? <u>sixteen</u>

The big chimes use big octave leaps starting on either the first or the fifth notes of C major scale (C or G). How many big leaps are there in the LH part of *Chimes*? <u>twenty-one</u>

Here is a connect-the-dots activity to illustrate the RH and LH chime patterns:

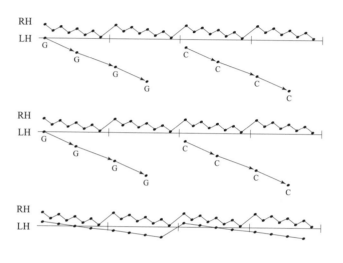

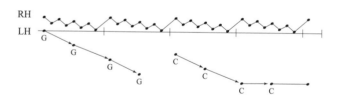

Playful Puppy

Linda Niamath (b. 1939)
Preparatory Student Workbook, p. 27

Play these tails (*codas*). How would you describe each of them? For example: long, short, pointy, or shaggy?

<u>short, stubby, thick</u>

<u>twitchy, pointy, thin</u>

<u>long and shaggy</u>

To Fly Like an Eagle

Anne Crosby (b. 1968)
Preparatory Student Workbook, p. 28

There are seven different intervals of a 5th played by the LH. Some are in the bass clef, and some are in the treble clef.

Write them here:

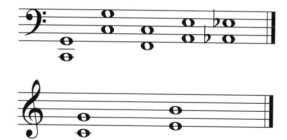

Shade in the area where the eagle flies in each measure of music.

1	High			▨	▨
	Middle		▨		
	Low	▨			
5	High				
	Middle				
	Low	▨	▨	▨	▨
9	High				
	Middle		▨		▨
	Low	▨		▨	
13	High			▨	▨
	Middle		▨		
	Low	▨			

First Waltz, op. 89, no. 5

Dmitri Kabalevsky (1904–1987)
Preparatory Student Workbook, p. 29

Here are three squares. Color the first square a dark color (for strong) and color the next two squares a light color (for weak). This is the usual pattern for a waltz and compositions with a $\frac{3}{4}$ time signature.

Here is a chart of the piece. Color in all the strong beats.

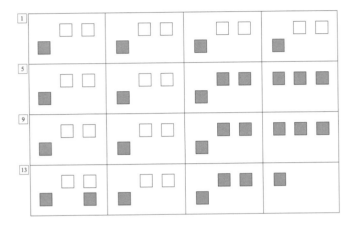

Sad Feelings

Daniel Gottlob Türk (1750–1813)
Preparatory Student Workbook, p. 30

Which of these cookies would you like to have? Color in the biggest cookie:

Draw a circle around the cookie parts that add up to a complete cookie (♩). How many complete cookies there are on each plate?

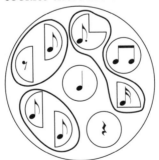 

<u>six</u> cookies   <u>five</u> cookies

A Carefree Fellow

Daniel Gottlob Türk (1750–1813)
Preparatory Student Workbook, p. 31

The carefree fellow in this piece began his musical journey in G major (notice the F sharp in the key signature). Then, he took a little detour into another key—can you tell which one? (HINT: Which key signature has both F sharp and C sharp? <u>D major</u>) As he continued along, the carefree fellow left the C sharp behind and went back to G major.

Now play each of these melodies on the piano to find out what keys the carefree fellow visits on his next journey!

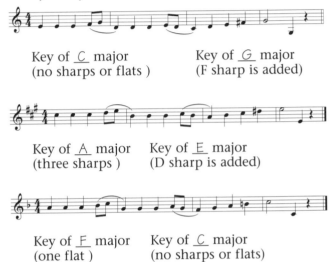

Key of <u>C</u> major   Key of <u>G</u> major
(no sharps or flats)   (F sharp is added)

Key of <u>A</u> major   Key of <u>E</u> major
(three sharps)   (D sharp is added)

Key of <u>F</u> major   Key of <u>C</u> major
(one flat)   (no sharps or flats)

Describe this carefree fellow:

Is he happy or sad? <u>happy</u>

Is he moving slowly or quickly? <u>moderately quickly</u>

On a Greek Island

Mark Mrozinski (b. 1964)
Preparatory Student Workbook p. 34

There are many rhythmic treasures to be found on this island. Clap the following rhythms while saying the words. These are clues:

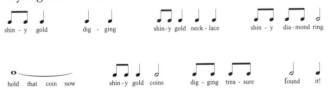

Find and circle each clue on the Treasure Map, using a different color for each rhythm.

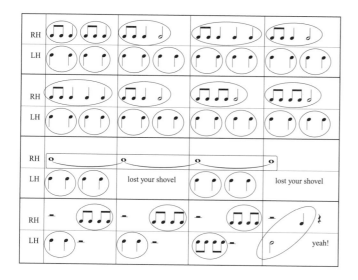

By the Mill Pond

Joan Last (1908–2002)
Preparatory Student Workbook, p. 35

For this piece, imagine a story about a family of ducks playing in little ponds. Here are some rhythms found in your music:

float-ing lit - tle ducks   quack!

Tell the story by shading in parts of the circular ponds wherever you see these two rhythms.

Sparklers

Linda Niamath (b. 1939)
Preparatory Student Workbook, p. 36

Matching Game
Here are some words and symbols that Linda Niamath has used to create her piece.

Write the number beside the matching words or symbols.

1. time signature	6	gradually getting quiet
2. *mezzo piano*	8	𝅘𝅥𝅭
3. gradually getting louder	9	𝄾
4. accent	2	moderately quiet
5. dotted quarter rest	10	loud
6. ⟋	4	>
7. key signature	1	**6/8**
8. *staccato*	12	***ff***
9. eighth rest	5	𝄽·
10. *f*	3	⟍
11. play *legato*	7	seven sharps at the beginning of each line
12. very loud	11	phrase

Olie the Goalie

Stephen Chatman (b. 1950)
Preparatory Student Workbook, p. 37

Try taking these four-note patterns and moving them up to each of these different "starting" notes. Let your ear help you find which notes to play.

What instrument does the rhythm of the ***ff*** section remind you of? _a trumpet_

Student Workbook 1 Answers

Minuet in G Major

attr. Franz Joseph Haydn (1732–1809)
Student Workbook 1, p. 4

Chord Shapes in the Melody

Draw a line to connect each of the melody fragments with its matching solid (blocked) chord shape.

Melody fragment   Solid (blocked) chord

The Sound of a Minuet

List the other measures where the RH repeats and the LH moves: mm. _9, 11, and 13_

The Form of a Minuet

On the staff below, write the first RH note of each measure that is indicated.

Andante in G Minor

Georg Philipp Telemann (1681–1767)
Student Workbook 1, p. 6

A Mystery Title

When was Telemann born? _1681_
Which century was that? _17th_
What is the time signature? _$\frac{3}{4}$_
What is the tempo marking? _♩=66–72_
Is there an upbeat? _yes_
How many notes? _2_
What kind? _quarter_

Articulation Fun

The first note you play comes on what beat? _3_
All the slurred notes are _eighth_ notes.

How should they be played: ☑ smoothly

How many half notes are there? _20_

Keeping Both Hands Busy

There are two places where both hands play a succession of notes with the same touch. They are in mm. _6–7_ and _10–11_.

Keys and Character

Telemann's *Andante* is in the key of _G minor_.

What mood does this key suggest? Check one or two: ☑ serious ☑ sad

Now change the chord to G major by removing the _B flat / key signature_ .

How does the key change make the piece feel?
Check one or two: ☑ more excited ☑ happier

Arioso in F Major

Daniel Gottlob Türk (1750–1813)
Student Workbook 1, p. 8

Playing a Song on the Piano

In Türk's *Arioso*, which hand plays the part of the singer? _RH_

Which hand plays the part of the accompanist? _LH_

What instrument might play the accompaniment?

cello ✓ double bass ✓ bassoon ✓ tuba __

Slurs

Do these slurred notes move ☑ by step or ☐ by skip?

Here is a chart of *Arioso*. Each box represents one measure. For each slurred pair of quarter notes in the music, draw a slur sign in the corresponding measure box.

Draw an arrow beside the slur to show whether the notes go up ↑ or down ↓.

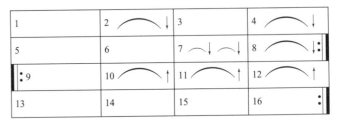

Look at the direction of the arrows.
The slurs in mm. 10–12 go _up_ .
The slurs in the rest of the music go _down_ .

Moving in Two Directions

Compare the melodies of mm. 1–2 and 9–10, noticing whether the notes go up or down.

In m. 1, the two eighth notes move _up_ .
In m. 9, the two eighths move _down_ .
In m. 2, the quarter notes move _down_ .
In m. 10, the quarter notes move _up_ .

Now look at mm. 3–4 and 11–12.
Does the same thing happen here?   ☑ yes

Minuet in D Major, T 460

Jeremiah Clarke (*ca* 1674–1707)
Student Workbook 1, p. 10

Minuet Rhythm

What is the time signature of this minuet? $\frac{3}{4}$
How many beats are there in a measure? _3_

Which note gets one beat? _quarter note_

On which beat of the measure does *Minuet in D Major* begin? third ✓

Circle the rhythm that Clarke uses in this minuet.

List each measure that has this rhythm.
mm. _1 and 5_

Variation

Find a variation of the rhythm you circled. Copy it below.

This variation of the rhythm is used in which measures? mm. _9, 11, and 13_

Important Notes in a Scale

Write a D major scale on the staff below:

Write the names of the first two LH notes: _D_ and _A_ .

On your scale above, circle the notes that have those names.

These notes are the first and _fifth_ notes of the scale of D major.

Two Sections

What other notes does the LH play? _F, E, and G_

In which measures? mm. _11, 18, and 19_

How many measures long is this section? _12_

Which section is longer—the first / (the second?)

Minuet in C Major, op. 38, no. 4

Johann Wilhelm Hässler (1747–1822)
Student Workbook 1, p. 12

Imitation

Play mm. 9–12 hands together. Where in m. 12 does the LH **imitation** stop? (beat 1)

If you imagine the melody (RH) of mm. 1–8 being played by a violin, what might the other part (LH) be played by? Circle your choice: (bassoon) / (cello) / piccolo / viola.

If you imagine the melody (RH) of mm. 9–14 being played by a flute, what might the other part (LH) be played by? Circle your choice: (double bass) / trumpet / (clarinet) / violin.

Where does the small orchestra join in? m. _15_

Triads

Play the RH notes of the first two measures together in solid (blocked) form.

What triad does this create?
Triad of _C Major_ .

Now play the LH notes of the first three measures all together. What triad does this create?

Triad of _C Major_ . Name the notes of the triad _C, E, and G_ .

In the scale of C major, these three notes are the first, _third_ , and _fifth_ notes of the scale. Which inversion of the triad is Hässler showing us in the RH melody in the first two measures?
☑ second inversion

Variation

One extra note appears! Circle the note on the example below:

What kind of notes do you see on the second and third beats of m. 9? _eighth_

Can you find another example of variation in this minuet? mm. _11–12_

Bourrée in D Minor

Christoph Graupner (1683–1760)
Student Workbook 1, p. 14

Time for a Bourrée!

This music should be felt as:

☑ 2 beats to a measure
What type of note gets one beat? <u>half</u>
A note that leads us over the bar line to the downbeat is called an <u>upbeat</u>.

Finding a Form

There are four phrases in Graupner's *Bourrée*. Write the measure numbers of the second and fourth phrases in the "Measures" column of the chart below. One of the four phrases is quite different from the other three. Find this phrase and label it "b" in the "Names" column of the chart. Label the other three phrases "a."

Phrases	Measures	Names
first	mm. <u>1–4</u>	<u>a</u>
second	mm. <u>5–8</u>	<u>a</u>
third	mm. 9–12	<u>b</u>
fourth	mm. <u>13–16</u>	<u>a</u>

The A and B sections are divided by what musical sign? <u>repeat signs</u>

Slurs and Articulation

Find the **upbeat**. Draw a circle around it.
Find the notes joined by slurs. Draw a box around them.

Minuet in A Minor

Johann Krieger (1651–1735)
Student Workbook 1, p. 16

Clues and Patterns

Listen to the effect as the hands answer each other in **contrary motion**. Contrary motion describes movement in opposite directions. The opposite of contrary motion is **parallel motion**.

Find a spot where parallel motion occurs: m. <u>13</u>

Identical Twins?

Are they identical or similar? <u>similar</u>

The melody of mm. 3–4 has the same shape as the melody of mm. 1–2 but the notes are one step <u>lower</u>. Now compare mm. 9–10 with mm. 11–12. Are these also twins? <u>yes</u>

Look through the rest of the music. Find more examples of this type of repetition.
mm. <u>17–18</u> and <u>19–20</u>

Repeated Sections

What sign is used to show this division? <u>a repeat sign</u>

How long (in measures) is the first section?
<u>8 measures</u>

How long (in measures) is the second section?
<u>16 measures</u>

Are both sections repeated? <u>yes</u>

Within the second half there is another repetition of <u>A</u>.

Fill in the measure numbers below the chart:

A :‖: B   A :‖

mm. <u>1 – 8</u>   mm. <u>9 – 16</u>   mm. <u>17–24</u>

Aria in F Major, BWV Anh. 131

Johann Christian Bach (1735–1782)
Student Workbook 1, p. 18

A Song with Accompaniment

In this Aria, which hand plays the part of the singer? <u>RH</u>

Moving from One Key to Another

Look at the second line of the music (mm. 5–7), which ends the A section. There's a note that wasn't in the first line. What is it? <u>B natural</u>

Write a C major scale and circle the **tonic** notes.

Name the leading note of C major and circle it in your scale. <u>B</u>

Did you notice that the leading note of C major and the note you named at the start of this activity are the same note? <u>yes</u>

Aria is in F major. It has a key signature of one flat: B flat. Bach had to write a <u>natural</u> sign in front of the B's in mm. 5–7 in order to cancel the flat in the key signature.

An Arching Melody

A section, mm. 1–7 highest note <u>G</u> m. <u>5</u>
B section, mm. 8–15 highest note <u>F</u> m. <u>13</u>

Burlesque in G Major

Anon.
Student Workbook 1, p. 20

Joking Rhythm

Look at the whole LH part.
What type of notes do you see? <u>quarter notes</u>

Meter and Rhythm

How many beats in a measure are there in this piece? <u>2</u>

Running Onstage

How many notes are in the group? <u>5</u>
What kind of notes are they? <u>sixteenth and 1 eighth</u>
Are they all the same? <u>no</u>
Which one is different? <u>the last</u>

Copycats in Contrast

Fill in the dynamic markings for the phrases.
First phrase <u>*mf*</u> Third phrase <u>*f*</u>
Second phrase <u>*mp*</u> Fourth phrase <u>*p*</u>
What happens at m. 13, second beat? <u>*mf*</u>
Which phrase is this? <u>the first</u>

Minuet in F Major, K 2

Wolfgang Amadeus Mozart (1756–1791)
Student Workbook 1, p. 22

Dancing the Minuet

How many minuets are there in your *Piano Repertoire 1*? <u>five</u>

Which measures have this ♩ ♩ resting rhythm?
mm. <u>4</u> <u>8</u> <u>12</u> <u>16</u> <u>20</u> <u>24</u>

Chord Shapes

Which position is indicated in the RH in m. 1?
<u>2nd inversion</u>

A Treasure Hunt for Mozart's Gold Nuggets

Nugget no. <u>5</u> : broken triad of C major in root position (m. <u>5</u>)
Nugget no. <u>4</u> : there is a pause in the music (m. <u>20</u>)
Nugget no. <u>2</u> : three notes are played in the time of two (m. <u>7</u>)
Nugget no. <u>3</u> : a slightly stressed note that "relaxes" onto a note a step below (m. <u>8</u>)
Nugget no. <u>1</u> : a slightly stressed note that "relaxes" onto a note a step above (m. <u>4</u>)
Nugget no. <u>6</u> : a short motive that is repeated lower (mm. <u>10–11</u>)

Chord Shapes

Which position is indicated in the RH in m. 1?
<u>second inversion</u>

Gremlins

Lorna Paterson (b. 1953)
Student Workbook 1, p. 25

The Hands Run Around Together . . .

Draw arrows from one note to the next to indicate whether notes move up or down.
Notice the distance, or interval, from one note to the next. In these measures, the notes move in 2nds.

Compare your markings for each hand. What similarities do you see? <u>The hands always move in the same direction; and always move by step.</u>

Find three other measures that have parallel motion: mm. <u>2, 6, 9</u>

. . . and Sometimes Jump Together

Draw arrows to show the direction of each leap.

In mm. 10–12, the hands are leaping in <u>contrary</u> motion.

Find the one leap where our gremlin doesn't make it quite as far as an octave.
It's in m. <u>10</u> in the <u>right </u>-hand part.

Hunting for a Key

Clue no. 1: the key signature.
The key signature has <u>one sharp</u> .
This means the music is either in <u>G</u> major or <u>E</u> minor.

Clue no. 2: how the music begins and ends.
Which of the two notes named in your major-or-minor answers appears most often in both the first and last measures? <u>E</u>

This means that the piece is likely to be in the key of _E minor_.

Write an E minor scale in its natural form.

Paterson uses not only F sharp, but also _D_ sharp. This raised note is note number 1 2 3 4 5 6 ⑦ within the scale.

The Bronze Bear

Yvonne Adair (b. 1897)
Student Workbook 1, p. 27

Fairy Tale Bear

What sign in the first measure tells us that? _f_

Bear Walking

How can you tell that the bear is not running? _quarter notes; no eighth notes; tempo marking_

Draw the four types of notes used in the piece.
1 beat ♩ 2 beats ♩ 3 beats ♩. 4 beats 𝅝

What would running notes look like? ♪♪♪♪

Keeping a Consistent Tempo

Name one way of using your whole body that would imitate the bear. _walking_

How would you count this piece? (Write the numbers.) _1 2 3 4_
Would you need to count with ands? _no_

Bear Steps (Articulation)

What articulation marks tell you that the bear is taking bouncy steps? _staccato_

Find two places where the bear walks smoothly: mm. _7–8_ and _13–16_ .

Circle the articulation mark on beat 3 of m. 2.

Its full value in this measure is _2_ beats.

Chords

This piece is in the key of G minor. Find and name another piece in your *Piano Repertoire 1* in that key.

Name _Andante in G minor by Telemann or Where did the Sun Go? by Markow_ Page number _5 or 38_

In *The Bronze Bear*, find a bass clef G minor triad in root position. m. _13_

Find a bass clef D major triad in root position. m. _7_

Play the RH in m. 13. There are ties on the G minor triad. For how many beats do you hold this chord? _10_

The dynamic marking for mm. 13–16 is _p_ .

Listen to the change of sound in m. 21. What is the name of the different note? _B natural_

Dream Journey

Christine Donkin (b. 1976)
Student Workbook 1, p. 30

Pattern no. _3_ : This pattern is played seven times by the _left_ hand.

Pattern no. _5_ : Harmonic 3rds on white keys, played only by the _left_ hand.

Pattern no. _2_ : Rising melodic 3rds on black keys, played only by the _right_ hand.
Which pattern has harmonic 3rds with the same letter names? _1_

Pattern no. _1_ : Harmonic 3rds on black keys, played only by the _right_ hand.

Pattern no. _6_ : This is the opening LH pattern. However, it is changed a little. It starts a whole step /(half step) higher than at the beginning of the piece. It is played twice in this new version.

Pattern no. _7_ : Falling melodic 3rds on black keys, played only by the _right_ hand.
Which pattern has harmonic 3rds with the same letter names? _1_

Pattern no. _4_ : Rising melodic 3rds on white keys, played only by the _left_ hand.
Which pattern has harmonic 3rds with the same letter names? _5_

Folk Song

Alfred Schnittke (1934–1998)
Student Workbook 1, p. 32

Accidentally on Purpose

Play the RH and LH notes together. Describe what you hear. _a clash / ugly sound_

Write the names of the notes in the following examples.

E♭

E♮

E♭   E♮   D   D♯

Name the RH notes that begin each slur. <u>E♭ D♮</u>
Name the LH notes that begin each slur. <u>E♮ D♯</u>

Articulation and Phrasing

Find three places (two in the RH and one in the LH) where the ends of the slurs do *not* finish with *staccato*.
mm. <u>4 and 8</u>

Coda

The song finishes in m. 8, but then the composer "tacks on" another repeat of motive <u>9</u>.

Does this match the idea of *coda* described in the Glossary? <u>yes</u>

Spooks

Clifford Poole (1916–2003)
Student Workbook 1, p. 34

Chapters of a Story

Look first at the music in mm. 1–16. What do you see?

☑ short slurs   ☑ staccato notes

Label this section Chapter A in your "book" below.

On the second page of the music, find a group of measures that look the same as Chapter A. Are these measures exactly the same as mm. 1–16?

☑ no

Label this section Chapter A1 and write the measure numbers on p. 2 of your "book." (The A1 indicates that they are almost the same as Chapter A.)

Now look for a group of measures that are different from the A chapters. Label this section Chapter B and write the measure numbers.

Chapter <u>A</u> mm. 1–16	
Chapter <u>B</u> mm. <u>17</u> – <u>30</u>	Chapter <u>A1</u> mm. <u>31</u> – <u>42</u>

Name two things that make Chapter B different from Chapter A.
1. <u>legato notes instead of staccato notes</u>
2. <u>the melody is not split between RH and LH</u>

Here is a list of markings he uses to add to the spookiness. Write the number of the correct definition for the terms that have a space provided.

misterioso	<u>3</u>	1.	getting excited
pp		2.	suddenly very loud
legatissimo	<u>4</u>	3.	mysteriously
staccato		4.	very smoothly
tenuto	<u>7</u>	5.	sad and expressive
mf		6.	getting faster
fermata	<u>9</u>	7.	hold the note for its full value
ff		8.	return to original tempo
mesto espressivo	<u>5</u>	9.	pause
crescendo			
ff subito	<u>2</u>		
agitato	<u>1</u>		
8va			
accel.	<u>6</u>		
a tempo	<u>8</u>		

A Spook's Favorite Intervals

Name the two notes in m. 2. <u>A in both hands</u>
How far apart are these two notes? <u>one octave</u>

Play the RH notes of m. 7 and the LH notes of m. 8 together.

How far apart are your hands? <u>one octave</u>

These spooks must like: ☑ octaves

In the RH of mm. 5–6, there is the interval of a 2nd.

How far apart are the two notes? ☑ a whole tone

Now look at the bottom RH note (A flat) and the LH note in mm. 5–6.

Is the interval between these two notes also a 2nd? <u>yes</u>

How far apart are the two notes? ☑ a semitone

Play these two 2nds one after the other. Listen to the difference between the whole tone and the semitone.

Which one sounds more spooky? <u>the semitone</u>

Silly Argument

Stephen Chatman (b. 1950)
Student Workbook 1, p. 36

An Argument between the Hands

Notice that the hands never play together, except for one place: m. <u>8</u>.

This music is always jumping from one hand to the other.

What dynamic marking does the LH have? <u>ff</u>

What dynamic marking does the RH have? <u>pp</u>

As you see, the hands are indeed arguing with each other, and it's the <u>left</u> hand that speaks the loudest.

Dots Everywhere

What does a dot above or beneath a note tell you to do? <u>play detached</u>

What is the Italian word for these dots? <u>staccato</u>

A Rhythmic Argument

How would you describe the rhythm of this piece?
☑ sharp and biting

Write out the rhythm of the whole piece in the diagram below.

The Argument Finally Ends

What is the highest note that the RH plays and the lowest note that the LH plays? Write these two notes on the staff below and name them:

At what point in the piece are the hands playing these notes? <u>mm. 11–16</u>

Robots

Anne Crosby (b. 1968)
Student Workbook 1, p. 38

Finding Patterns

Get your hands set on the first two notes of *Robots*.

Name the two keys under your fingers. <u>C and G</u>

What is the distance between the first note and the second note? <u>a 5th</u>

The RH always plays 5ths when the LH does, except in m. <u>12</u>.

Feeling the Keyboard under your Fingertips

Compare the two long passages of 5ths in mm. <u>1–4</u> and <u>7–10</u>.

Now look at the rest of the cluster chords.

How many different chords are there? <u>three</u>

Hunting for Scales

Stretch out the cluster chords in m. 4. Start with middle C and write all the notes separately, like a scale.

What is the distance between the first and second notes of your scale? ☑ a whole tone

Are all the notes that distance from each other? <u>yes</u>

In m. 5, each hand plays a scale.

How far apart are the first two RH notes?
☑ a semitone

How far apart are the first two LH notes?
☑ a semitone

Are all the notes in both scales the same distance apart? <u>yes</u>

A Starry Night

Italo Taranta (b. 1928)
Student Workbook 1, p. 40

A Triple Pulse

The time signature of this piece is? $\frac{3}{4}$.
Name three other pieces in your *Piano Repertoire 1*
that have the same time signature:
<u>Where Did the Sun Go?</u>
<u>Minuet in G Major</u>
<u>Minuet in A Minor</u>
<u>Mist</u>
<u>Minuet in D Major</u>
<u>Minuet in F Major</u>
<u>A Ball</u>
<u>Minuet in C Major</u>
<u>Duet for One</u>
<u>She's Like the Swallow</u>

Write in the subdivisions below the rhythm of the
first two measures of *A Starry Night*:

Find the Musical Sentences

Look through the piece, then write the letter name
of the description that matches each phrase.

This phrase is repeated exactly (although the LH
changes a little at the end).
Phrase <u>a</u>

This phrase is repeated a step higher / (a step lower).
Phrase <u>b</u>

A Duet inside the Left Hand

The LH part has two voices, like a duet. The stems
of the lower voice of the duet go <u>down</u> and the
stems of the upper voice go <u>up</u> . Play the bass part
through with one hand on each part in order to
hear both voices well.

The <u>upper</u> voice plays pairs of notes, either
together (harmonically) or one after the other
(melodically).

The <u>lower</u> voice plays in single notes, each lasting
for the entire measure.

Notice that the LH lower voice almost never plays
on beat 3.

Would this piece sound different if the bass played
on beat 3 throughout the piece? <u>yes</u>

Hide and Seek

Linda Niamath (b. 1939)
Student Workbook 1, p. 42

Getting Ready

In the first two measures, notice the notes going
from below the bass staff to above the treble staff.

What is the time value of each note? <u>one beat</u>

Name the starting note. <u>F</u>

Name the highest note. <u>C</u>

Keyboard Geography Experiment

Place your LH on the first two notes of *Hide and
Seek*. Count the white keys under your hand
(lowest, highest, and all those in between).
How many keys are under your hand? <u>5</u>

Now keep your LH resting lightly on the keys, and
play the RH notes in the first measure.
What is that interval? <u>5th</u>

Measuring:
Were your hands still in their original interval
shape? ☑ yes

Hand crossing:
Hide and Seek indicates a <u>staccato</u> touch on the
quarter notes.

Now play the same intervals backwards, moving
from the top note back down.

Which hand starts? <u>RH</u> What is the first note? <u>C</u>

3rds and 5ths Together

Play mm. 3–4 RH alone. Each interval is a <u>3rd</u> .
Do the 3rds move ☑ up By ☑ half step?

Now play mm. 3–4 LH alone.

Look carefully at m. 4. Does the interval look like a
3rd? ☑ no

Play the interval. Does it sound like a 3rd? ☑ yes

Now play mm. 3–4 hands together.
In which measures are 3rds and 5ths used together?
mm. <u>11–12</u>

Compare the sound of these measures played hands
together to the sound of mm. 3–4. Describe the
difference in sound that you hear.
<u>In mm. 3–4, the combined chords are more distant; in
mm. 10–11, they are major triads</u> .

Jumping Out

You began by jumping up and down the keyboard
with your fingers, hands, and arms. What does the
composer tell you to do at the end of the piece?
<u>Suddenly accent the last two chords in ff, with a sf in
m. 16</u> .

The Flea

Mel. Bonis (1858–1937)
Student Workbook 1, p. 44

Finding Sections

We often use letters to show the different sections of a piece. Label the beginning section with a letter A. In this opening A section, almost all of the notes are marked with staccato dots.
What kind of sounds will you be making?
 separated / short

Now look for a section that looks really different. It begins at m. _9_. Label it B.

Instead of staccato dots, there are _slurs_. The sounds here will be _smoother_.

The A section returns at m. _16_. Label it again in your music.

As you see, the overall form of the music is quite clear. Which section (A or B) sounds most like fleas? _A_

Hunting for Patterns

As you saw in the activity you just did, different ways of writing (and playing) create different sections in a piece. *Within* each section, there are interesting patterns to discover. The following quizzes will help you do just that!

Quiz 1

Here are mm. 1–2. On the blank system, rewrite the notes a 3rd lower. The first two notes have been done to help you get started.

In the piece, find the lower notes that you just wrote. They begin at the **upbeat** to m. _3_.

Quiz 2

Write the letter names of the first four notes of m. 7, and group them in pairs.

 _D_ & _A_   _F_ & _B_

Now, write them again, but reverse the order of the notes in each pair.
 _A_ & _D_   _B_ & _F_

Quiz 3

Here are the notes with upturned stems from mm. 9–12. The RH plays these notes, and they fall in steps. Mark "H" or "W" between the notes to show whether they are falling by a half step or a whole step. (The first two have been done to help you get going.)

Observe the large rising leap marked near the end of the m. 10. The pattern begins again here, except it is written lower _____ / higher _✔_ than the first time. Congratulations! You've just found another sequence.

Speeding Up or Slowing Down

Accel. is short for _accelerando_, which means _gradually faster_.

Rit. is short for _ritardando_, which means _gradually slower_.

Crafty Card Tricks

Christine Donkin (b. 1976)
Student Workbook 1, p. 46

Some Tricky, Some Not

In the scale of D minor, which note is sharp? _C_

In *Crafty Card Tricks*, there is a G sharp in the _left_ hand in mm. _2–3_ and _18–19_. The composer has "thrown in" this accidental like a wild card.

Do a "crafty" experiment. Write the scale of D minor, but change the G to a G sharp:

Plan the fingering and write the finger numbers under the notes.

Fill in the rest of the scale in the example below. Play the scale.

Scale of A minor harmonic

Tricky Rhythm

The LH has a "skipping" rhythm organized with a time signature of $\frac{6}{8}$.

Don't use the metronome at m. 9. The *accel.* tells you to _gradually increase the tempo_.

Duet for One

Christopher Norton (b. 1953)
Student Workbook 1, p. 48

Playing a Duet

Piano duets are usually written for _two_ people playing one piano.

The higher part is called *Primo* and the lower part is called *Secondo*.

Why does the composer call this a duet when only one person is playing?
Is this a duet between your hands? _yes_
Which hand has the melody? _RH_

A Conversation for your RH

Notice that the RH phrases have a question-and-answer quality, like a conversation.

What markings does Norton use to divide the RH questions from the answers?
slurs and _dynamics_

Notice that the questions and the answers always begin on beat _3_ of the measure.

Find two examples of this in your piece.
(**Remember:** The first complete measure is m. 1.)
  question: mm. _1–2_ answer: mm. _3–4_
  question: mm. _5–6_ answer: mm. _7–8_

The slurs indicate that you should play the melody *legato*.
Legato means you play how? _smoothly_ .

The rhythm of the melody has a short–long feeling.
What is the note value of the first note? _1 beat_
What is the note value of the second note? _2 beats_

A Duet for your LH

The LH part has two voices, like a duet within a duet.

The stems of the lower voice go _down_ and the stems of the upper voice go _up_ .

Play the bass part through with both hands so that you can follow each voice.
The lower voice of the LH plays only one note: _E_ .

The upper voice of the LH has a pattern that repeats every _4_ measures.

Name the four notes: _B_ _C_ _D_ _C_

How many times is this pattern played? _4_

A Triple Pulse

The time signature is $\frac{3}{4}$. Name three other pieces in your *Piano Repertoire 1* that have the same time signature:
Where Did the Sun Go?
Minuet in G Major

Minuet in A Minor
Mist
Minuet in D Major
Minuet in F Major
A Ball
Minuet in C Major
A Starry Night
She's Like the Swallow

The Jolly Fiddler, op. 41, no. 5

Grigori Frid (b. 1915)
Student Workbook 1, p. 50

Finding Sections

The double bar line divides this music into two sections. Look at the first section.

How many measures are there in this section? _8_
(HINT: Don't count both versions of m. 8.)

Is this section repeated? _yes_

When do you play the second version of m. 8?
after the repeat of mm. 1–7

Now look through the second section.

Where is the A music repeated in this section?
mm. _17–24_

Is it *exactly* the same? _no_

Will you label these measures A or (A₁) in your music?

Finally, look at mm. 9–16.

Is the fiddler playing a different tune here? _yes_

Tuning Up

The fiddle plays an important role in the folk music of many cultures.

What is the other name for this instrument? _violin_

Have you ever heard a violinist tuning a violin or fiddle? If you have, mm. 1–4 will sound familiar.

Name the four different notes in these measures:
_A_ _E_ _G_ _D_

Take a close look at these notes.

What kind of notes are marked *staccato*? _eighth_

Describe how to play *staccato*. _separated / short_

The _quarter_ notes are marked *tenuto*. Hold them for their full value.

Did you notice that the RH rhythm is a backwards version of the LH rhythm?
The RH quarter notes are on beat _1_ .
The LH quarter notes are on beat _2_ .

A Lively Melody

How many different rhythmic groupings can you find in this piece that equal a quarter note? Write each group in a box:

What other musical sign for touch can you find? <u>slur</u>

How will you play these notes? <u>smoothly, connected</u>

A Drone

In mm. 4–8, two of the open-string notes are used as an accompaniment for <u>nine</u> beats.

The LH in *The Jolly Fiddler* starts a drone on m. 9.

For how many beats does the fiddler hold these notes? <u>four</u>

Square Dance

Dale Reubart (b. 1926)
Student Workbook 1, p. 52

Find that Key

Here is the beginning of *Square Dance*. Write the letter name under each note:

E F# G# A B C# D# E

Now add the sharps after the letters (e.g., F#) as shown by the key signature.
These notes create the scale of <u>E</u> major.

Dancing to the Sounds of Triads

Write the names of the notes that form an E major triad.
<u>E G sharp A</u>

List the measures of the LH that use only the notes belonging to the E major triad: mm. <u>3 4 7 8 9 10 13 14 17 18 19 20 21 22</u>

Now let's find more places where Reubart uses E major. On the following staff, write the last RH note of each of mm. 3, 4, 7, and 8:

Name the chord that these notes make when played together: <u>E major</u>

Which other measures use a similar pattern in the RH? <u>17 18 19 20</u>

It's Good to Know

Let's use a C major chord to review triads and their inversions:

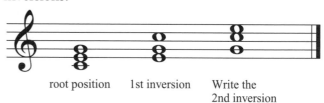

root position   1st inversion   Write the 2nd inversion here

Now write the root position and two inversions of the E major triad on the staff below:

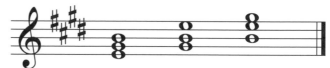

root position 1st inversion 2nd inversion

One of the inversions of the E major triad is used three times in the RH of *Square Dance*.

It is used in mm. <u>9</u> , <u>10</u> , and <u>13</u> . (HINT: It may be in a different place on the keyboard from the way you wrote it above.)

A Lively Mood

Find a set of five measures where you will only play *staccato*:
mm. <u>9</u> – <u>13</u> .

Find three pairs of measures where you will use accents (>) to make the rhythm more exciting:
mm. <u>3 – 4 7 – 8 17 – 18</u> .

In mm. 19–20, the *tenuto* sign (—) is used instead of the earlier accents. It suggests a calmer, gentler accent.

Several other markings also appear in the last four measures.

What is the effect of these markings? <u>tempo slows; dynamics become softer</u>

The Alligator

Veronika Krausas (b. 1963)
Student Workbook 1, p. 54

Sharing Space

If you were to write a piece about an alligator, where would you put it on the musical staff?

low ✓

Compared to the way other pieces are written in this book, what is different in the way *The Alligator* is written? <u>It is written on only one staff — in the bass clef.</u>

Usually music for piano is written on a grand staff, but here your hands have to share one staff. The trick is to watch the direction of the note stems.

Your RH plays the notes with the stems that go <u>up</u> .

Your LH plays the notes with the stems that go <u>down</u> .

Alligator Time

How many different time signatures are used? <u>6</u>
Write them here. <u>6</u> <u>7</u> <u>4</u> <u>8</u> <u>2</u> and <u>5</u>
(bottom: 4 4 4 4 4 and 4)

Do all the time signatures have the same bottom number? <u>yes</u>

What does this bottom number tell you? <u>The quarter note gets one beat.</u>

What does the top number of a time signature tell you? <u>The number of beats in one measure.</u>

Alligator Rhythms

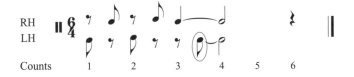

How many quarter-note beats are there in m. 1? <u>six</u>
How many quarter-note beats are there in m. 2? <u>seven</u>

Are the first three beats the same in both measures? <u>yes</u>

Does the alligator hold still for a longer time in m. 2? <u>yes</u>

Jazzy Alligator

Look at the rhythm of m. 1 again. Which hand plays a note between two beats, and holds it into the next long beat? <u>LH</u>

Circle this note in the example above.

"Croc" the Curmudgeon

Pierre Gallant (b. 1950)
Student Workbook 1, p. 56

Crocodile Mood

Is the alligator in a good mood? <u>yes</u>
How can you tell? <u>He dances a jazzy dance.</u>

Feeling the Scaly Bits

The crocodile begins low down on the keyboard.
Is this the same as the alligator? <u>yes</u>

Snaps and Bites

Does the accent (>) sign on the G tell you to snap? <u>yes</u>

Croc Crossing

There are two places where the hands cross over in this piece. Look at m. 5.

Which hand starts the pattern? <u>RH</u> Which hand crosses over? <u>RH</u>

Now look at m. 9.
Which hand starts the pattern? <u>LH</u> Which hand crosses over? <u>LH</u>

What touch is used in m. 11? <u>staccato</u>

Reptile Rhythm

You will recognize the $\frac{6}{8}$ time signature. What other piece in your *Piano Repertoire 1* uses that same time signature? <u>Crafty Card Tricks</u>

Count and clap mm. 5–6 and mm. 9–10.

What rhythm is this? <u>three beats to the measure</u>
How is he moving in mm. 7–8? <u>in two groups of three</u>

Mist

Clifford Poole (1916–2003)
Student Workbook 1, p. 58

Misty Triads

The RH plays a melody, and the LH plays only triads all the way through the piece. The triads move up or down by step except in two places. They jump a little in mm. <u>8–9</u> and jump a lot in mm. <u>15–16</u> .

Play the LH from the beginning to m. 4.
In which position are these triads? <u>root</u>

The triads with accidentals are in mm. <u>10</u> and <u>12</u> .
The name of the note that has an accidental is <u>B♭</u> .
Name the triad notes in m. 10: <u>B♭</u> <u>D</u> <u>F</u>
Name the triad notes in m. 12: <u>G</u> <u>B♭</u> <u>D</u>

Major or Minor

The triad in m. 1 has a <u>major</u> sound.
The triad in m. 2 has a <u>minor</u> sound.

Melody and Balance

In m. 1, there is a <u>mp</u> dynamic mark between the staves.

There is also a <u>p</u> dynamic mark below the bass staff.

In which other measure do you see the same markings? m. <u>13</u>

Where in the piece do the dynamic markings change? m. <u>9</u> m. <u>13</u> m. <u>17</u>

24

Watch for all the dynamic markings as you play the piece.

The loudest dynamic in *Mist* is _mf_ . The softest dynamic is _ppp_ .

What happens to the mist at the end? _It thins out and fades away / disappears._

On the Right Lines

Christopher Norton (b. 1953)
Student Workbook 1, p. 60

A Jazzy Rhythm

Write the beats below the music, counting them as *1 and 2 and* (1 & 2 &).

1 & 2 & 3 & 4 &   1 & 2 & 3 & 4 &

Rock 'n' Roll Triads

In the LH of m. 2, circle the three notes that form a triad:

Find the measure where the LH pattern moves to a new spot. m. _6_

Write the pattern on the staff and circle the three notes that form a triad:

The Blues Pattern

The key signature has one _sharp_ .
This means that the music is in either _G_ major or _E_ minor.

What is the lowest LH note at the very beginning and the very end? _G_

This piece must be in the key of _G major_ .

On the chart below, write in the first LH note of each measure, starting with m. 2, and also which note it is in the G major scale.

m. 2	m. 3	m. 4	m. 5
G – note 1	G – note 1	G – note 1	G – note 1
m. 6	m. 7	m. 8	m. 9
C – note 4	C – note 4	G – note 1	G – note 1
m. 10	m. 11	m. 12	m. 13
D – note 5	C – note 4	G – note 1	G – note 1

This is the pattern of a basic twelve-bar blues. Twelve bars, of course, means the same as twelve measures.

This pattern is used in many music styles, including traditional blues and early rock 'n' roll. (*Rock around the Clock* would be a great piece for you to listen to, to hear the twelve-bar blues.)

A Bluesy Tune

Norton gives the music an extra "bluesy" flavor by introducing a few special notes. Write the letter names of all the notes in mm. 10–13 that have accidentals in front of them: _C♯, C♮, B♭, F♯_ .

Now, write the scale of G major going up one octave (the starting and ending **tonic** notes are already there for you).

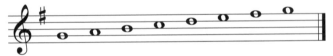

The third note of the G major scale is _B_ . The seventh note is _F♯_ .

March, op. 39, no. 10

Dmitri Kabalevsky (1904–1987)
Student Workbook 1, p. 62

Marching to the Sound of Triads

Shown below is the triad of C major in root position (with C on the bottom). Write the first and second inversions next to it.

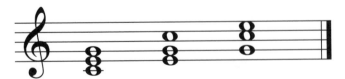

root position   1st inversion   2nd inversion

Find each triad shape and write it in its measure. You may write the triads in solid or broken form.

25

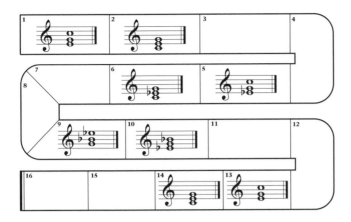

Left-Hand Copycat

What does the LH do that it didn't do in the first half of the piece? _It copies some of the RH triad shapes._

Write the RH of m. 9 and the LH of m. 10 together in the same measure:

Find two other measures in *March* that have imitation similar to that in mm. 9–10: mm. _13_ and _14_.

Dotted Marching Rhythm

Complete the following chart to see how these rhythms fit into the $\frac{2}{4}$ beat of this piece:

The Snake

Renée Christopher (b. 1955)
Student Workbook 1, p. 64

Gliding Smoothly Along

Where does the thumb act like a snake when it creeps under your hand?
RH m. _1_ LH m. _4_

The title mentions only one snake, but the music looks like there might be _two_ snakes.

Descriptive Dynamics

In the score, there are *crescendos* when the direction of the music goes _up_, and *diminuendos* when the music goes _down_.

Key Signature? Really?

The name of the flat is _B flat_.
The name of the sharp is _C sharp_.

The music is centered around the note A.
It begins and ends on _A_. Most of the long notes are _A's_.

You can form a scale using the notes of this piece. Write these notes *in order* on the staff below:

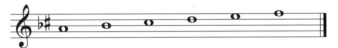

Carol in Canon

Christopher Norton (b. 1953)
Student Workbook 1, p. 66

Hiding Chords inside a Canon

On the pair of staves below, write the first note played by each hand at the start of every measure.

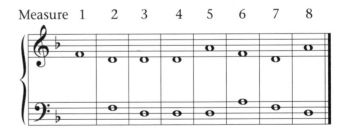

What single triad do *all* of these notes belong to? _D minor_

Have you found the mystery triad? It's the triad of _F major_.

The note that does not belong is _G_.

The passage whose notes contain the triad goes from m. _9_ to m. _12_.

Describe what happens right after this passage:
Part of the original opening passage returns.

A Change in Timing

Write the RH of mm. 15–16 on the staff below:

Now, write out the same music, but make each sound last twice as long.
Instead of two measures, you will now fill how many measures? _four_

This is called **augmentation.**

Where does Norton use this effect in _Carol in Canon?_ mm. _19–22_

What effect does this have on the listener? _The music sounds slower._

A Ball

Irena Garztecka (1913–1963)
Student Workbook 1, p. 68

Playing Ball

Which direction are the balls going in mm. 1–4?
up–down

Which direction are the balls going in mm. 5–8?
down–up

Two Kinds of Notes

There are only two different note values in this piece. Circle the correct ones:

Does the LH always follow the RH pattern? _no_

Two Kinds of Dots

What does a dot _above_ or _beneath_ a note tell you to do? _Play the notes detatched or short._

What are these dots called? _staccato_

In this piece, what kinds of notes have these dots?
quarter notes

What does a dot _beside_ a note tell you to do? _Add half the value of the note._

In this piece, what kinds of notes have these dots?
half notes

Do you think the ball is bouncing on the _staccato_ notes? _yes_

What happens on the dotted half notes? _One ball is being held still._

Two Kinds of Accidentals

Name these signs. What do they tell you to do?

♭ _flat_   _Lower a note by a semitone._

♯ _sharp_   _Raise a note by a semitone._

Name the notes that have a ♭: _E and A_

Name the notes that have a ♯: _F_

Bouncing Triads

Be a detective and find the hidden triads in the bouncing quarter notes!

	G major triad	D major triad	A♭ major triad	A major triad
mm.	1, 2, 9, 10	3	5 and 13	12

Where Did the Sun Go?

Andrew Markow (b. 1942)
Student Workbook 1, p. 70

Dialogue between the Hands

How would you describe this invention?
Both hands play the melody. ✓

The RH starts the piece. How far behind is the LH?
3 beats / 1 measure

Compare the LH in m. 2 with the RH in m. 1.

Are the letter names of the notes in each hand
☑ the same or ☐ different?

This style of writing, called **imitation**, continues for most of the piece.

In which measure does the LH stop playing what the RH just played? m. _5_

A Scale Creates a Mood

In the opening portion of the melody shown below, circle all the notes that form a G triad.

Because of the B flat, the triad is G <u>minor</u>, which is also the key of the piece.

Does the key of the piece match the mood of the title? <u>yes</u>

Style of Playing
Is this piece written in a ✓ *legato* or __ *staccato* style?

Sur le pont d'Avignon
On the Bridge at Avignon

arr. Pierre Gallant (b. 1950)
Student Workbook 1, p. 71

Hang on to the *Tenutos*
What do these marks tell you to do? <u>Hold the note for its full value</u>.

Are all the *tenuto* marks on repeated notes? <u>yes</u>

Are there any *staccato* notes in this piece? <u>no</u>

Slide along the Slurs
What is the mark over the RH melody in mm. 3–4? <u>a slur</u>

What does it tell you to do? <u>play the notes connected</u>

Is this touch a contrast to the *tenuto* notes? <u>yes</u>

Two Rhythms
There are two main rhythms in *Sur le pont d'Avignon*. Write them here:

Rhythm a (RH, m. 1)

Rhythm b (RH, m. 3)

She's Like the Swallow

arr. David Duke (b. 1950)
Student Workbook 1, p. 73

This song is divided into phrases, which follow the punctuation of the sentences. Write the phrase marks above the music.

How many phrases did you find? <u>four</u>

A Canon
Which hand is the leader? <u>RH</u>

How far behind is the second part? <u>two measures</u>

Teapot Invention

Andrew Markow (b. 1942)
Student Workbook 1, p. 75

Follow that Teapot
The RH starts the song. How long does the LH wait before joining in? <u>two measures</u>

The LH is identical to the RH until m. <u>10</u>. How is the LH different in this measure?

notes: <u>RH holds the G for two beats</u>
<u>LH plays G and B</u>

rhythm: <u>RH plays one half note</u>
<u>LH plays two quarter notes</u>

Student Workbook 2 Answers

Entrée in A Minor

Anon.
Student Workbook 2, p. 4

Find the Meter

This piece, like all other pieces with the same title, is in <u>duple</u> meter. This is one of the things that make it sound like a procession.

Major and Minor Relatives

Three semitones up from A is <u>C</u> . This new key, <u>C</u> major, will have the same key signature as *Entrée*.

Finding a Musical Form

Clue no. 1: The circled notes create the triad of the starting key. Write the triad in the staff beside the excerpt. In your music, label this section A.
Clue no. 2: Look for a new triad here. Once again, the circled notes are your clues.

This triad suggests the key of <u>C major</u> . How is this key related to the starting key? <u>relative major</u> In your music, label this section B.

Clue no. 3: *D.C. al Fine.* Consider how this will affect your playing. Is the key named using Clue no. 2 the last one you will hear in this piece? Or, will you now be returning to the starting key? <u>returning to the starting key</u>

Measure: <u>1–2</u>
Triad:
Key: <u>A minor</u>

Measure: <u>9–10</u>
Triad:
Key: <u>C major</u>

Measure: <u>16</u>
Triad:
Key: <u>C major</u>

Is the overall form of *Entrée* AB or ABA? <u>ABA</u>

Harmonic or Melodic Minor?

Now look at the section of *Entrée* that is in A minor. Is the composer using harmonic or melodic minor? <u>melodic</u>
Which hand gives you the best clues for your answer? <u>left</u>

Écossaise in G Major, WoO 23

Ludwig van Beethoven (1770–1827)
Student Workbook 2, p. 6

Dance Character

In this piece:
- the tempo is *Allegro*, which means <u>fast, cheerful</u>
- the time signature is $\frac{2}{4}$
- the touch is mostly <u>staccato</u>

Syncopation in the Melody

Write the rhythm of m. 2.

Write the rhythm of m. 4.

Form

This dance is divided into two sections of equal length, each ending with a double bar line with a repeat sign. How many measures are in each section? <u>8</u>

You will see instructions on the score over m. 16 that say *D.C. al Fine (Da Capo al Fine)*. The *Fine* sign is in m. <u>8</u> .

Articulation Technique

Prepare your fingers with a curved shape to play the sixteenth notes evenly, firmly, and smoothly, even though the dynamic marking is <u>p</u> .

Broken octave bounce

At m. 9, you will see a pattern that leaps up an octave four times in a row:

Circle the lower notes of each pair on the diagram. You will see that the octave pattern is a four-note chord of D major.

Dance Dynamics

There are only two dynamic markings in the score: <u>p</u> and <u>f</u> .

Menuetto I in C Major

Wolfgang Amadeus Mozart (1756–1791)
Student Workbook 2, p. 8

An Accidental Key Change?

Menuetto has two sections and you can see clearly where they are.

Write in the measure numbers below and label the sections A and B in your music.
A: mm. _1_ – _8_   B: mm. _9_ – _16_

We know this music is in C major for two reasons.
1. There is a key signature of _no sharps or flats_ .
2. The first and last notes of the piece are both _C_ .

Look at the accidentals in the A section.

What is the accidental in m. 2? _C sharp_
m. 4? _D sharp_ m. 6? _D sharp_

These two accidentals do not change the key. Mozart has added them to enrich, or decorate, the melody.

Name the accidental in m. 5. _F sharp_

How many times do you see this accidental in mm. 5–8? _three times_

This accidental *does* change the key.

Name the new key at m. 8. _G major_
(HINT: Which key signature has only this accidental?)

Now fill in the blanks to explain the accidentals and the key change in the B section.

This section opens in the key of _G major_ . At m. 11, the music returns to the key of _C major_ . The clue is that in this measure, the note _F_ no longer has a sharp. In m. 14, the accidental _G sharp_ is used to enrich the melody. It does not change the key.

Repetition of an Idea

Look for the same similarity and difference between mm. 9–10 and mm. 11–12.

What is the same? _the rhythm_

What is different? _the intervals_ Is this repetition another example of a sequence? _yes_

Now compare mm. 5–8 and mm. 13–16.

The rhythm is: ☑ the same

The melodic shape is: ☑ different

Chamber Music

Violinists have to change their bow direction frequently to play smoothly. Now look at the printed music. What do you see in the melody that suggests where the violinist does this? _two-note slurs_

Dancing Partners

Which hand plays a *legato* line with a rich *cantabile* tone? _the RH_

Which hand plays *detached* notes? _the RH_

What instrument would you choose to play the LH part?
☑ Cello   ☑ Harpsichord
☑ Bassoon   ☑ Double bass

Impertinence, HWV 494

George Frideric Handel (1685–1759)
Student Workbook 2, p. 10

A Dance?

Compare the opening measures of *Entrée* and *Impertinence*:
What similarities can you find?

1. The time signatures: The sign ¢ (*alla breve*) is another way of writing the time signature $\frac{2}{2}$. How many beats are in each measure? _2_

2. The note values: Look through both pieces and check off the note values you find in both pieces.
☑ half notes ☑ quarter notes ☑ eighth notes

3. The key: Each of these pieces is in a _minor_ key.

Rhythmic Patterns

The following rhythmic patterns appear in *Impertinence*:

How many times can you find these patterns in the music?
pattern no. 1: in RH _1_ in LH _1_
pattern no. 2: in RH _6_ in LH _0_
pattern no. 3: in RH _1_ in LH _3_

Equal Partners

The RH and LH seem to be equal partners in this dance.
The LH is just as busy as the RH, except in mm. _13–15_ , where the LH seems to "sit down" for three measures!

The first phrase in the RH is two measures long.

Draw a bracket above this phrase. (Remember to include the upbeat.)

Now draw a bracket above the first phrase in the LH.

The LH imitates the RH but the two phrases are not exactly the same.

Circle the LH notes that are different from the RH.

A Minor Mystery
The key signature is two flats (B flat and E flat).

What key does this suggest? _Bb major_

If F sharp is the leading note, what is the **tonic** _G_

In this piece, the first note is _D_ and the last note is _G_ .

The key signature of this music (two flats) indicates _Bb_ major.

The relative minor is _G_ minor.

Ornaments
Impertinence contains two **ornaments** called trills. They are in mm. _7_ and _19_ .

Allegretto in C Major
Christian Gottlob Neefe (1748–1798)
Student Workbook 2, p. 13

A Familiar Melody
Did the melody of Neefe's *Allegretto in C Major* seem familiar to you the first time you heard it? This might be because one phrase is almost the same as the fourth phrase from the English folk song *Early One Morning:*

Which phrase? mm. _5_ – _8_

A Melody to Sing
Imagine how this melody would sound played on another instrument. Which instruments will best bring out the gracefulness and beauty of this melody?

Trombone	Cello	(Flute)
Bassoon	(Violin)	French horn
(Oboe)	Timpani	Trumpet

Two Contrasting Sections
This piece is divided into two sections. Find each section in the music and write the measure numbers below. (HINT: Look for the double bar lines.)

mm. _1_ – _8_   This section is _8_ measures long.

mm. _9_ – _24_   This section is _16_ measures long.
Is each section repeated? _no_

Take a look at the melody of the first section. Where else in the piece does Neefe repeat this melody? mm. _17_ – _24_

Now look at the melody of mm. 9–16. This melody begins with a two-measure figure, starting on the note _G_ .

Where does Neefe repeat this figure? mm. _11–12;_ _13–14_

Are the repetitions exactly the same? _no_

Write the starting note of each repetition. _E_   _D_

Phrasing
Play the melody in mm. 1–8 without observing the slurs.

Where would you take a breath?
at the ends of mm. 2, 4, and 8

In your score, make a light pencil mark at every breathing point. Now draw in long phrase lines connecting the measures that go together in one phrase.

Did you mark a phrase beginning at m. 5? _yes_

How long is this phrase? _four_ measures

Minuet in B Minor
Johann Ludwig Krebs (1713–1780)
Student Workbook 2, p. 15

Triads in the Minuet
In the RH of mm. 1–2 in Krebs's *Minuet*, the notes form the B minor _triad_ .

Which inversion of the triad appears in m. 2? _2nd_

Triads in Triplets
If you play each triplet in m. 7 in a solid (blocked) position, you will hear the two triads.

What is the name of the first? _D major_

What is the name of the second? (HINT: It's in an inversion.) _E minor_

Ornaments
Another ornament appears in the last measure. You will see it "realized" (written out) at the bottom of the page as footnote (b). What is the name of the note indicated by the sharp sign under the ornament? _A sharp_

Menuet en rondeau
Minuet in Rondo Form

Jean-Philippe Rameau (1683–1764)
Student Workbook 2, p. 17

Repetitions: Over and Over Again

There are two measures that have words written above them. Write the measure numbers and the words below.

m. <u>8</u> <u>Fine</u>

m. <u>16</u> <u>D.C. al Fine</u>

First you play the A section (mm. <u>1–8</u>).
At the end of the B section, the sign tells you to go back to <u>the beginning</u> and play to the <u>Fine</u> sign.

A Flowing Sound

Write all the different note values you can find in this piece, one in each box:

Which note value does Rameau use the most often? <u>the eighth note</u>

Similarity and Difference

This piece is in the key of <u>C major</u> .

Play the RH part of the A section.

Where does the first long-line phrase end? m. <u>4</u>

Where does the second long-line phrase end? m. <u>8</u>

Now compare the two phrases.
They are both: ☑ the same length
☑ similar with some differences

In what ways is the second phrase different from the first?

1. <u>The LH rhythm is different in the second phrase.</u>

2. <u>The RH notes in m. 7 are different from m. 3; in</u>
    <u>m. 3 they go down, in m. 7 they go up.</u>

3. <u>The notes in the last measures of the phrases are</u>
    <u>different.</u>

The B section has an accidental. It is <u>F sharp</u> .

Name the scale that has this accidental and you will know the key of the B section. It is the scale of <u>G major</u> .

Describe the difference in sound between the A section and the B section.

The A section is <u>higher</u> in pitch and has a brighter sound.

Gavotte in C Major, op. 12, no. 2

Samuel Arnold (1740–1802)
Student Workbook 2, p. 20

Find a Phrase That Returns in a New Key

On the staff below, write out the opening phrase but begin with the given starting notes. Have your notes rise or fall the same intervals as in the example above.

What measures in the music match what you have written? mm. <u>8–10</u>

You will notice that there is an added accidental in the LH on the note <u>F</u> . Which scale has this accidental? <u>G</u> major.

Therefore, the phrase that you played in C major at the beginning has been transposed to the key of <u>G</u> major.

Phrases and Repeats

Look at the beginning of *Gavotte* in the first example above. This phrase appears in three other places. You have already found one; now find the other two and mark them on this chart.

	Measure	Key
Opening phrase	1	C major
First repeat	<u>5</u>	<u>C major</u>
Second repeat	8	G major
Third repeat	<u>13</u>	<u>C major</u>

Each time, the melody starts on beat <u>3</u> of the measure. Therefore, we hear <u>2</u> beats before the first beat of the next measure.

Finding a Form

Look at the double bar lines in the music. Do they divide the piece into two or three sections? <u>two</u>
Where does the opening phrase return to C major?

☑ at the start of the second section

Minuetto II in F Minor, H 196 / 2

Carl Philipp Emanuel Bach (1714–1788)
Student Workbook 2, p. 22

How Melody Creates Musical Sentences

Below is a map of the sixteen measures of *Minuetto*. Write each of the patterns shown above in the appropriate measure of the map, exactly as it occurs in the music:

Fill in the blanks below:

First Half

Phrase 1: _2_ measures; phrase 2: _2_ measures; phrase 3: _2_ measures

Second Half

Phrase 1: _2_ measures; phrase 2: _2_ measures; phrase 3: _4_ measures

Discover New Keys

Follow the clues to discover triads and keys in the music.

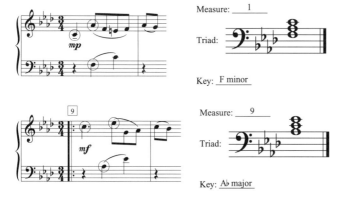

Measure: _1_

Triad:

Key: _F minor_

Measure: _9_

Triad:

Key: _A♭ major_

The last measure uses the notes of one of the triads you discovered earlier.

Minuetto ends in the key of _F minor_ .

A Cheerful Spirit

Daniel Gottlob Türk (1750–1813)
Student Workbook 2, p. 24

Character and Mood

Play the RH alone to the end of m. 8. How do you think Türk establishes a cheerful mood in this piece? Check all the things that set the mood:
- ☑ major key
- ☑ tempo
- ☑ direction of melody at the beginning

Two Best Friends

The RH begins the melody on an **upbeat**, running (or walking quickly) in _eighth_ notes. The LH follows a couple of steps behind, on _the second half of beat 1_ (which beat?) of m. 1.

What is the first interval leap in the RH melody? _perfect 4th_ What interval distance is shown between the bracketed RH and LH notes in the above example? _major 10th / major 3rd_

Articulation

Which hand does the hopping? _RH_

Different varieties of **articulation** show the different walking styles. Look for:
1. *walking or running smoothly:* in mm. _1, 3, 5, 7–8, 13, 15–16_

   (type of articulation) _legato_

2. *skipping:* in mm. _2, 4, 6, 10, 12, 14_

   (type of articulation) _slurs_

3. *hopping:* in mm. _9, 11_
   (type of articulation)
   detached eighth notes with rests

Fingering

To play scales that begin on black keys, do not begin with your thumb. Notice the starting fingers in each hand. RH begins on finger _2_ ; LH begins on finger _3_ .

Look at the RH beginning of the piece again. In m. 1, is the fingering the same as for the B flat major scale? _yes_

The Banshee's Ball

Anne Crosby (b. 1968)
Student Workbook 2, p. 31

Ghostly Manner

The composer has written "in a ghostly manner" for the tempo marking. What dynamic marking do you see at the beginning of the piece that might lead you to believe that this is about a ghost? _mp_

Are there any markings in the LH at m. 4 that might indicate a ghost on tip toe? _staccato_

Two Dance Rhythms at the Ball

What is the time signature at the beginning? $\frac{4}{4}$

Where does it change? m. _9_

What is the time signature in that measure? $\frac{3}{4}$

Ghostly Key and Phantom Triads

First play the LH in the second beat of m. 1.

Is this a major or a minor triad? _minor_

Name the triad. _A minor_

Now play the RH on the first beat of m. 1.

Is this a complete triad? _no_

Which note is missing? _the third_

Without the middle note, this is an interval of _a perfect 5th_ .

The key of the piece at the beginning is _A minor_ . Find and name some other solid (blocked) triads in the piece, for example, in m. 3 _F minor_ and m. _7_ , _D flat major_ .

The waltz section at m. 9 is different in its time signature and in its melody. It begins with a broken triad. If you play the notes in the RH (m. 9) all at once, you will hear the triad. Play the inversions to find the root position.

Where did you see this triad before? m. _3_

Banshee Voices

The dynamic markings in the score range widely. Write all the dynamic symbols first in the order they appear, and then in order from soft to loud.
_mp mf p f p f p mp pp_
_pp p mp mf f_

The bigger wails start in a pattern beginning at m. 9 and increase in strength until m. _16_ . There are two ways of indicating this effect in the music:

1. _poco a poco crescendo_ (which means: _getting louder bit by bit_)

2. ◁━━━━━━ (which means: _gradually getting louder_)

Where does their voice pattern start in a higher location? m. _13_

Are the banshees leaving at the end, or are they intending to come back and dance and shriek some more? _They are leaving._

March of the Goblins

Boris Berlin (1907–2001)
Student Workbook 2, p. 29

Tapping Time

There is a strong 1–2 pulse in each measure.

The time signature of this piece is $\frac{6}{8}$.

There are _6_ eighth notes in a measure.

The _eighth note_ gets one beat.

The six eighth notes in each measure divide into _two_ groups of _three_ .

A Musical Picture

Berlin uses several musical devices to create his musical interpretation of these marching goblins. The LH in mm. 1–4 imitates the bounce of their feet as they hop along. This repeating pattern or motive is called an **ostinato**.

Name the two intervals that form this pattern. _5_ th and _6_ th

Where else can you find the *ostinato?* mm. _9–13_ mm. _21–25_

In the RH, what marking tells you to play with a bounce? _m. 16_

Find other sets of measures where a melody is repeated an octave higher or lower: mm. _5–7_ mm. _16–18_ mm. _25–26_

Can you find a place where the goblins land on both feet? _m. 16_

How does the march end? _quietly, low_

Describe what happens during the last quick change from *forte* to *piano.* _The RH moves into the bass clef._

Skeleton Dance

Nancy Telfer (b. 1950)
Student Workbook 2, p. 31

At what time of year do you usually think of skeletons? <u>Halloween</u>

What's the first image that comes to your mind when you think of a skeleton? a lot of <u>bones</u>

These skeletons are dancing in $\frac{2}{4}$ time (or meter). The composer shows us through the music how they move around and shake themselves.

Skeleton Effects in Sound

Grace notes
Where does the first grace note appear? <u>m. 1</u> Find all the grace notes. How many are there in the piece? <u>9</u>

Sliding pattern
Skeleton ribs are close together, and they move from side to side. In m. 9, you will see four-note groups of sixteenth notes running down close together in a pattern:

How far apart are the notes? ☑ semitone

What is the pattern called? <u>chromatic</u>

You need to play these patterns smoothly. Be careful that the ribs don't slide "out of joint"!

Which notes should *not* be played smoothly?
<u>the staccato eighth notes</u>

Accents and *staccatos*
The short *staccatos* that Telfer mentions in her list of "skeletal effects" above occur mostly on what type of note values? <u>eighth</u>

Where do *staccatos* occur on a different type of note? mm. <u>18–19</u>

The *tremolo*
Accents occur mostly on the beginning of the "shake" (**tremolo**), but there is one single note that has an accent. It is in m. <u>12</u> .

Count the number of the thirty-second notes in the diagram. Is this the correct number of notes to play with the LH note? <u>yes</u>

Skeleton Partners
How far does the chromatic scale go before it turns around? <u>1 octave</u>

What is the length of this chromatic scale? <u>12 notes</u>

What note do you need to add to make a complete octave? <u>E</u>

Autumn Leaves

Linda Niamath (b. 1939)
Student Workbook 2, p. 33

Melodic Shape
Notice the shape of the RH melody in mm. 1–3. It has a curved shape like the slur over it. Play this melody with the given dynamics and listen to the change in color. As the phrase rises, there is a small *crescendo* from <u>mp</u> to <u>mf</u> where the color becomes more intense.

What happens to the sound at the end of the curve when the phrase falls?
It gets <u>softer</u> .

How many times do you hear this happening? <u>3</u>

The end of each curved line in the RH melody (e.g., mm. 3–4) ends in an interval that often represents a "sigh" in music.

What is the interval called? <u>minor 2nd</u>

How many times do you hear it? <u>4</u>

Patterns Falling
1. Each RH melodic phrase begins a step lower than the previous one:

   What is the interval distance between the starting notes of each RH phrase? <u>major 2nd</u>

2. The LH pattern falls gradually every other measure.

Circle the first note of the LH pattern in your score every time it changes.

What is the interval distance between the starting notes of each LH phrase? <u>minor 2nd</u>

The interval distance *between both hands* at the start of each pattern is a <u>perfect 5th</u> .

Hidden Triads
All the triads in similar phrases are in the same inversion.

What inversion is it? <u>2nd</u>

Are these triads major? or (minor)?

Name the key of each triad. <u>E</u>

Melody and Balance

The RH melody in this piece has a beautiful shape. The LH must be played in balance so that it does not overpower the melody. The composer has indicated directions on the score for creating this effect. Write these directions here:
<u>LH legato – mp throughout</u>

Phrase Length

It looks as though the phrases are only <u>3</u> measures in length because that is the length of the curved lines. But what happens in m. 4? There is a reference to m. 3 using the same note: (note name <u>C sharp</u>). It imitates the falling "sigh effect" with a wider interval leap of <u>one octave</u>.

You will notice that most phrases are four measures long, but there is one that is a different length. Can you find it? mm. <u>9–13</u>

What different clef appears in m. 15? <u>bass</u>

The Clock

Janina Garścia (1920–2004)
Student Workbook 2, p. 36

Tick, Tock, Tick, Tock

A pattern that is repeated over and over again throughout a piece is called an **ostinato**. Here, Garścia uses an *ostinato* pattern to imitate the steady ticking of the clock.

Which hand plays the *ostinato*? ☑ LH

Is the rhythm of the *ostinato* exactly the same all the way through? <u>yes</u>

Are the notes exactly the same all the way through? <u>yes</u>

Which measures are different? mm. <u>9–12</u>

Which note is added to the *ostinato* in these measures? <u>A sharp</u>

The Clock Struck . . .

This music actually tells you what time it is!

Where does this happen? mm. <u>9–12</u>

What time is it? Draw the hands on the clock.

In mm. 9–12, the LH plays the bottom note of the RH chords.

These chords have two markings.

What does > ♪ mean? <u>accent-emphasize</u>

What does the abbreviation *sf* stand for? <u>sforzando</u>

A Rhythmic Melody

The RH plays a short melody that is based on the motive in mm. 2–4:
Can you find a longer phrase based on this motive? mm. <u>14–18</u>

Can you find a shorter **variation** of part of this motive? mm. <u>6–8</u>

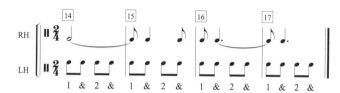

Write the beats (1 & 2 &) below each measure.

Sometimes a note is played on the last beat of the measure and held into the next measure. Find two places where this happens:

mm. <u>5</u> – <u>6</u>

mm. <u>11</u> – <u>12</u>

Finally, compare the sixteenth notes in mm. 4 and 8.

In mm. 3 and 4, you will play <u>2</u> sixteenth notes in the time of one eighth note.

The *3* under the sixteenth notes in m. 8 indicates that <u>3</u> sixteenth notes are to be played in the time of one eighth note. This type of note grouping is called a <u>triplet</u>.

Sailing by Moonlight

Joan Last (1908–2002)
Student Workbook 2, p. 38

A Rocking Rhythm

What is the time signature of *Sailing by Moonlight*?
<u>6/8</u>

Both hands contribute to the rocking motion, but the LH repeats the same rhythm for <u>16</u> measures. Where does this rhythm return? mm. <u>25–29</u>

Circle other words that you think describe the motion of the sailboat:
(swaying) galloping (lilting) riding dancing

A Broken-Chord Accompaniment

Look at the LH accompaniment. Do you see a single line of notes or a series of chords?
a series of chords

An Expressive Melody

Now look at the RH melody. The composer has marked this music *sempre legato*.

What do these Italian words mean? always smoothly

Find the marking *cantabile* in the score. m. 17
What does this Italian word mean? in a singing style

Which hand is playing the melody here? LH

Name three ways in which the accompaniment in mm. 17–24 is different from the accompaniment at the beginning of the piece.

1. The accompaniment is in the RH.

2. The rhythm is completely different.

3. The notes are played solidly rather than broken.

Pedal Language

For each term, write the meaning of the marking and the measure or measures where you found it.

simile: played the same way m. 4

ped. come prima: pedal like the start m. 9, m. 25

senza ped.: without pedal m. 16

A Little Song, op. 27, no. 2

Dmitri Kabalevsky (1904–1987)
Student Workbook 2, p. 40

A Russian Song

Look at the opening measures:

Find and circle the notes of a triad in m. 1.
Write the notes and name the triad. E G B
E minor

Where does Kabalevsky use this triad as a solid (blocked) chord? mm. 16–17

This piece has a key signature of 1 sharp(s).
This music could be in G major or E minor.
Which do you think it is? E minor

The melody begins with part of a scale. Complete the scale using notes that occur in the melody in the next few measures:

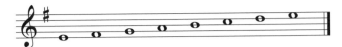

Does Kabalevsky's scale have any accidentals? no

Matching Game

Match the fragment with the description, and fill in any missing words.

Fragment no. 3
The bottom note of the first LH triad is the second note of the E minor scale, but it is lowered by a semitone / half step . This creates a surprising new harmony.

Fragment no. 2
The harmonic background is created by similar intervals sliding downward in **parallel motion**. The harmony seems suddenly strange, as though there is no key. Your fingers will have to crawl very smoothly along the keyboard.

Fragment no. 1
Here we have a quick visit to G major , the relative major of E minor. The transition is easy because both scales use the same notes.

Shaping the Melody

Now draw a gentle curve in the box to show the dymanic shape of the melody.

Rag Time

Christopher Norton (b. 1953)
Student Workbook 2, p. 43

The Musical Ingredients

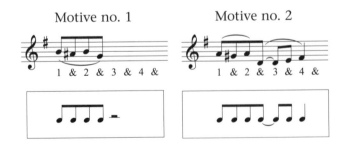

Write the beats (1 & 2 & etc.) under each motive.

Which motive features a note played on an "and" and then held onto a beat? Motive 2 . This is an example of syncopation, which gives this music a jazzy effect.

Sometimes Norton uses *both the melody and the rhythm* of a motive. Sometimes he uses *just the rhythm*. Write the rhythm of each motive in the boxes under the staves above.

Follow a Musical Path

Here's a map to help you trace the path of Norton's two motives from the beginning to the end of the piece. Look through the music, one measure at a time, and plot the appearances of the motives on the map. You can use the following symbols:

1 or 2   the number of the motive

↑   the motive starts higher than the first time

↓   the motive starts lower than the first time

R   only the *rhythm* of the motive is used (or the rhythm and a few of the notes)

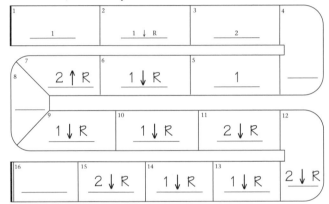

The Mouse in the Coal Bin

Clifford Poole (1916–2003)
Student Workbook 2, p. 45

A Story with Pictures

Write in the meanings of these dynamic markings and find their signs in the score.
piano _soft_ m. _1_
mezzo piano _moderately, soft_ m. _15_
forte _loud_ m. _13_
sforzando (forzando) _strongly accented, forced_ m. _21_
crescendo _gradually louder_ m. _6_
diminuendo _gradually softer_ m. _13_

Composers use markings to guide your decisions about touch.

Write the meanings and signs for these markings below, and find them in the score.

legato _smoothly_ m. _15_

staccato _detached_ m. _1_

tenuto _hold for full value_ m. _2_

Which measure contains the highest notes in the piece? m. _11_

Which measure contains the lowest notes in the piece? m. _14_
What is the marking that changes the pitch of a note? _8va_

In this piece, does this marking tell you to play:
☑ lower?

Tempo is an important painting tool for composers. There are a number of Italian tempo markings in *The Mouse in the Coal Bin*. Write the meaning of each term.

accel. (accelerando) _getting faster_

rit. (ritardando) _slowing down_

presto _very fast_

accel. molto _getting much faster_

poco accel. _getting a bit faster_

Tempo I _back to the first tempo_

Hands Far Apart and Close Together

At the beginning of the music, both hands play the same notes at the interval of an _octave_ .

In mm. 11–12, your hands play close together. The LH note fits in between the two RH notes. Name these notes.

RH _D flat E flat_   LH _D natural_

How many octaves do you cover in the move? _four_

A Drama in Three Scenes

The story of this mouse is divided into three scenes, or sections. Find these sections in your score, and write the measure numbers below.

A: mm. _1_ – _14_

B: mm. _15_ – _28_

A: mm. _29_ – _42_

The B "scene" presents a contrast to the two A "scenes." The composer does this by using different colors from his paint box. Look at the markings in this section.

How does the composer create a contrast with dynamics? _It starts mp followed by crescendos (including one crescendo to fz with a decrescendo immediately after)_ .

How does the composer create a contrast with touch? _This section is almost entirely legato._

The melody of this section is marked *cantabile*. What does this Italian word mean? _in a singing style_

How does the composer create an atmosphere of suspense in the last two measures? _By switching from eighth notes to quarter notes, and by delaying the final note with a half rest._

Madrigal

Mel. Bonis (1858–1937)
Student Workbook 2, p. 48

Melody and Dance

Look at the time signature of the piece, which is $\frac{3}{4}$.

What type of dance does this accompaniment pattern remind you of? <u>a waltz</u>

Articulation

What does a slur indicate? <u>smoothness</u>

What does a *staccato* indicate? <u>separation / shortness</u>

Transposition

The first accidental in the piece is in m. <u>13</u>. Every time you see an accidental in a piece, it is a reminder about possible key change. With the <u>C#</u> accidental as the seventh note of a new key, the composer is moving to the key of <u>D major</u> at m. 15.

The little melody that begins the middle section appears in mm. 15–19 in the key of <u>D</u> major. Beginning with beat 3 of m. 19, the same melody is immediately repeated in the home key of <u>G</u> major.

Penguins

Linda Niamath (b. 1939)
Student Workbook 2, p. 50

Musical Waddling

Look at the score as you listen to *Penguins*. Niamath has marked this music "Waddling." Which measures represent the penguins waddling along? mm. <u>1–7</u> <u>10–14</u> <u>18–25</u>

Which hand plays the pattern of their footsteps? <u>LH</u>

How are these notes marked? <u>staccato</u>

Sliding Down Icy Slopes

These penguins like to slide down two different slopes. Find these two slides in the music. mm. <u>8–9</u>

mm. <u>14–17</u>

How long, including the stop, is the first slide (in beats)? <u>8</u>

This slide seems to go down a small dip and then up again.

How can you tell this from the music? <u>The music goes down, then up.</u>

Does the second slide start from the same spot? <u>yes</u>

How long is it (in beats)? <u>16</u>

Does this slide go straight down? <u>yes</u>

A Musical Slide

Let's take another look at these slides.

In a major scale or a minor scale, some of the notes are a <u>whole</u> tone apart, and some are a <u>semi-</u> tone apart.

What is the distance between each note in the penguin slides? <u>a semitone</u>

Write a chromatic scale on the staff below, starting on middle C and going up an octave. Use sharps to raise each note.

Faraway Regions

István Szelényi (1904–1972)
Student Workbook 2, p. 52

Three Staves and Three Sharps

Which hand has the melody? <u>the RH</u>

Is the melody always on the top staff? <u>yes</u>

Why does Szelényi need two staves for the accompaniment in the first two lines? <u>The accompaniment is in two octaves</u>.

Have you ever seen a key signature that looks like this?

Name the three sharps. <u>F</u> <u>G</u> <u>A</u>

What is unusual about them? <u>There is no key with these three sharps.</u>

On the staff below, write the scale found in m. 9 starting on middle C.

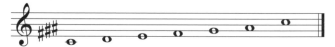

On the staff below, write an ascending C major scale.

Now compare these two scales.

A major scale has <u>seven</u> different notes.

Szelényi's scale has <u>six</u> different notes.

Mark all the semitones. Does Szelényi's scale have any semitones? _no_

Mark all the whole tones. Szelényi's scale has only _whole_ tones.

A Floating Rhythm

Now look at the rhythm of the melody. Does the rhythm stay the same, or are there frequent changes? _it changes_

New Pedal Effects

What marking tells you to use the pedal in this piece? _con pedale_

The LH of m. 4 begins with a _rest_ .

Szelényi uses this pedaling pattern to create a mysterious "breathing" sensation in the music. Look for at least three other places where a similar pedal change is suggested by the writing. mm. _7_ _12_ _15_

The louder notes seem to shine through a blanket of sound, just like stars. Where does Szelényi use an effect like this in *Faraway Regions?*

mm. _2–3, 5–6, 8–11, 13–14_

The Silent Moon

Nancy Telfer (b. 1950)
Student Workbook 2, p. 55

A Musical Companion

Compare *The Silent Moon* to *Sailing by Moonlight*, another piece in this volume. Both pieces are clearly associated with night.

Do these two pieces create a calm or an excited mood? _calm_ Will the sound in these pieces be smooth or detached? _smooth_

Now, rewrite the first four measures of *The Silent Moon* as two measures of $\frac{6}{8}$:

A Calm Key and Accompaniment

What major key has only an F sharp in its key signature? _G_ major

What is the relative minor key of the major key you just named: _E_ minor

Which of the two notes named in your previous answers appears in both the first and last measures? _E_ This means that the piece is likely to be in _E minor_ .

Notice how simple and regular the rhythm of the LH part is. It is written entirely in _quarter_ notes.

Pattern no. 1   Pattern no. 2

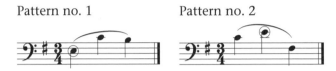

Starts at m. _1_   Starts at m. _9_

Circle the note E in each pattern.

The E is at the top and is played by the thumb in pattern no. _2_ .

The E is at the bottom and is played by the fifth finger in pattern no. _1_ .

Mazurka

Isak Berkovich (1902–1972)
Student Workbook 2, p. 57

The Mazurka Rhythm

The eighth note is marked _staccato_ .

The half note is marked with an _accent_ .

Variations on a Rhythm

List all the measures where you can find each of these variations.

Variation no. 1: mm. _3, 7, 15, 19, 23_

Variation no. 2: mm. _9–10, 13–14_

Major to Minor and Home Again

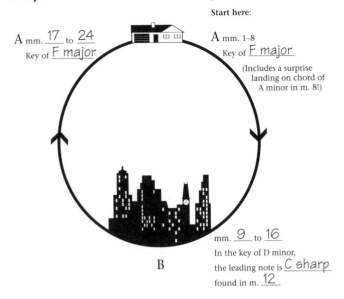

A mm. _17_ to _24_
Key of _F major_

Start here:

A mm. 1–8
Key of _F major_

(Includes a surprise landing on chord of A minor in m. 8!)

mm. _9_ to _16_
In the key of D minor, the leading note is _C sharp_ found in m. _12_.

B

So Long, See You Tomorrow

Yoshinao Nakada (1923–2000)
Student Workbook 2, p. 59

Create a Flowing Bass Line

On the staves below, write out the *lowest* notes played by the LH throughout the piece.

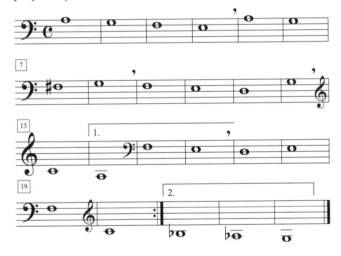

Place a comma at the end of each group of four measures. Within each phrase, do the notes you have written move mostly by step or by skip? _step_

Turkish Bazaar

Mark Mrozinski (b. 1964)
Student Workbook 2, p. 60

An Exotic Musical Destination

From the music examples below, decide which instruments best suit each one, then write your choice on the line beside the example:

percussion

percussion with fifes

fifes

A Special Scale

In a major or minor scale, you will see and hear a mixture of whole tones and semitones (half steps). How far apart are the notes in these scales? _one semitone / half step_

Write a descending chromatic scale on the staff below. Use flats when you need to lower a note:

A Trip through the Bazaar

Think of this music as taking you along a winding pathway through the bazaar. Your trip along this pathway is made up of a number of musical events, listed as a, b, c, etc. Place the letter that best describes what happens in the measures along the path.

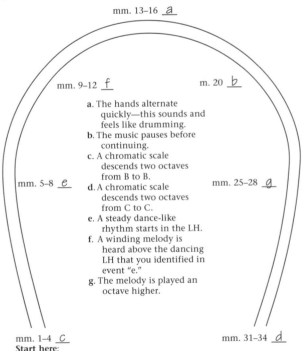

mm. 13–16 _a_

mm. 9–12 _f_

m. 20 _b_

mm. 5–8 _e_

a. The hands alternate quickly—this sounds and feels like drumming.
b. The music pauses before continuing.
c. A chromatic scale descends two octaves from B to B.
d. A chromatic scale descends two octaves from C to C.
e. A steady dance-like rhythm starts in the LH.
f. A winding melody is heard above the dancing LH that you identified in event "e."
g. The melody is played an octave higher.

mm. 25–28 _g_

mm. 1–4 _c_
Start here:

mm. 31–34 _d_

The Argument

Gordon A. McKinnon (b. 1952)
Student Workbook 2, p. 62

The Story
This "argument" between your two hands has a miniature story you can tell through music. Let's call the two voices Right and Left. Here's how the story begins.

 Right makes a statement in mm. 1–2. The first three notes form an E minor triad.

 Left interrupts Right in m. 2 with a B major triad that imitates Right 's statement.

Play these two statements separately. They are similar but not exactly the same.

How do they differ? The RH statement is in a minor key the whole time, whereas the LH statement starts out in a major key, then swithces to minor.

In mm. 4–6, the argument heats up. Left interrupts right again. Their voices become higher and shorter as they struggle to make themselves heard. Compare these short fragments to the original statement. What is the relationship? They are like the last four notes of the original statement.

Finally, in mm. 7–10, right finally drowns out left .

While Left stubbornly holds one long note, Right calms down (*decrescendo* to *mezzo piano*), to make one last point. The sharp in the final measure turns the music from E minor to E major.

Invention in A Minor

Frederick Silvester (1901–1966)
Student Workbook 2, p. 63

Rhythm Game with Metronome

The warmup
Where in the music does this back and forth rhythm stop? m. 13

Two Sections
The invention is divided into two sections. In the first section, the RH has slurs indicating the length of the melodic line.

How many measures does the first slur cover? 4

Is the next melody the same length? yes

Silvester has based his piece on the A minor melodic scale. Write this scale going up (ascending) on the staff below:

A longer melody with a slur returns in m. 13.

Is it the same melody as the first? no

Is it the same length in measures? yes

Does it contain the dotted rhythm? yes

Is the overall rhythm of the melody the same? no

On which beat of the measure does the melody enter for the last time? 2

Invention in C Major

Renée Christopher (b. 1955)
Student Workbook 2, p. 66

Looking for Canon
This little invention can be neatly divided into two four-measure phrases—mm. 1–4 and mm. 5–8. One of these two phrases features strict **canon** between the hands.

Which four-measure phrase has the strict canon? mm. 1 – 4

Which hand begins the canon? right hand
How many beats behind is the other hand?
 2 beats

Compare the starting notes of each hand. How far apart are they? ☑ one octave

Here's an Invention Puzzle to help you discover some of the other fascinating things about how this piece is put together.

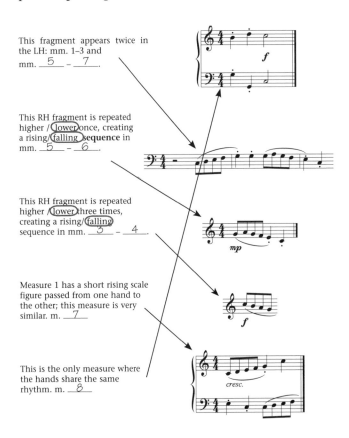

This fragment appears twice in the LH: mm. 1–3 and mm. 5 – 7 .

This RH fragment is repeated higher / (lower) once, creating a rising/(falling) sequence in mm. 5 – 6 .

This RH fragment is repeated higher / (lower) three times, creating a rising/(falling) sequence in mm. 3 – 4 .

Measure 1 has a short rising scale figure passed from one hand to the other; this measure is very similar. m. 7

This is the only measure where the hands share the same rhythm. m. 8

Moderato in C Major, op. 38, no. 5

Johann Wilhelm Hässler (1747–1822)
Student Workbook 2, p. 68

Where does the title *Moderato* come from? <u>the tempo marking</u>

What does *moderato* mean? <u>at a medium (moderate) speed</u>

Looking Closely at Two Melodies
In the first section, which hand plays first? <u>LH</u>

Play the LH (theme A) from mm. 1–4 (only to the first beat). Listen to the sound and look carefully at the notes.

Now play the RH beginning at m. 8 up to the first beat in m. 11:

The notes look a bit different because they are now in the treble clef, but what do you hear? <u>They are the same notes.</u>

Now play theme B with your RH mm. 1–4 (to the first beat). Find this same theme repeated in Section 2: mm. <u>8–11</u>. It is played by the <u>left</u> hand.

By playing the two themes, A and B, you will notice two main differences between them.

1. Direction: A <u>up</u>   B <u>down</u>

2. Major scale pattern: <u>A</u>

   Chromatic scale pattern: <u>B</u>

How many notes are grouped together by each slur? <u>4</u>

Look closely to see if the melodies continue to be upside down later. Look at the LH (theme A) from m. 4 (third beat) to m. 8. Now look at the RH (theme A) from m. 11 to the end.

Where does theme A change in Section 2? m. <u>11 beat 3</u>

Where does theme B change in Section 2? m. <u>11 beat 2</u>

Imitation

What is the interval leap marked with a bracket? <u>perfect 4th</u>

What is the note value circled in the RH? <u>half note</u>

Is the combined value of the tied notes in LH equal to those RH notes? <u>yes</u>

Petit canon No. 2

Claude Champagne (1891–1965)
Student Workbook 2, p. 70

Strict Canon—Or Not?
In this piece, the hands are equal partners. The RH begins the canon.

How far is the LH behind the RH? <u>4 beats</u>

How far is the LH below the RH? <u>one octave</u>

In a strict canon, both parts are exactly the same, at least almost until the end.

Is this a strict canon? <u>yes</u>

Play through the piece, starting both hands at the same time. Are your hands playing the same music throughout? <u>yes</u>

A Smooth Style, but Some Offbeat Rhythm
Mark the beats above the measures printed below, and label each one either S (strong) or W (weak).

Look for notes played on weak beats, but tied or held onto the following strong beats. Circle these notes.

Canon

Cornelius Gurlitt (1820–1901)
Student Workbook 2, p. 71

A Canon

The two voices in Gurlitt's *Canon* are very polite.

Which hand leads the **canon**? _the RH_

In a strict canon, both parts are exactly the same. Is this a strict canon? _no_

Triad Discovery

In the key of A minor, the two most important notes are _A_, the **tonic** (the first note of the scale), and _E_, the **dominant** (the fifth note of the scale).

Look at mm. 1–2. In the example below, some of the notes are circled. These notes form an _A_ minor triad. Write these triads in the blank staff.

Look at mm. 5–6. Find and circle the notes of the E major triad, and write the triad in the blank staff.

A Space to Breathe

Can you find a place where both voices are silent? m. _4_

Now look for spots where one voice is silent. Write the measure numbers below.

RH mm. _1, 3, 4, and 7_

LH mm. _1, 2, 4, 5, and 8_

Jazz Inventions Nos. 1 and 2

Pierre Gallant (b. 1950)
Student Workbook 2, p. 73

Jazz Invention No. 1

A Jazz Sound

A look at the key signature and the final measure will tell you that this piece is (at least partly) in the key of _C major_. But the composer has added several accidentals, and in this invention he gradually adds more of them throughout.

What is the name of the accidental introduced in the first two measures? _D sharp_

What comes next in m. 3? _B flat_

Where does the first accidental disappear? _m. 4_

How long does the second accidental continue? _to the end_

What is the name of the new accidental at m. 5? _G sharp_

Can you find and name two more accidentals near the end? _E flat_ _G natural_

Jazz / Blues Hand Position

If you have tried to play the opening two measures, you will notice that the hands lie on the keyboard in a triad position that represents the key of the piece.
What is the name of the triad? _C major_

Later at m. 5, the hands lie over a new triad. Can you name it? _F major_

The piece starts to move to this new position in m. 3, and gradually in m. 4, the hand stretches out to arrive at m. 5. What is the interval distance from the first triad to the second? _perfect 4th_ Blues melodies are often repeated this same distance higher.

Jazz Imitation

Which type of imitation does Gallant use here? _free_

Jazz Invention No. 2

A Jazz Sound

The key is <u>C major</u> .

Play the last measure.

How many notes in the RH? <u>1</u>

How many notes in the LH? <u>2</u>

Compare the last measure with m. 8 in *Jazz Invention No. 1.*

Is the total number of notes the same? <u>yes</u>

Are the note names the same? <u>yes</u>

Where is the interval of a 3rd here? <u>in the LH</u>

Which note is missing from the triad of the tonic key? <u>the 5th / dominant (G)</u>

Look through the piece, and make a list of all the accidentals you see. List them in the order they appear in the music.
<u>D sharp; E flat; D natural; G sharp; B flat</u>

Play each one to hear how they sound. What do you notice in the first three measures?

Two of these notes sound the same. Which ones?
<u>D sharp and E flat</u>

Are all the accidentals from *Jazz Invention No. 1* used in *Jazz Invention No. 2*? <u>no</u>

Name any that are different: <u>D natural</u>

Can you find two exceptions where accidentals are approached *and* followed by a leap?
m. <u>5</u> and m. <u>7</u>

Jazz / Blues Hand Position

Just as in his first invention, Gallant begins in the triad position of the **tonic** key, which is <u>C major</u> . There is a change afterwards too, but in a slightly different measure.

Where do you see and feel a change of hand position, and what triad position is it? <u>m. 4, F major</u>

Is this the same hand shift as in *Jazz Invention No. 1*? <u>yes</u>

Offbeat Rhythm

Which beats usually share a tied note? <u>2 and 3</u>
Copy one of these rhythms into the staff below. Line up the notes with the beat numbers.

Which measures contain offbeat rhythms in both hands at the same time?
mm. <u>4 and 6</u>

Jazz Imitation

Which type of imitation does *Jazz Invention No. 2* show? <u>free</u>

Where do you think the imitation in *Jazz Invention No. 2* is the most different from its RH motive?
m. <u>6</u>

Student Workbook 3 Answers

Bourrée in D Major

Johann Philipp Kirnberger (1721–1783)
Student Workbook 3, p. 4

Bourrée Dance Character

If you have played a *bourrée*, you will recognize some of the characteristics that *bourrées* have in common. Here is a short list. How many apply to Kirnberger's *Bourrée*?

Popular 18th-century dance   ☑ yes

Lively tempo   ☑ yes

Dance in duple meter with time signature of ¢
☑ no

Quarter-note upbeat   ☑ yes

Four-measure phrases   ☑ yes

Binary form   ☑ yes

Continuing to Count

Clapping is very different from playing, and there are two spots in the RH that make m. 2 tricky to play. Name each tricky feature and the beat it falls on:

<u>trill</u> beat <u>1</u>

<u>dotted rhythm</u> beats <u>3–4</u>

Classical Clues

Kirnberger has added two features to *Bourrée* that are common in Classical style: scales and chords. Find the scales, and identify the key of each scale. Be aware that the scale passages might not begin on the tonic of the key. The accidental <u>G#</u> in the first section suggests a clue to the new key of <u>A major</u> that ends the first section.

m. <u>3</u>	key <u>D major</u>
m. <u>5</u>	key <u>A major</u>
m. <u>6</u>	key <u>A major</u>
m. <u>13</u>	key <u>D major</u>
m. <u>14</u>	key <u>D major</u>

How many different scales did you find? <u>2</u>

Chords are formed by combining notes in many different ways. Notice the RH at m. 9, the beginning of the second section. What is the interval played? <u>3rd</u> Play the two hands together. Name the two chords formed that are circled in the following diagram:

<u>A major</u>   <u>D major</u>

Gavotte in G Major, HWV 491

George Frideric Handel (1685–1759)
Student Workbook 3, p. 7

A Home Run

How many sections are there in *Gavotte in G Major*?
<u>2</u>

Write the measure numbers for the sections below.

A   mm. <u>1</u> – <u>8</u>

B   mm. <u>9</u> – <u>20</u>

Are both sections repeated? <u>yes</u>

The leading note of G major is <u>F sharp</u>.

Fill in the blanks on the diagram to hit a home run.

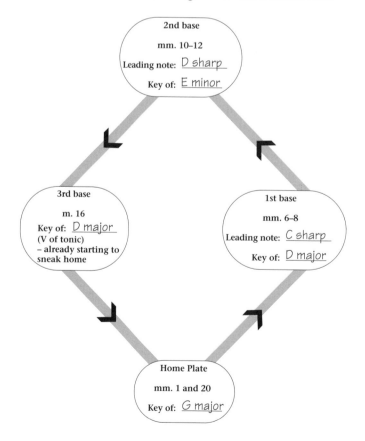

2nd base
mm. 10–12
Leading note: <u>D sharp</u>
Key of: <u>E minor</u>

3rd base
m. 16
Key of: <u>D major</u>
(V of tonic)
– already starting to sneak home

1st base
mm. 6–8
Leading note: <u>C sharp</u>
Key of: <u>D major</u>

Home Plate
mm. 1 and 20
Key of: <u>G major</u>

46

Now, hunt for triads to double check the keys you have chosen. Here's how:

Find three different letter names in all the notes on the first beat of m. 8: <u>D</u>, <u>F sharp</u>, and <u>A</u>.

Now arrange these notes into a triad in root position on the staff:

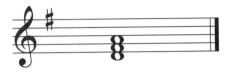

This is the triad of <u>D major</u>. Does this match the key you chose on 1st base? <u>yes</u>

Do the same for m. 12. Write your triad in root position here:

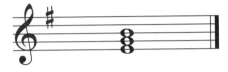

This is the triad of <u>E minor</u>.

An Answering Phrase

Here is the melody of mm. 9–12. Write the beat numbers (1, 2, 3, 4) below the staff.

There are two phrases in this excerpt. How long are these phrases (in beats)? <u>8</u>

A Rising Sequence

Play mm. 17–19, then look again at the score. Notice the repeating patterns in both hands.

On the bass staff below, write in the LH notes on beats 1 and 3 of mm. 17–18, plus beat 1 of m. 19. On the treble staff, write in the RH notes for the same beats.

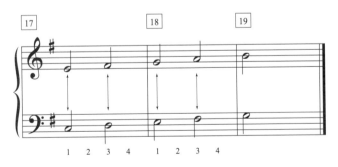

Harlequinade

Johann Ludwig Krebs (1713–1780)
Student Workbook 3, p. 10

Fun Key

Name the flats in this key signature:
<u>B flat</u>   <u>E flat</u>   <u>A flat</u>.

Name the first LH note in m. 1: <u>E flat</u>.

Name the LH note in m. 20: <u>E flat</u>.

These clues will tell you that the piece is in the key of <u>E flat major</u>.

Scale Tricks and Black Key Magic

Find this scale in your music, then circle the notes of the scale on the following diagram.

Is the fingering in the music the same as in the scale? <u>yes</u>

A Leaping Left Hand

What is the interval leap in LH mm. 3 and 6?
<u>one octave</u>

Harlequinade Harmony

Find and name the **triads** in the middle section.

<u>B flat major</u>

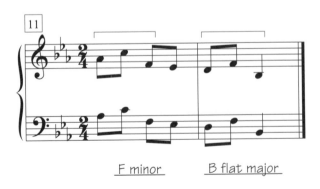

<u>F minor</u>   <u>B flat major</u>

Now write these triads in root position. Identify them by name underneath.

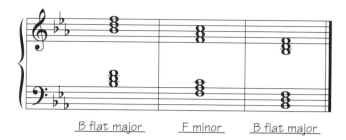

B flat major   F minor   B flat major

Another Clown Piece

In your *Piano Repertoire 3*, you will find a piece called *Clowns* on p. 32. Compare the two pieces and you will find some similarities:

1. Time signature $\frac{2}{4}$

2. LH leaping intervals <u>octaves</u>

3. Rhythmic motive <u>♪♫</u>

4. LH articulation <u>staccato / detached</u>

5. Anything else? <u>slurs, sixteenth notes</u>

Musette in D Major, BWV Anh. 126

attr. Johann Sebastian Bach (1685–1750)
Student Workbook 3, p. 13

A Rhythmic Drone

Which hand plays the drone notes? <u>LH</u>

How many different drone notes are there? <u>three</u>

Besides the D's at the beginning, what are the other drone notes? <u>A</u> and <u>E</u>

The composer has used repeated notes to sustain the sound, and these repeated notes in turn provide a basic rhythm for the dance.

How would you describe this rhythmic drone?

☑ bouncy and energetic

A Boomerang Form

Musette has two sections. Write the measure numbers below.

A   mm. <u>1</u> – <u>8</u>

B   mm. <u>9</u> – <u>20</u>

The A section is in the key of <u>D major</u>.

The B section is in the key of <u>A major</u>.

Does this piece end at m. 20? <u>no</u> When you see the Italian phrase *D.C. al Fine (Da Capo al Fine)*, you know you're not finished yet.

What does this Italian phrase mean in English?
<u>Go back to the beginning and play to Fine</u>.

Where is the end of the dance? m. <u>8</u>

The A section is like a <u>boomerang</u> because it comes back again! This means that this *Musette* actually has three parts: AB <u>A</u>.

Minuet in G Major, BWV Anh. 114

Christian Petzold (1677–1733)
Student Workbook 3, p. 15

A Partnership of Hands

The minuet is a graceful dance in a moderate tempo, with three beats to the measure. In Petzold's *Minuet*, each hand plays an important role.

The <u>left</u> hand provides rhythm for the dancers and creates a harmonic plan for the melody. The <u>right</u> hand provides the melody for the dancers to follow.

There are only two solid (blocked) triads, in m. <u>1</u> and m. <u>32</u>.

Compound Intervals—Just Add Octaves!

The intervals in the following example are parallel 3rds:

Now look at these notes from m. 27:

The notes are the same, but the spacing is different. These intervals are parallel <u>10ths</u>.

Play the intervals in both examples, and listen to the difference in tone.

Do you think the 10ths have a rounder, fuller sound?   ☑ yes

A Melody in Phrases and Sequences

The well-known melody of this minuet has a singing quality. Look at the first two phrases, mm. 1–2 and mm. 3–4.

How are these phrases similar?
<u>The both begin with a descending interval, followed by an ascending scale pattern.</u>

Play through the melody, listening for sequences. Write the measure numbers for each sequence.
mm. 1–4, mm. 5–6, mm. 9–12, mm. 13–16, mm. 17–19, mm. 25–26

Look at the rising eighth-note pattern in m. 1 and in m. 3.
The notes form which major scale? G major

Matching Game

Here are three excerpts from Petzold's *Minuet.* Find each excerpt in the score and write the measure numbers below the excerpt. Play each excerpt, then match it with the description that fits it best.

Excerpt no. 1

mm. 13–16

Excerpt no. 2

mm. 21–24

Excerpt no. 3

mm. 1–4

Excerpt no. 3:
The repeated notes in this excerpt suggest the elegant small steps of a minuet.

Excerpt no. 1:
Petzold uses a sequence to extend the melody all the way to a **cadence** on the **tonic**.

Excerpt no. 2:
An accidental that appears three times in this excerpt takes the music away from the home key. Circle those notes. The accidental is the **leading note** of the new key and rises to the tonic of the new key.

The new key is D major.

Hornpipe in B flat Major, Z T683

Henry Purcell (*ca* 1659–1695)
Student Workbook 3, p. 18

Rhythms for Dancing

The energetic RH rhythms in m. 1 set a bright tone for this dance. Write out the rhythm of m. 1 in this box:

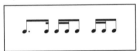

In which other measures does this rhythm reappear exactly?
mm. 1, 2, 3, 5, 6, 7, 11

In which two measures is this rhythm changed slightly? mm. 9 and 10

Write out this rhythmic variation in this box:

Cadences Shape the Music

As you play this piece, listen for the measures you did *not* name in the activity above. In these measures, does the rhythm have mostly shorter or longer rhythmic values? longer

These measures are resting places in the music and contain cadences. A **cadence** is like punctuation at the end of a musical sentence or phrase.
In *Hornpipe*, cadences occur at mm. 4, 8, and 12.

Write out the scale of B flat major, going up one octave, on the staff below (the **tonic** notes are already written for you):

A Perfect Cadence

Here's how to write a perfect cadence of your own.

1. In the RH, write the leading note of B flat major in the first measure, and the tonic (B flat) in the second measure.

2. In the LH, write the **dominant** (the fifth note of the scale of B flat major) in the first measure, and the tonic in the second measure.

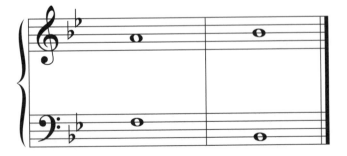

Celebration Series Perspectives® Answer Book

A New Key

When composers want to establish a new key within a piece, they will nearly always do it with a cadence to confirm the key. The second cadence you spotted was in m. _8_, where the last two notes of the RH are _F sharp_ and _G_. Find the scale in which these two notes are the leading note and the tonic. The scale is _G minor_.

This new key is the: ☑ relative minor of B flat major.

Sequences: Patterns Repeated in New Places

In mm. 1–3, a **motive** is presented _three_ times at different pitches. This type of repetition is called a **sequence**. Since each starting note is higher/(lower) than the previous one, this is a rising/(falling) sequence.

Find a group of three measures that contains a rising sequence:
mm. _9_ – _11_

Andantino in A Major, op. 38, no. 31

Johann Wilhelm Hässler (1747–1822)
Student Workbook 3, p. 20

Feeling the Tempo

Let's start with some facts about Hässler's piece:

1. Time signature. _$\frac{3}{8}$_

2. Metronome mark (and note value). _♩.=46-50_

3. Is there a melody? _yes_

4. What is the fastest note value?
   thirty-second notes

The time signatures of $\frac{3}{8}$ and $\frac{6}{8}$ usually imply a lilting pulse. For a swaying or moving tempo in $\frac{3}{8}$, it's necessary to think of the entire measure as one beat. Does the metronome mark indicate that? _yes_

Play the RH melody in mm. 1–8. Does the sixteenth-note scale pattern sound like part of the melody? _yes_

Phrasing and Form

Play motive 1. What happens in mm. 3–4?
The motive is repeated one step lower.

The motive begins again in m. 5, making us think that motive 1 will be repeated. What happens instead? _There is a scale pattern that runs over the bar line_. This is an indication that a new phrase starts in m. 5, and that the phrases are four measures long.

Name the key at the end of the first section.
A major

At m. 9, does the key change? _no_

How does the RH motive at m. 9 and m. 11 compare to m. 1 and m. 3?
They are both repeated a step lower.

Does the melody of mm. 1–8 return in mm. 17–24 (even if not exactly)? _yes_

The double bar lines suggests binary form, but the length of phrases, the return of the A melody, and the cadences in the same key (mm. 8 and 24) suggest _ternary_.

Harmony

The first motive of *Andantino* with its LH accompaniment is built on intervals of a _10th_.

If you move the RH down an octave, what does the interval become? _a 3rd_

Do the two intervals have a similar sound? _yes_

Now look at mm. 17–18.

The RH melody is the same as in mm. 1–2, but the LH looks different. Play only the notes that fall on the beats. What do you hear?
The same sound as in m. 1.

The last two measures (mm. 23–24) are a wonderful example of close harmony in the RH:

The top voice moves stepwise from **dominant** up to **tonic**, and the lower voice moves down by (interval of) _semitones_.

Sonatina in G Major

attr. Ludwig van Beethoven (1770–1827)
Student Workbook 3, p. 23

First Movement: *Moderato*
Sonata Form

What musical sign divides this movement into sections? _repeat sign_

Label the beginning of the music A. This exposition section includes mm. 1–8.

How many themes do you hear? _one_

What is the key of this theme? _G major_

Now label the development section (mm. 9–16) B.

What is the key of the B section? _G major_

Are there any key changes? _no_

Find where the theme returns and label this section A.

Is this recapitulation the same length as the exposition? _yes_

What is the key of this section? _G major_
Label the final section (mm. 25–34) *coda*.

What is the key of this section? <u>G major</u>
Does it reinforce the tonic of the home key? <u>yes</u>

A Musical Patchwork Quilt

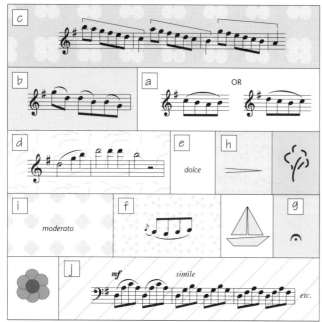

a) This pattern has a note above and below a middle note. It is called a turn and is indicated by the symbol ∿.

b) This pattern forms a falling G major chord.

c) This figure forms a falling sequence.

d) This pattern forms a rising G major chord.

e) This means sweetly.

f) This note is tucked in just before the beat.

g) *fermata*—hold the note longer than its written value

h) *diminuendo*—gradually getting softer

i) Play at a moderate pace.

j) This LH accompaniment pattern of broken chords, rising and falling.

Second Movement: *Romanze*
Smooth Melody . . .

This melody seems smooth because it moves mainly by <u>steps</u>.

What does *cantabile* mean? <u>in a singing style</u>

Explain the touch Beethoven asks for in m. 9.
<u>slightly detached</u>

. . . and Varied Accompaniment

A song usually has an accompaniment.

Which hand plays the accompaniment in this *Romanze*? <u>the LH</u>

The examples below include a divided chord, a rolled chord, and a broken chord. For each example, write in the appropriate description and the measure numbers where it is found in the score.

<u>divided chord</u>
mm. <u>1–2</u>

<u>rolled chord</u>
mm. <u>17–19</u>

<u>broken chord</u>
m. <u>5</u>

A High Note and a Chord

In mm. 16–19, the melody builds toward a climax, or high point. The highest note is emphasized with two signs.

How should you play this note?
<u>longer and with emphasis</u>

Look for a repeating pattern (or **motive**) in the buildup to this note. Mark each repetition of this motive with a bracket:

How many notes make up the motive? <u>four</u> Circle the highest note inside each repetition of the motive.

How far apart are these notes from each other? (3rd)

This is an example of **sequence**. Is it a rising or falling sequence? <u>rising</u>

The LH plays a four-note chord under each of the quarter notes that you identified earlier.

Examine this chord without its top note. The remaining three notes are a triad.
Is it major or minor? <u>major</u>

Now put the top note back on the original chord.

What is the interval between this note and the upper note of the triad? (3rd)

Including the highest and lowest pitches and all the notes in between, how many pitches are there?
<u>seven</u>

The *Coda*

• Compare mm. 27–29 with mm. 37–40. Notice the similarity. What does Beethoven do at the very end to give the movement a sense of completion?
<u>He repeats the tonic chord</u>.

Does this *coda* have a similarity to the *coda* of the first movement? <u>yes</u>

Menuetto II in F Major

Wolfgang Amadeus Mozart (1756–1791)
Student Workbook 3, p. 27

Contrary vs. Parallel Motion

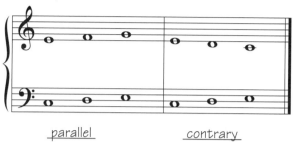

parallel   contrary

In one of the examples above, the hands are moving in opposite directions, or **contrary motion**. In the other, they are moving in the same direction, or **parallel motion**. Place the appropriate label under each example.

Draw arrows between the circled notes in the following example, showing whether the notes rise or fall.

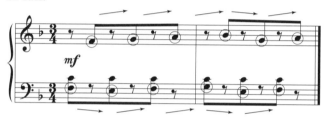

Are the hands moving in mostly parallel or contrary motion? _parallel_

Other Patterns: Sequences . . .

A **sequence** is a fragment of music repeated at a higher or lower pitch level. Here's an example:

Is this a rising or falling sequence? _falling_

. . . and Pedal Tones

A beautiful effect is created when one hand stays on one note (by either holding or repeating it) while the other keeps moving. The stationary note is often called a **pedal tone**.

Find one example in the first half of the *Menuetto*: m. _6_ .

The _right_ hand has the pedal tone.

Is this a repeating or a sustained pedal tone? _repeating_

Finding Cadences

Cadences are resting points in the music; they occur fairly regularly in dance pieces. There are many ways of spotting them. As you might expect, the melody slows down or stops. Often, the LH will play a pattern similar to one of the two following examples:

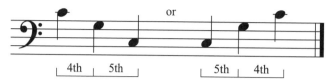

Mark the intervals inside each of the patterns, within the brackets provided.

What is the interval between the highest and lowest notes in each example? _octave_

Complete the *Menuetto* Map

Now it's time to see how Mozart has put together all of these patterns to create a piece of music. Each time one of these patterns occurs, mark it in the correct place on the map. Some of your terms will fit inside one measure; others will stretch over two measures. Choose from the following list of terms:

Parallel motion
Contrary motion
Pedal tone
Sequence
Cadence

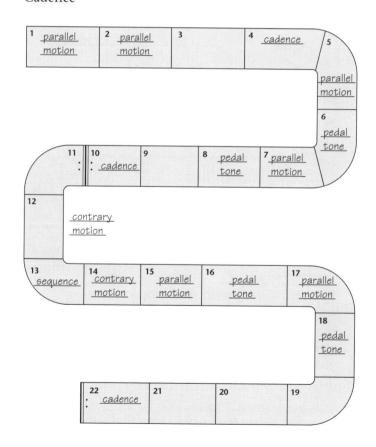

Sonatina in C Major, op. 36, no. 1

Muzio Clementi (1752–1832)
Student Workbook 3, p. 30

First Movement: *Allegro*
Two Themes

Each theme is made up of two **motives** in which you can find a broken triad (T) and a scale passage (S).

Which hand has the T idea in the second theme?
the LH

A Musical Road Map

Using the road map below, see if you can find in your score the landmarks that are the special characteristics of sonata form.

Write the motive letters in the measure blocks for each appearance of the two themes. You will be asked to fill in a few other guideposts along the way as well.

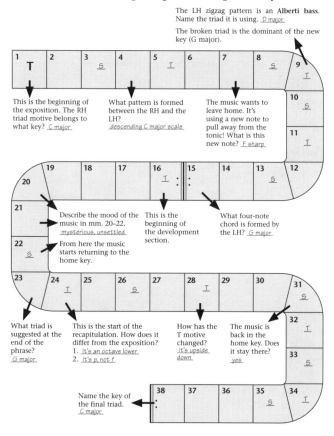

The LH zigzag pattern is an **Alberti bass**. Name the triad it is using. D major

The broken triad is the dominant of the new key (G major).

| 1 T | 2 | 3 S | 4 | 5 T | 6 | 7 | 8 S | 9 T |

This is the beginning of the exposition. The RH triad motive belongs to what key? C major

What pattern is formed between the RH and the LH? descending C major scale

The music wants to leave home. It's using a new note to pull away from the tonic! What is this new note? F sharp

| 10 S |
| 11 T |

19	18	17	16 T	15	14	13 S	12
20							
21							
22 S							

Describe the mood of the music in mm. 20–22. mysterious, unsettled

This is the beginning of the development section.

What four-note chord is formed by the LH? G major

From here the music starts returning to the home key.

23	24 T	25	26 S	27	28 T	29	30	31 S
								32 T
								33 S
38	37	36	35 S	34 T				

What triad is suggested at the end of the phrase? G major

This is the start of the recapitulation. How does it differ from the exposition?
1. It's an octave lower
2. It's p, not f

How has the T motive changed? It's upside down

The music is back in the home key. Does it stay there? yes

Name the key of the final triad. C major

Second Movement: *Andante*
Singing Triplets

What is the time signature of this movement? $\frac{3}{4}$
In this time, eighth notes usually fall into three groups of two, but in this movement, there are three groups of three.

This is because Clementi uses triplet eighths. The italic "3" below the eighth notes in the first measure indicates that three eighth notes are to be played in the time of two. The Italian word simile in m. 2 indicates that this triplet rhythm continues

in the same way through the entire movement. The triplets keep the tempo moving. Which measure has no triplets? m. 12

Accompaniment and Melody

In the opening measures, triplets appear in the LH as a broken triad accompaniment. In m. 4, the accompaniment becomes the melody as well, creating an arpeggio shared between the hands.

In some measures, the melody divides into two voices. Write down the measure numbers where this happens, and name the interval distance between the two voices.

m. 9   3rd apart
m. 11   6th apart
m. 16   3rd apart
m. 23   3rd apart

Third Movement: *Vivace*

What single word would you choose to describe the character of this third movement? lively

Melodic Shapes

Do you notice a melodic pattern that rises and falls many times? yes

Now look at mm. 17–24.

First, look for repeating patterns.

Does the rhythm in mm. 19–20 seem to "answer" the rhythm in mm. 17–18? yes

The rhythm in mm. 17–18 is repeated in mm. 21–22.

The rhythm in mm. 19–20 is repeated (partly) in mm. 23–24.

Of these two "answer" phrases (mm. 19–20 and 23–24), does one sound more like a question? yes

Which one? mm. 19–20 Why?
The notes continue upward.

Which sounds more like an answer? mm. 23–24
Why? It ends on the G

An Interesting Dominant Chord

The bass seems to stay on one note in mm. 24–34.

What is the key through most of these measures?
G major

What note of the scale is this long bass pedal note?
tonic

When does the key begin to change back to the original? m. 30 (HINT: Look for F natural.)

In C major, which note of the scale is this long bass note? dominant

In mm. 34–35, two things happen.

The bass moves from G to C.

The theme from m. 1 returns.

Playing a Complete Sonatina

When you have filled in this chart, you will have a useful summary of what you have learned about Clementi's *Sonatina in C Major*, op. 36, no. 1.

Sonatina in C Major, op. 36, no. 1	Movement 1	Movement 2	Movement 3
Tempo marking	Allegro	Andante	Vivance
Key	C major	F major	C major
Meter	¢	3/4	3/8
Character or mood	Happy, energetic	Sweet and calm	Lively playful

Sonatina in C Major, op. 36, no. 20

Alexander Gedike (1877–1957)
Student Workbook 3, p. 36

Two Contrasting Characters

Here's the first phrase of the "a" theme:

Which words best describe this theme?

☑ sharp and rhythmic ☑ bright

☑ energetic

Where is the second phrase of this theme?
mm. 3–4

Listen to the way the second phrase answers the first.

Can you find the "b" theme? Copy the RH part on the staff below.

What are the measure numbers of this theme?
mm. 5–8

Which words best describe this theme?

☑ gentle ☑ smooth and singing

Mapping the Themes

Now that you are acquainted with these two characters from mm. 1–8, you can complete the sonatina map. Indicate where each theme appears by placing its letter in the measure space on the road. Watch out for variations of the two themes—places where the rhythmic style of a theme reappears but with different notes. Label these "a varied" or "b varied."

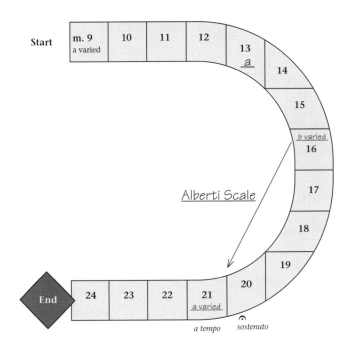

Along the Road

F major C major G major C major

This LH accompaniment pattern is called an Alberti bass.

Does Gedike use it with theme "a" or theme "b"? *b*

Play these triads in solid (blocked) form, and write the name of each triad below the staff.

Where does the following Alberti bass pattern appear? mm. 17–20

Circle the notes on the first and third beats of each measure.

Do these notes move by step? *yes*
What type of scale do they create? *chromatic*
Indicate this pattern as "Alberti scale" on your map.

Coconut Rag

Christopher Norton (b. 1953)
Student Workbook 3, p. 38

The Sound of 4ths and 5ths

Look for other perfect 5ths that occur in the LH throughout the piece. Now, write them on the staff below, starting with the lowest one and placing the others in rising order.

How far is it from each 5th to the next?
☑ up a half step

You will discover that Norton gives an interesting twist to these 5ths. When we **invert** an interval, we turn it upside down so the bottom note becomes the top note. To invert the 5th shown below, simply move the bottom note up an octave, leaving the other note where it is. The new interval is a 4th .

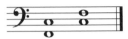

Examine the clues written below, and draw a line from each to the bit of music that it best describes:

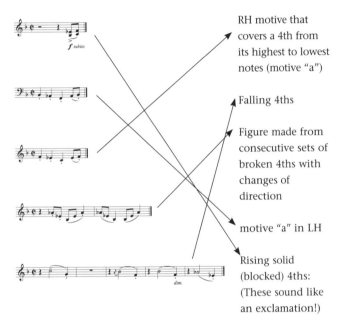

RH motive that covers a 4th from its highest to lowest notes (motive "a")

Falling 4ths

Figure made from consecutive sets of broken 4ths with changes of direction

motive "a" in LH

Rising solid (blocked) 4ths: (These sound like an exclamation!)

Blue Notes

Coconut Rag has a key signature of one flat, and the first and last notes are F . This suggests the key of F major.

Write the ascending scale of this key, but add accidentals to the notes that are consistently flat in the music.

Spiky Rhythms

How would you describe the rhythms of *Coconut Rag*? ☑ biting and sharp

What is the time signature of this piece? ¢

Which note gets the beat? 𝅗𝅥

How many beats are there to a measure? two

Observe the four rhythmic figures shown below. In one of them, a note is played on a weak part of the measure. This shifts the emphasis from the beat to the offbeat, creating an effect called **syncopation**. This offbeat sound is typical of much music written in a jazzy style.

Find this rhythm and circle it. Feel the swing within it, and give full value to the quarter rest.

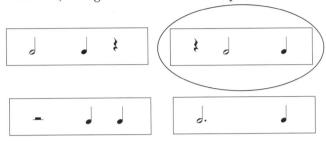

After the Ball, op. 98, no. 13

Alexandr T. Grechaninov (1864–1956)
Student Workbook 3, p. 41

A Dancing Rhythm

One of the most popular ballroom dances is the waltz. At first glance you might think this piece is a waltz because the time signature is $\frac{3}{4}$. However, the tempo marking is *tempo di mazurka* , and the rhythm has a special character. This piece is not a waltz; it's a mazurka.

Play the first eight measures of the RH melody. Which beat of the measure seems to be emphasized? 2

How does Grechaninov do this?
 by using a half note

In *After the Ball*, Grechaninov uses both a long dotted rhythm and a short dotted rhythm. Find these measures in the music and write the measure numbers beside each example:

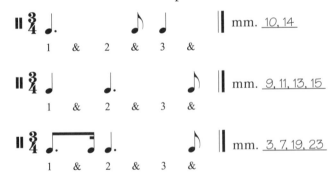

mm. 10, 14

mm. 9, 11, 13, 15

mm. 3, 7, 19, 23

Jumping!

This little exercise will help your LH land in the right place in mm. 9–14.

Keep your second finger on A and use your wrist to swing your hand from side to side.

Name the intervals below and above A:
below <u>6th</u>　above <u>5th</u>.

Clues for Keys

What is the key of *After the Ball*?

Clue no. 1:
The first clue to finding the key of a piece of music
is to look at the key signature.
The key signature is <u>F sharp, C sharp</u> so the major
key would be <u>D major</u>.

Clue no. 2:
The second clue for finding a key is the presence of
accidentals.
The accidentals in mm. 1–3 are <u>E sharp</u> and
<u>A sharp</u>.

An accidental often—but not always—indicates that
the music is in a minor key. The accidental could be
the raised note (the leading note) of the minor scale.

If the accidentals occur near the beginning of the
piece, that minor key is very likely related to the
major key with the same key signature. You can
find the relative minor of a major key by counting
<u>down</u> three semitones.

Clue no. 3:
The third clue for finding a key is seen in the first
and last notes of the music, especially in the bass.
Music usually starts and ends on the **tonic** or on a
note of the tonic triad.

Name the notes in m. 1 <u>D, F sharp</u>.

Name the notes in m. 24 <u>(B), D</u> and circle the lower
bass note.

Now, put all these clues together.
The key of *After the Ball* is <u>B minor</u>.

To confirm your answer, take another look at the
two accidentals in mm. 1–3.

Which one is the leading note of B minor? <u>A sharp</u>

The Song of Twilight

Yoshinao Nakada (1923–2000)
Student Workbook 3, p. 43

Paint the Picture with a Scale . . .

Write out each of the LH bottom notes in mm. 1–4
and in beat 1 of m. 5. Write each note only once,
even though they are repeated in the music.

Which scale do these notes form? <u>A major</u> Does
the scale rise or fall? <u>fall</u>

How might this scale suggest twilight? <u>It makes you
imagine the sun setting</u>.

. . . and a Change of Key

Play the piece through m. 12 (the end of the first
ending).

Did you hear a slight change of mood or color from
m. 9? <u>yes</u>

Nakada has changed the key of the music in this
section. To find out what this new key is, look for
telltale triads. At the beginning, the two hands
form a triad.

Write it here:

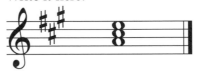

This is the triad of <u>A major</u>.

Now go to m. 9, and name the notes of the LH
chord. <u>C sharp, F sharp, A</u>

Write these notes as a root-position triad (with notes
on successive lines or spaces):

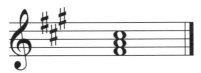

This is the triad of <u>F sharp minor</u>.

Nakada has used a new key in mm. 9–12. He is able
to create this new key without using any accidentals
because this key is the relative minor of the
opening major key. The two keys share the same
key signature.

This <u>F sharp minor</u> triad occurs frequently in
mm. 9–12. It is the **tonic** triad of the key of <u>F sharp</u>
minor. The movement of the RH in m. 12 from C
sharp (**dominant**) to F sharp (tonic) reinforces this
key.

This first ending serves as a contrasting middle
section of the piece. This music, therefore, has three
sections.

Write the measure numbers below.

A　mm. <u>1</u> – <u>7</u>

B　mm. <u>8</u> – <u>12</u>

A　mm. <u>1</u> – <u>7</u> and 2nd ending

The Elegant Toreador

Seymour Bernstein (b. 1927)
Student Workbook 3, p. 45

Tambourines and Stamping Feet

What are the two intervals used in RH mm. 1–3?
_2nd_ and _3rd_

Why does the first interval catch your attention?
Pieces often do not begin on 2nds.

Toreadors stamp their feet while they wave their capes. Spanish dancers also stamp their feet a lot.

Find a stamping rhythm in two places on the first page of the music.

mm. _4–5_   mm. _8–9_

How are these notes marked, and what does this marking mean?

accents — play these notes with more emphasis

Glissandos and Suspense

What might the toreador be doing during the _glissando?_ _jumping out of the way_

Notice the fermata in m. 20. This measure of silence is a very dramatic. What might be happening?
waiting for the bull to charge

Final Elegance

It is appropriate for music about an elegant toreador to have an elegant ending. Bernstein has decorated the last chord with a written-out ornament, a turn. The notes turn above and below the principal note in a very elegant manner.

What Spanish instrument does this ending sound like? _guitar_

Douce amie

Sweet Friend

Mel. Bonis (1858–1937)
Student Workbook 3, p. 47

Melody and Accompaniment . . .

Look for the melody in the first few lines of the music. Is it in the RH or LH? _LH_

The other hand has a background of repeating tones. Repeated notes can be played in various ways. Which style might best contribute to the mood of this music?
☑ smooth, connected sounds

Where do the melody and accompaniment switch hands? mm. _10_ – _16_

Now find the place where the melody and accompaniment return to their original hand.
m. _18_

. . . Create a Form

Based on the patterns of the melody and accompaniment, which one of the following patterns best describes _Douce amie?_
☑ A B A₁

A Closer Look At the Accompaniment

On the staff below, write the top notes played in the RH from m. 19 to the end. Write each note only once; don't write the repeated notes.

There is one passage in this piece where the accompanying hand seems to divide into two parts:
mm. _12_ – _14_

One of the parts continues with the accompaniment while the other plays a short melody in longer notes moving stepwise in an ☐ ascending or ☑ descending pattern.

Play

Béla Bartók (1881–1945)
Student Workbook 3, p. 49

Melody and Rhythm

Look at the melody and rhythm of the opening four measures. In the first eight measures, the _staccato_ chord plays on beat _2_. Play this LH pattern and then try using your feet to imitate the rhythm. You will notice that you have to _jump up_ on beat 1 in order to land on beat 2.

Write the tonic triad here:

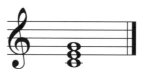

Where do you see part of a scale pattern? m. _3_

A Dramatic Change

Something exciting must be happening in mm. 19–32.

Does the Italian marking _più mosso_ mean that the tempo gets faster or slower? _faster_

Can you find the measures where the children might be clapping their hands together or stomping their feet? mm. _21_ – _22_ and _25_ – _26_
The accidentals indicate new triads. Composers often use accidentals to create intensity or to highlight a particular idea. Play the LH triads in mm. 27–28.

On the staff below, write these triads in root position and name them:

B flat major   A major

The triads move: ☑ down

By what distance? _a semitone_

What might the children be doing here?
playing hopscotch or leapfrog

What does *Tempo I* mean? _back to the first tempo_

Touch
Bartók gave precise indications for touch. There are very few notes in *Play* that do not have some form of marking.
How many different markings do you see? _4_

Match the name of the touch with its definition:

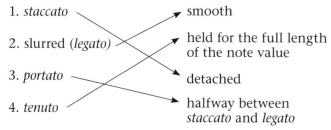

1. *staccato*   smooth
2. slurred (*legato*)   held for the full length of the note value
3. *portato*   detached
4. *tenuto*   halfway between *staccato* and *legato*

Call and Echo
There are many short call-and-echo places in the piece. Find them and write their measure numbers below. One example is written in for you.
1. mm. 9–10 *mf*: mm. 11–12 *p*
2. _mm. 13–14 mf: mm. 15–16 p_
3. _mm. 41–42 p: mm. 43–44 pp_
4. _mm. 45–46 p: mm. 47–48 pp_

Now, have a second look at the measures you have noted. Is the echo an exact copy, or are there small differences? _There are small differences_.

What are the differences?
The LH accompaniment changes in the echo.

The Sleeping Dragon
Nancy Telfer (b. 1950)
Student Workbook 3, p. 51

The Breath of a Dragon
As the music begins, you have just come across a sleeping dragon. Play mm. 1–6 and listen to the shape of the rhythm. Can you hear the dragon breathing in and out?

Can you see his chest rise ↑ and fall ↓ with each breath?

Is each breath the same length? _no_

Rhythm
Notice that the piece is in three sections.

How does the composer show the division of the sections? _double bar lines_

What happens in the last section?
It sounds like the beginning of the piece.

The large middle section is very different from the first and last sections. Name three differences.

1. _Time signature $\frac{3}{4}$_
2. _Staccato touch_
3. _Triads_

In the middle section, the rhythm becomes more definite, and the pulse quickens.

The phrase created by this short rhythmic motive is four measures long. The composer shows the building of excitement by lengthening the phrases.

How long are they? _8 measures_

Harmony
What is the key of the piece? _A minor_

When the dragon starts to dream, you will see and hear 3rds (double notes or partial chords) in the bass clef.

What happens at m. 11?
The 3rds become triads as the RH joins in.

At m. 15, the composer begins to "spread out" the chords as the action becomes more and more intense. The chords are based on triads but they have four notes. In a four-note chord, one note of the triad is doubled. The chord in m. 15 is A minor. The name of the doubled note is _C_.

In your score, write the name of the lowest note in each measure from m. 15 through m. 30. Play the chords and listen to the sound.

Do you hear any major chords in this section? _no_

58

Chromatic Movement

Measures 31–34 show **chromatic** movement in the RH. This pattern is often used to describe something happening in the story.

What do you think is happening here?
<u>The dream is ending.</u>

Clowns, op. 39, no. 20

Dmitri Kabalevsky (1904–1987)
Student Workbook 3, p. 53

Alternating Moods

Draw a line from each of the musical moves shown below to the "clown move" that best describes it:

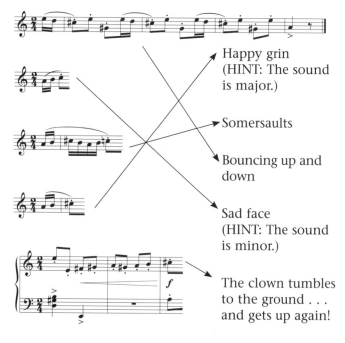

Happy grin
(HINT: The sound is major.)

Somersaults

Bouncing up and down

Sad face
(HINT: The sound is minor.)

The clown tumbles to the ground . . . and gets up again!

Alternating Notes

Kabalevsky has built *Clowns* on several repeating patterns in which one or more notes change back and forth. For example, in the repeating pattern in the RH, mm. 1–4, an accidental is alternately added and removed.

Name the two alternating notes in this pattern.
<u>C sharp</u> and <u>C natural</u>

Let's take a closer look at this pattern.

In the RH, mm. 1–4, the lowest note is <u>A</u> ;

the highest note is <u>E</u> .

Here are the two alternating groups of notes shown as triads:

The first triad is the **tonic** triad in the key of <u>A major</u> .

The second triad is the tonic triad in the key of <u>A minor</u> .

Now look at the RH of mm. 9–12.
The lowest note is <u>A flat</u> ; the highest note is <u>F</u> .

Here are the two alternating groups of notes shown as triads. (Notice that the high F has been lowered an octave in this example.)

The first triad is the tonic triad in the key of <u>F major</u> .

The second triad is the tonic triad in the key of <u>F minor</u> .

Left-hand Ostinato

The repeating LH pattern in mm. 1–8 is called an *ostinato.*

What two intervals are formed between the top E and the two lower notes?
<u>perfect 5th</u> and <u>perfect 8ve</u>

These two lower notes are the tonic and **dominant** of <u>A</u> major or <u>A</u> minor.

Where does the *ostinato* shift to a different pitch? m. <u>9</u>

These two lower notes are the tonic and dominant of <u>F</u> major or <u>F</u> minor.

In mm. <u>13–16</u> and <u>24–25</u> , the *ostinato* disappears.

In these measures, the LH plays <u>chords</u> instead of single notes, and the markings are <u>tenuto</u> , <u>staccato</u> , and <u>accent</u> .

Kabalevsky has cleverly combined all these features to create one of the most well-loved and often-played pieces in the piano repertoire!

Echoes of November

Stephen Chatman (b. 1950)
Student Workbook 3, p. 55

Atmosphere

The tempo marking <u>reflective</u> tells us something. Perhaps Chatman is thinking back and remembering something about November.

Musical Echoes

What musical signs indicate the echo?
dynamincs: p–pp

Can you find other echoes in the piece? _yes_

Where? _mm. 8–10, mm. 14–15_

In mm. 1–2, the RH notes look the same, but there is something different about the LH.

Is the echo exactly the same? _no_

Is there something different other than dynamics? _yes_

Think of mm. 1 and 2 as an introduction. How do these measures compare to the two-measure melody that begins in m. 3? There is a matching section at m. _14_. This is like an epilogue that ties up loose ends in a story. Is it exactly the same as the introduction? _no_

Atmospheric Key

You see a key signature with _five_ flats. What is the key of the piece? _D flat major_

Have you ever studied a piece in this key? _no_

Name the *flat* names of the black keys that you see on the piano keyboard, beginning with the first one after middle C: _D flat, E flat, G flat, A flat, B flat_

Are the names of the flats in the key signature the same as what you see on the piano? _yes_

In the key signature, are they in a different order from the scale? _yes_
Which notes are *not* flat? _C_ _F_

Name the LH notes in m. 2. _F flat, C flat_ Notice the accidentals. Play those LH notes. Both notes are played on black /(white keys)

Black and White Keys

Is the sound of Exercise 1 different from the sound of Exercise 2? _yes_

Which one sounds like the scales that you already know? _Excercise 2_

Melody

Chatman has chosen a time signature of _6/8_ and a _dotted_ rhythm to make sure the melody moves forward.

Accompaniment

Chatman uses many triads to accompany the melody, and some intervals of _6th_ and a _perfect 5th_. Most of these chords and intervals belong to the home (or **tonic**) key, D flat. Remember the "outsiders?" (note names) _F flat, C flat_ They have been waiting silently for most of the piece, but they appear at the end in m. _15_. What do these strangers add to the music? _tone color, dissonance_

The triads create a beautiful harmonic language in the piece. They appear in the LH first, then in the RH at m. _5_. The direction of the triads is always down /(up). What else about them is the same?
The notes appear in the same order.

White Sand

Christopher Norton (b. 1953)
Student Workbook 3, p. 58

Calypso Rhythm
Observe the following set of rhythms:

How would you need to alter the above to match the first measure of *White Sand*?

☑ Displace the note on beat 2 into the second half of the beat

Calypso Harmony—Follow Those Roots!
White Sand is written in the key of _B flat major_.

On the staff below, write each of the pitches indicated (the first is done as an example):

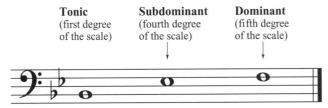

The pattern of the first measure in the LH starts on the _tonic_. Now, transpose the pattern so that it starts on each of the other two scale degrees you added above.

Pattern starting on _subdominant_   Pattern starting on _dominant_

Look for these patterns in *White Sand*. You should find the pattern in some form in mm. _1–8, 12–19, 21–22, 28–35._

As you learn the piece, you will notice that the music is grouped into four-measure phrases, and that these phrases are shaped, in large part, by the patterns you explored above.

How many phrases have a I–IV–V–I pattern? _4_
How many phrases have a IV–I–V–I pattern? _1_
How many phrases have a V–I–V–I pattern? _1_
How many phrases have a V–V–IV–I pattern? _none_

The Haunted Castle

Boris Berlin (1907–2001)
Student Workbook 3, p. 60

A Picture in Sound

As you listen to the piece, let the sounds suggest a picture.
Is the sound   ☑ high

How does Berlin create the sighing effect in mm. 2 and 4? <u>with a diminuendo, and moving from high chords to low</u>

Five Whole Tones Create Atmosphere

The *staccato* chords in mm. 1 and 3 create a floating, shimmering effect.

One reason for this is that they are based on a whole-tone scale. In a whole-tone scale, there are no semitones. On the staff below, write a five-note scale using the notes in the RH of m. 1:

Are these notes all a whole tone apart? <u>yes</u>

Intervals and Chords

In mm. 1–4, both hands play a series of parallel intervals.

The intervals are <u>3rds</u> .

When the hands are combined, you will hear beautiful chords. Look carefully at mm. 4 and 5.

Play each chord as written. Listen to the sound. Do they sound the same or (slightly different)?

Compare the notes of chord "a" and chord "b."

Which note in "b" does not appear in "a"? <u>G</u>

Which chord is the same as the first chord in the piece (m. 1)? <u>a</u>

Now look at chord "c."

Which one note in "a" and "b" does not appear in "c"? <u>D</u>

Is the sound of chord "c" more familiar than the others? <u>yes</u>

Pedaling *Staccato*

Berlin has written pedal markings throughout the score. The combination of pedal and *staccato* may seem unusual, but this pedaling technique gives the notes a bell-like quality. As an experiment, play a few of these chords *legato* with pedal, then *staccato* with pedal.

Can you hear the difference? <u>yes</u>
Now try longer and shorter *staccatos* with pedal.

Does the sound ring out even more with the shorter *staccatos*? <u>yes</u>

Morning Prayer, op. 39, no. 1

Pyotr Il'yich Tchaikovsky (1840–1893)
Student Workbook 3, p. 63

A Four-Part Choir

Have you ever sung in a choir or heard a choir perform? A choir is made up of different parts, or voices. The singers in the choir are divided into groups based on the range of their voices. A children's choir is often divided into Soprano 1, Soprano 2, Alto 1, and Alto 2.

Which voice is the highest?   <u>Soprano 1</u>
Which voice is the lowest?   <u>Alto 2</u>

Adult choirs are usually divided into four parts, but the names are different because men's voices are deeper.

What does the abbreviation SATB stand for?
S <u>Soprano</u> A <u>Alto</u> T <u>Tenor</u> B <u>Bass</u>

Which voice usually has the melody? <u>Soprano</u>

These four voices singing together produce the beautiful **harmony**.

Can you see four "voices" in *Morning Prayer*?

Which voices do the RH play?
<u>Soprano</u>   <u>Alto</u>

Which voices do the LH play?
<u>Tenor</u>   <u>Bass</u>

Singing the Melody

What is the Italian musical term that means "in a singing style"? <u>cantabile</u>

Place your RH fingers over the first notes. What is the interval? <u>3rd</u>

Sometimes one of the lower voices has an important melody. The lowest voice (bass) has its own melody in mm. <u>10–12</u> . The accented E flats in the tenor voice of mm. <u>17, 19</u> suggest the tolling of a bell.

Pedal and Pedal Point

The word "pedal" has another meaning.

What is the key of *Morning Prayer*? <u>G major</u>
What is the tonic of that key? <u>G</u>
What is the repeated note in mm. 16–21? <u>G</u>

When a bass note is repeated or held for several measures, it is called a pedal tone.

A pedal tone is usually on the tonic or the dominant of the key.

The pedal tone in this piece is on the <u>tonic</u>.

Funny Puppy

Anne Crosby (b. 1958)
Student Workbook 3, p. 65

Lively Refrains

The opening section of *Funny Puppy* returns several times, like a refrain.

How long is this refrain? <u>5 measures</u>

How many measures go by before you spot the opening measure again? <u>5</u>

Now, let's follow this puppy as he runs around the yard. Study these music examples and fill in the blanks below.

Opening refrain: mm. 1– <u>5</u>

Opening refrain repeated: mm. <u>6</u> – <u>10</u>

How is it different this time?
<u>It is two octaves lower, below the LH.</u>

Measures 11–14: Refrain . . . or something else?

mm. <u>15</u> –end. This is the last statement of the refrain, with a few extra measures added.

To find out if mm. 11–14 are the refrain, compare these measures with the beginning. Find the place in the musical fragments that matches the description best, and add the measure numbers:

Accompaniment of solid *staccato* chords: mm. <u>1–10</u>

Accompaniment of smooth broken chords: mm. <u>11–14</u>

Melody: *staccato* and jumpy: mm. <u>1–10</u>

Melody: smooth: mm. <u>11–14</u>

Your conclusion: mm. 11–14 are the refrain / (a new section.)

Some Funny Rhythms

Funny Puppy starts in a lively $\frac{4}{4}$ meter with four quarter-note beats, each of which can be divided into <u>two</u> eighth notes. Sometimes this simple rhythm is disrupted a little, as though the puppy was tripping over his small legs. What other time signature can you find in this piece? <u>$\frac{7}{8}$</u> It appears <u>4</u> (how many?) times.

Hybrid meter can be organized in a variety of ways. Three possible ways of grouping together eighth notes in $\frac{7}{8}$ time are shown below. Play one of the $\frac{7}{8}$ measures from *Funny Puppy*. How does the puppy organize his eighth notes? (Circle one.)

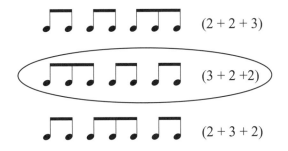

There's another hybrid meter that is not as obvious. It's in one of the $\frac{4}{4}$ measures between m. 16 and the end. Play this section and listen for a $\frac{4}{4}$ measure that seems somehow different. It's in m. <u>19</u>.

How are the groups of threes and twos organized?
<u>3+3+2</u>

Yes Sir!

Clifford Crawley (b. 1929)
Student Workbook 3, p. 67

March Beat and Rhythm

Play mm. 1–8 with the LH alone in a fairly slow tempo, using your RH to tap out the time signature of <u>4</u> beats in a measure.

Perhaps it is a hot day and the kids do not feel much like marching. Some of them are fooling around. The band is playing though, and you will recognize the thumping rhythm of low bass notes. Which percussion instrument might be used— (Bass drum) / Triangle?

The march continues at a steady pace until . . . Which measure contains nothing but a rest? _m. 9_ But wait, what is the time signature here? _2/4_

Musical Rhythm that Imitates Words

If you say the words "Yes Sir" out loud, you will hear a definite rhythm of equal beats because each word is short and contains one syllable only. Try *shouting* the words. Then look at m. 10. This looks like a question and answer.

Which hand speaks the loudest? _RH_

Which hand answers? _LH_

What is the interval between the slurred notes? _perfect 5th_

The hand speaking the loudest could represent the teacher shouting at one of the students in the group for not keeping in step. What kind of voice does the student use to respond: louder or (softer)? His little joke that he keeps to himself is that he only pretends to be respectful to the teacher. In m. 11, he falls back into line.

Does the march continue exactly like the beginning? _no_

What sign indicates a change? _8va_

The Rest Counts!

An unusual effect is created by the composer to indicate an interruption in the march (in two places): mm. _9_ and _20_. What is the time value of the rest in these places: does the rest represent two beats? _____ four beats? _____ a whole measure of rest? _✔_

March style in music usually continues steadily in a time signature of _4/4_ .

End of Story

How does the story end? After the measure of silence in m. _20_, there seems to be a little joke between the student and the teacher.

Student Workbook 4 Answers

Air in D Minor, HWV 461

George Frideric Handel (1685–1759)
Student Workbook 4, p. 4

Find a Sequence
On the staff below, write the highest and lowest notes of each measure. Write them in the order that they actually occur within each of the measures. The lowest note of m. 2 has been written as an example:

Observe the layout of the notes above.

In each measure, the interval between the two notes you have written is an _octave_ .
Overall, is this a rising or a falling sequence? _falling_

There are some interesting things to discover about the shape of the melody in the RH in this section. Look at the music again, then circle the appropriate word in each sentence below:
When the melody leaps an octave, it (rises)/ falls.
When there are added notes within the octave, the melody rises /(falls).

Rhythmic Excitement
Here is the rhythm of the RH in mm. _1_ – _2_ . Write the beats (1 & 2 & 3 &) under the second of these measures:

Which measure features a note played on "and" that is then held over onto the next beat? m. _2_

This is an example of **syncopation**. Listen for its effect as you play.

In Handel's *Air*, syncopation occurs throughout the (first half)/ second half.

A Steady Beat
Most of the time, the LH plays _quarter_ notes and _eighth_ notes underneath the melody.

Just to keep you on your toes, Handel has inserted a dotted quarter-note–eighth-note rhythm in three places: mm. _1_, _4_, and _6_ .

Try tapping the LH part alone and then together with the RH part in these measures.

Did the LH rhythm help you to keep the pulse steady? _yes_

Fantasia in E Minor, TWV 33:21

Georg Philipp Telemann (1681–1767)
Student Workbook 4, p. 6

Two-Part Form
This piece has two contrasting themes. Here is the first part of each theme. Match each theme to the description that fits it best, and fill in the rest of the blanks.

Theme A

Theme B

Theme _A_
This theme has a bouncy dance style characterized by _rising_ quarter notes in the _right_ hand. It first appears in mm. _1 and 2_, and it is repeated in mm. _11 and 12_ .

Theme _B_
This theme has a _playful_ mood. It is characterized by a rhythmic figure that the two voices toss back and forth.

In the beginning theme, energy is created by the interval of a rising 5th in the RH and then the falling 4th in m. 3. Both of these intervals reinforce the key of _E minor_ .

Now that you have found the two themes, you can make a chart of the form. Include all the repeats in your chart.

A	mm.	1	–	4
A	mm.	1	–	4
B	mm.	5	–	10
A	mm.	11	–	14
B	mm.	5	–	10
A	mm.	11	–	14

This type of form is called **rounded binary**. The form is binary because the music is divided into main sections by the _repeat_ signs. The binary form is called rounded because the _A_ theme returns part way through the second section to round it out.

Imitation and Sequence at the Same Time

Look again at theme B. The voices _imitate_ each other.

Let's look at what is different about the imitation in mm. 5 and 7.
The notes in m. 5 are _the same_, while the notes in m. 7 are _different_.

Which measure shows exact imitation? m. _5_

Now look at the melody in mm. 7–9:

Does this pattern repeat itself by rising? _no_ falling? _yes_

The interval between the first note of each measure (each repetition) is _minor 3rd_.

What is the name of the pattern created in the RH melody mm. 7–9? _sequence_

You have already seen imitation in the LH. Using the same rhythmic pattern for both sequence and imitation, Telemann combines them in mm. _5_, _7_, and _8_.

March in D Major, BWV Anh. 122

Carl Philipp Emanuel Bach (1714–1788)

Student Workbook 4, p. 9

March Time

What is the Italian name for the time signature of this march? _alla breve_
Which note gets one beat? _half note_

Mix and Match

1. Play each excerpt, then find where it is in the score.
2. Match the example with the description that fits best, and write in the measure numbers.
3. Answer the question about the excerpt.
4. Read the performance suggestion below the description, then practice the passage (as well as any similar passages).

Excerpt _3_: mm. _13–16_
- a rising **sequence**
- How many times is the motive repeated? _3_

Excerpt _5_: mm. _14–16_
- a rising **chromatic** passage
- What is a chromatic scale? _a scale that moves by semitones_

Excerpt _1_: mm. _1–2_
- a **syncopated** rhythm
- What is syncopation? _displaced accents_

Excerpt _6_: m. _7_
- an ornament added for emphasis near the end of the first section
- Name this ornament. _trill_

Performance suggestion: Play the ornament quickly, then play it more slowly. Which way highlights the cadence best? _slowly_

Excerpt _4_: mm. _10–11_
- the opening motive repeated in the key of _A major_
- The **tonic** note of this new key is the _dominant_ of the home key.

Excerpt _2_: mm. _21–22_
- the sound of trumpets and drums

Minuet in D Minor, BWV Anh. 132

attr. Johann Sebastian Bach (1685–1750)

Student Workbook 4, p. 11

A Minuet in Binary Form

Like most dance forms, this minuet has two sections.
Write the measure numbers here.
A mm. _1_ – _8_
B mm. _9_ – _16_

Melody and Harmony

Before you play the piece, look for clues in the printed music that will indicate the character and style of the minuet. Each hand plays one independent voice, or line of music.

Which hand plays the more song-like, melodic line?
 _RH_

Do you notice the short and long slurs marked in the RH? Imagine this line played by an instrument other than a keyboard.

What might it be? _flute, violin_

How can you imitate the sound of that instrument in your own playing?
 legato or cantabile playing; observe the phrasing

The other hand plays an equally important role. This voice provides a foundation for the melody. Together with the RH, its notes create harmony. What instrument could you imagine playing the lower part? _cello, bass, bassoon_

Find Some Important Notes

Look again at the LH part.
What do you notice about the first five notes?
 They resemble a scale.
If you were to continue going up after the fifth note, what scale would you be playing? _D minor_

Notice that the rising LH pattern ends on the fifth note, the _dominant_ of the scale, in m. 3.
Notice that m. 4 contains the first note of the scale, the _tonic_ .

Cadences in Two Keys

As you play through this minuet, you will also hear a cadence at the end of the A section and at the end of the B section.

In D minor, the tonic note is _D_ , the dominant note is _A_ .
In F major, the tonic note is _F_ , the dominant note is _C_ .

Now look through *Minuet in D Minor* and identify the cadences and the keys at each of the following points:

Cadence: _Perfect_
Key: _D minor_

Cadence: _Perfect_
Key: _F major_

Cadence: _Perfect_
Key: _D minor_

A Leaping Right Hand

The B section opens with a leaping figure in the RH, mm. 9–10.

This figure is repeated in mm. _11_ – _12_ .

How much lower or higher is the repeated figure?
 3rd lower

When a figure is repeated at a different pitch, this repetition is called a _sequence_ .

Rigadoon in A Minor

William Babell (*ca* 1690–1723)
Student Workbook 4, p. 14

A Rigadoon

1. Time signature: The ¢ indicates _two_ beats per measure. This means fewer beat divisions in the measure than ⁴⁄₄, giving the feel of freer, easier movement.
2. Starting on an upbeat: Try this experiment:
    a) Begin the first four-measure phrase on beat 1 (omitting the upbeat) and end on m. 4, beat 3.
    b) Begin the first four-measure phrase as written, on the upbeat.

Which version gives the beginning of the phrase more energy and movement? _b_

There is another reason why the listener hears a "push" from the upbeat toward the first beat of m. 1. The piece is in A minor.

What degree of the scale (and its name) is the upbeat? _5 (dominant)_

What degree of the scale (and its name) is the first note in m. 1? _1 (tonic)_

Two Phrases, Two Textures

Here is the opening motive of the first phrase:

The LH copies the RH _2_ beats later.

Now, find a measure where the RH and LH notes together form a C major triad: m. _9_.

What is the length (in measures) of a single imitative phrase? _4_

What is the length of a single triadic phrase? _6_

Ternary Form

A musical structure that has three parts is called a **ternary form** (ABA). Fill out the following chart: list each phrase (noting measure numbers and letter name A or B); identify the type of upbeat, and name the key. Notice that all the phrases appear in pairs, like twins.

Phrase	Imitation (A) or Triads (B)	Type of Upbeat	Key
mm. 1–4	A	♩	A minor
mm. _5–8_	A	♩	_A minor_
mm. _9–14_	B	♫	_C major_
mm. _15–20_	B	♫	_C major_
mm. 21– _24_	A	♩	_A minor_
mm. _25–28_	A	♩	_A minor_

A Surprise Ending

There are small differences between the four A phrases in this piece, but the last one has a big difference. Play the last phrase.

What note do you hear that is not part of the A minor key? _C sharp_

Write the triads of A minor and A major on the staff below.

A minor triad   A major triad

Which triad does Babell use in m. 28? _A major_
In a minor triad, the interval between the two lower notes is a _minor_ 3rd.

In a major triad, the interval between the two lower notes is a _major_ 3rd.

Allegretto in E Minor, op. 38, no. 24

Johann Wilhelm Hässler (1747–1822)
Student Workshop 4, p. 16

Looking at a Piece

1. _key signature — one stamp_
2. _time signature — $\frac{6}{8}$_
3. _imitation_
4. _sixteenth notes running up and down_
5. _chords at the end_

Comparison of Character

Compare the time signatures of all the List A pieces in your *Piano Repertoire 4*. You will notice that this is the only one with a time signature of _$\frac{6}{8}$_ . What are the time signatures of the others?
$\frac{3}{4}$, $\frac{4}{4}$, $\frac{2}{2}$

Musical Style

The RH melody shown here is in the form of a question and answer. The imitation in the LH follows closely behind the RH.

How far behind? _one measure_

Is the imitation exact? _yes_

A **sequence** is the repetition of a melody at a different pitch level, higher or lower.

In the first section of *Allegretto*, where does the imitation between the hands come closer together? m. _5_ You can also find a sequence in the melody here. How far does it continue? to m. _6_

Practicing for Security

Play the opening LH imitation (mm. 2–3) and imagine that the score is marked *f*. Lift your fingers high at first, to work for complete finger independence.

Is there a need for you to shift position? _no_

How far can you go in the same hand position without shifting? m. _7_

Once you shift your hand position, the rest will be easy if you remember the fingering.

Work in a similar way with the RH. You will notice the benefit of good fingering immediately. The first two measures lie under the five-finger hand position; then with the strategic use of finger _4_, you are able to shift so that you can stretch (in m. 4) down to the note _B_.

Sonatina in B flat Major, op. 4, no. 8

Samuel Wesley (1766–1837)
Student Workbook 4, p. 18

Form

If you did not see the title *Sonatina* as you played through the piece, you might think this was a dance from List A. The form is similar: two sections of unequal length, with repeats and a return of the first theme at the end.
What is the name of this familiar form?
rounded binary

We usually think of another form when we think of a sonatina.
What is the name of that form? _sonata form_

What aspects of a typical sonatina does this piece contain? _scale fragments in sixteenth notes; fast tempo_

Key

Write a one-octave scale with the RH beginning on the first RH note in the piece and the LH beginning one octave below the first LH note in the piece.

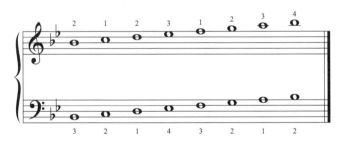

Now add fingering to your scale. In the RH ascending, the rule is that the thumb passes under immediately after a black key. In the LH ascending, the thumb comes just before crossing over to a black key. (Start with the finger numbers on the first notes in the *Sonatina* score.)

Is there a change of key at the end of the first section? _no_
In the second section? _no_

Melody

Name the note values that you see in the RH of the first section.
quarter note; eighth note; sixteenth note

Which of these note values is the shortest?
sixteenth note

These short notes are characteristic of sonatinas, and their presence is one of the ways to justify the title of the piece. You see groups of four of these notes throughout the piece. Notice how they turn in different directions:

In m. 1, you see a turn (over and under the main note, B flat).
In m. 3, the direction is the (same) / different.
In m. 7, the direction is up–down / (down–up).
In m. 9, the direction is up / (down).

What do you notice in the LH at mm. 9–10?
imitation and sequence

Harmony

The harmonic structure of *Sonatina* is based closely on the **tonic–dominant** relationship.

The symbol for tonic is _I_.

The tonic triad in this key is _B flat major_.

The symbol for dominant is _V_.

The dominant triad is _F major_.

Write these two triads in the key of B flat on the staff below:

There is another version of the dominant triad in this piece. By adding an extra note to the dominant triad (count seven notes up from the bottom) you are adding the 7th to the chord, so this chord is called a **dominant 7th**. Write it on the staff above.

There is a dominant 7th chord on the first beat of mm. 8 and 24. In the RH, Wesley leaves out one note of the chord. Which one? _F (the root)_

There are **cadences** at the end of almost every four-measure phrase. There is one exception. When you are counting the phrases, look for the place where the music runs on (mm. _12–13_). All the cadences in *Sonatina* are either **perfect** (V–I) or **imperfect** (I–V).

Sonata in F Major, Hob. XVI:9
Third Movement: Scherzo
Franz Joseph Haydn (1732–1809)
Student Workbook 4, p. 21

A Simple Structure

Do you see scales and chords in mm. 1–4? <u>yes</u>

Haydn has used sixteenth-note figures to decorate the framework of a simple scherzo. Let's have a look at this framework.

What is the name of the sign that divides the music into two sections? <u>repeat</u>

Where are these signs? mm. <u>8</u> and <u>24</u>

In your score, label the first section A and the second section B.

This scherzo is in **rounded binary form** because there are two sections, with the theme of section A returning at the end of the B section.

Where does the A theme come back in B? m. <u>16</u>

Simple Harmony

What is the key of the music? <u>F major</u>

Write each triad that is implied in the RH and LH, as a solid (blocked) chord, in root position:

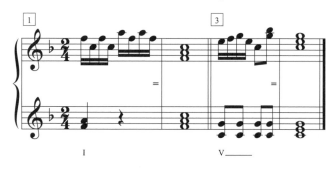

In m. 3, there is an extra note in the RH at the end of the measure: <u>B flat</u>.

How would you describe the sound?
<u>unfinished, incomplete</u>

Half an Alberti Bass

Does Haydn use an Alberti bass in this *scherzo*? <u>no</u>

In mm. 9–13, there is a pattern that is almost, but not quite, an Alberti bass.

Can you make this into a full Alberti bass pattern? Change the notes in this example, then play it with Haydn's right-hand part.

Answering Phrases

Haydn cleverly repeats musical ideas in this piece. Chart the measures where you find the following motive:

mm.	<u>1–2</u>
mm.	<u>5–6</u>
mm.	<u>17–18</u>
mm.	<u>21–22</u>

and the following rhythmic figure:

mm.	<u>9–10</u>
mm.	<u>11–12</u>
mm.	<u>13–14</u>

Sonatina in G Major, op. 36, no. 2
Third Movement
Muzio Clementi (1752–1832)
Student Workbook 4, p. 24

Clementi's Sonatinas

This joyous *Allegro* is the third of three movements that make up Clementi's *Sonatina in G Major*. The last movement of a sonatina usually has a quick tempo and a lively, spirited character.

What is the tempo marking of this movement?
<u>Allegro</u>
What does this Italian word mean? <u>fast, spirited</u>

Scales in Music

Here are three examples from this sonatina movement. Play each example a few times and decide which note sounds like the tonic of the scale.

Key: <u>G major</u>
Tonic: <u>G</u>

Key: <u>A minor</u>
Tonic: <u>A</u>

Key: <u>G major</u>
Tonic: <u>G</u>

Write the key of each scale under the excerpt, and name the tonic.

Keys and Sections

2. Is there any repetition within these sections? <u>yes</u>

3. List the themes by letter in the order they appear in the music.

Write the measure numbers beside each letter.

Section A:	mm. 1–16
Section A₁:	mm. <u>17</u> – <u>31</u>
Transition:	mm. 32–40
Section <u>B</u>:	mm. <u>41</u> – <u>56</u>
Section <u>B₁</u>:	mm. <u>57</u> – <u>74</u>
Section <u>A</u>:	mm. <u>75</u> – <u>90</u>
Section A₁ + *coda*:	mm. 91–104

Usually a change of key indicates a new section. In mm. 38–40, the key changes from <u>G</u> major to <u>D</u> major.

Is m. 41 the beginning of a new section? <u>yes</u>
In which measures did you find a **variation** of the theme from section B? mm. <u>57</u> – <u>74</u>

Would you call this form (ternary) / **binary** / theme and variation?

German Song

Daniel Gottlob Türk (1750–1813)
Student Workbook 4, p. 26

Melody and Rhythm

Which hand has the most rhythmic motion? <u>RH</u>

When you are learning a piece with complex rhythms like *German Song*, it is helpful to first subdivide the beats.

Imagine this piece with four beats in each measure. Which rhythm value would get the beat in this case? <u>eighth</u> note

Draw lines to match each of the following sets of notes to the correct description:

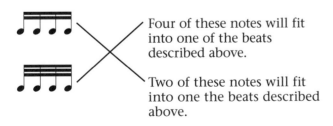

Four of these notes will fit into one of the beats described above.

Two of these notes will fit into one the beats described above.

Here are some of the rhythmic figures that occur in *German Song*. For each, mark in the four beats where they occur. The first has been marked as an example:

m. <u>11</u> mm. <u>2</u> and <u>10</u> m. <u>1</u> m. <u>7</u>

A Singer's Phrases

Find the phrases in *German Song*. There are four measures in which the RH note vaules are noticeably longer: mm. <u>4</u>, <u>8</u>, <u>12</u>, <u>16</u>.

These measures are phrase endings, and there is a pattern as to where they occur within the piece. Look for this pattern as you construct a map of the phrases using the following layout:

Phrase 1: mm. <u>1</u> – <u>4</u>

Most of the notes in m. 1 belong to the **tonic** triad of the key of the piece. Write this triad in root position on the staff above. This piece is in the key of <u>E flat major</u>.

Phrase 2: mm. <u>5</u> – <u>8</u>

At another of the phrase endings, the LH plays a different triad (in root position). Write this triad inside the box where it occurs. This is the triad of <u>B flat major</u>.

Is it the triad on the **tonic**, **subdominant** or **dominant** of the home key? Write the answer below the triad.

Something in your music indicates that this particular phrase ending is also the end of a section; mark this at the close of the correct box.

This triad is part of a **cadence** that is like phrase 1:

Phrase 3: mm. <u>9</u> – <u>12</u>

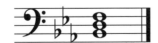

The notes of the LH in the last measure also form a triad. This is the triad of <u>E flat major</u>.

Phrase 4: mm. _13_ – _16_

Overall, is this piece divided into two or three sections? _two_

Based on your answer, is it written in
☑ **binary form** or ☐ **ternary form**

Sonatina in F Major, op. 168, no. 1
First Movement

Anton Diabelli (1781–1858)
Student Workbook 4, p. 28

Can you name at least one other composer who lived in Vienna during the first twenty-five years of the 1800s? _Beethoven, Haydn, Schubert_

Diabelli's Sonatinas

What is Diabelli's tempo marking?
Moderato cantabile

How will you interpret this marking?
moderately, in a singing style

Step 2: Find the Two Themes

The first theme is in the **tonic** key of _F major_.
The second theme is in the **dominant** key of _C major_.

Step 3: Take a Closer Look at Theme 1

In m. 1, the LH notes form a _F_ major triad. Which melody note does not fit in with the accompaniment? _D_

In m. 2, the LH notes form a _G_ minor triad. Which melody note does not fit in with the accompaniment? _A_

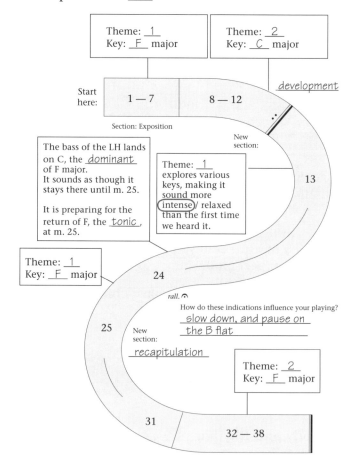

Pairs of slurred notes like you see on the first two beats of mm. 1–4 are often described as musical "sighs." Diabelli has used these notes to add an expressive tension to the melody. The second note of the "sigh" is the resolution—where the music relaxes. Look through the rest of theme 1.
Can you find other "sighing" notes? _yes, mm. 3–4_
Do these notes fall on a weak beat or a strong beat? _strong_

Step 5: Winding It All Up

In the recapitulation of a sonata-form movement, theme 1 and theme 2 are presented once more, but with an important difference: the return of theme 2 is always in the home (tonic) key. Be sure to mark the themes and their keys on the map.

Sonatina

Erkki Melartin (1875–1937)
Student Workbook 4, p. 31

Relative Major and Minor Keys

Which major scale has a key signature with two flats? <u>B flat major</u>

For every major key, there is a minor key that has the same key signature. These keys are each other's relative major and minor. To find the relative minor of a major key, simply count down three semitones.

The relative minor of the major key named above is <u>G</u> minor.

Write the major scale and its **tonic** triad here:

Write the relative minor scale (harmonic form) and its tonic triad here:

Let's Take a Musical Journey

mm. 1–2

This phrase is played <u>three</u> times in a ☑ descending sequence.

Does *Sonatina* begin in the ☐ major or the ☑ minor key?

mm. 7–8

Circle the lowest LH note in each of these two measures; these two notes move from the <u>dominant</u> to the <u>tonic</u>. This motion creates a **perfect cadence**, which acts as a musical punctuation mark at the end of the first eight-measure phrase.

mm. 9–10

marcato

The melody is heard in the <u>left</u> hand.

mm. 16–19

What event described earlier occurs again here? <u>perfect cadence</u>

Now, it marks the end of the first section of *Sonatina*.

mm. 21–23

The interval between each pair of circled notes in the RH and LH is a <u>10th</u>.

The motion between the hands in this section is ☑ parallel.

The notes at the start of m. 21 form a triad. Write it here:

This is the triad of <u>B flat major</u>.

mm. 35–36

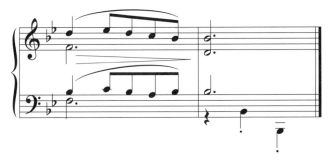

What event described earlier occurs here?
perfect cadence

In what key? _B flat major_
This marks the end of the second section of *Sonatina.*

mm. 37–end
Examine this section—it should give you the information you need to figure out the overall form.

Circle the set of letters that matches the structure of *Sonatina*:
ABAC   (ABA₁)   ABAB

Dancing on the Green

Cornelius Gurlitt (1820–1901)
Student Workbook 4, p. 34

Form

You will notice a thin double bar line on the first page at the end of m. _16_ .
This is the first section, which we can call A. Write A in your music at the beginning of the piece. Include the upbeat.

What is the key? _F major_

How many measures are in section A? _16_

The next section begins at m. _17_ and ends at m. _32_ . Write the letter B in your music. What key is indicated by the chord at the beginning of this section? _B flat major_

What is the key of the perfect cadence at the end of the section? _F major_

How many measures are in this middle section? _16_

The final section occurs at m. _32_ . What happens here? _The first section is repeated._

Which letter is most appropriate for the music for this section? _A_

How many measures are in the final section? _16_

What is the only difference between this and the first section? _the dynamics_

If we look at the structure of the piece in chart form:

A section is _16_ measures.
B section is _16_ measures.
A section is _16_ measures.

Rhythm

Continue tapping at mm. 8 and 9. What musical concept do you discover? _imitation_

Can you tap this easily? Will it be easier to play after you've practiced tapping it? _yes_

Clarity of Articulation

To play this dance with the right *scherzando* quality (what is the meaning of *scherzando*? _jokingly / playfully_), you need to follow the articulation marks closely, and play with firm strong fingers.

How many types of articulation marks do you see? _four_

Name each one, and give an example (measure number) of each:
slur mm. 21–24
staccato mm. 10–11: short and crisp
tenuto m. 4
staccato-tenuto m. 17: held and lifted

In the case of detached notes, be specific in your description of the types. For example: short and crisp; slow lift; hold for full value, then lift.

Dreamcatcher

Anne Crosby (b. 1968)
Student Workbook 4, p. 36

Establishing Atmosphere

Movement
Play the LH separately in the first two measures. Immediately you will notice a pattern in the rhythm that shifts the emphasis forward from the strong beat to the weaker half of the beat.

What is the name of this pattern of rhythmic shift?
syncopation

In the time signature of $\frac{4}{4}$, this pattern allows a rocking or swaying effect to take place. The rocking aspect might portray an image of a _cradle_ and the swaying effect could portray an image of _feathers in a breeze_ .

Whatever idea you have in your imagination, it is important to keep the tempo consistent. The composer has indicated a slight change of tempo in only one place: m. _15_ . What is the full name and meaning of the term written at this place in your music? _ritardando — gradually slower_

Color

What is the key of the piece? _D major_

Does the LH in m. 1 outline the key? _yes_

Is it a broken triad? _no_ Solid (blocked) triad? _no_

Other? (Describe.) _melodic perfect 5th_

Now look at m. 2. Does the LH accidental create a key change? _no_

The composer herself answers the question in m. 3. The key is still _D major_.

Match the number of each motive with the correct description below.

Opening motive of first phrase: no. _7_

LH statement of opening motive: no. _3_

Closing motive of first phrase: no. _10_

LH rocking rhythm: no. _6_

Rocking rhythm with two types of accidentals: no. _2_

Melody with one type of accidental: no. _4_

Similar melody beginning in reverse direction: no. _9_

Hand-over-hand: no. _5_

Closing motive of first phrase in 3rds: no. _8_

Accompanying motive in 6ths (quarter notes): no. _11_

Closing motive of first phrase in 6ths (eighth notes): no. _1_

The Wild Horseman, op. 68, no. 8

Robert Schumann (1810–1856)
Student Workbook 4, p. 39

Musical Imagery

In the first section, which hand sounds like the galloping of horses' hooves? _RH_

Musical Ingredients

Here is a list of musical ingredients. Check the ones that Schumann uses to create a clear picture that you can express in your performance.

- ☑ triads, solid (blocked) or broken
- ☑ *sf* markings
- ☑ staccatos
- ☑ a steady rhythm
- ☑ a rhythmic value heard throughout
- ☑ short slurs

The melody is written in _eighth_ notes. Most of these notes are marked _staccato_. A few are marked with _slurs_.

The _sf_ markings indicate bright accents. Schumann places these accents in a definite pattern, on the _first_ beat of the measure. The notes of the melody outline broken _triads_, and the melody moves by _skip_ rather than by step. Schumann also uses solid (blocked) _triads_ in the accompaniment, which provide strong rhythmic energy.

Celebration Series Perspectives Answer Book

Exploring Triads

Let's have a closer look at some of the triads Schumann uses.
What is the key of this piece? _A minor_

Write the scale of this key and circle the first and fifth notes. (Don't forget to raise the leading note.)

Now write the **tonic** and **dominant** triads for this key:

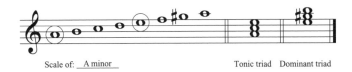

Scale of: _A minor_   Tonic triad   Dominant triad

The tonic triad first appears in root position in m. _1_.

The dominant triad first appears on beat 1 in the LH of m. _3_.

In mm. 9–16, Schumann switches the melody to the LH and moves to a new key, but he keeps the same triad structure.

What is the new key? _F major_

Write the tonic and dominant triads in this key:

Tonic triad   Dominant triad

Key: _F major_

Nocturne

Paul Sheftel (b. 1933)
Student Workbook 4, p. 42

Patterns in the Accompaniment

Observe the first measure of the LH accompaniment in the examples shown below. Three notes have been circled, and another set of three notes is enclosed within a box. Follow these steps:
What is the interval between the first and third circled notes? _perfect octave_
What is the interval between the first two circled notes? _perfect 5th_ Write this interval as a harmonic interval in the space provided.

Observe the notes inside the box. Write them as a solid (blocked) chord in the space provided.

Write the   Write the
interval here: chord here:

This is something you have played before, the __tonic__ of __E__ minor.

Now go through a similar set of steps with the next two measures. (You can use the Accompaniment Map on the next page.) As you will see, the composer has created a pattern that is repeated on different pitch levels.
This type of pattern is called __sequence__.

Your Accompaniment Map

It's now time to complete the LH part of Nocturne in the measures shown on the map. For each measure, write the notes that correspond to the size of interval and the type of chord that you observed above. Look for a few clues and questions along the way. (You will also have to change the clef from time to time.)

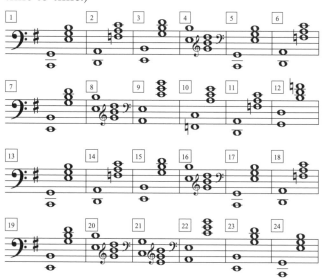

m. 4: This measure is an __octave__ higher than the previous one.

m. 5: The pattern of measures __1__ – __4__ starts again here.

mm. 13, 17: There are two different places where the exact notes of the opening measures return. Mark these spots on the map.

mm. 23–24: Each note of the two closing measures is a __4th__ (name the interval) higher than the previous one.

Play It Again

Christopher Norton (b. 1953)
Student Workbook 4, p. 44

Meet the Musicians in the Jazz Combo

Here are four excerpts from *Play It Again*. Find each excerpt in the music, and play it. Then write the excerpt number beside the description on the next page that fits it best.

Excerpt __D__
A pair of trombones play a falling "slide."

Excerpt __A__
The bass moves from the **dominant** to the **tonic**. (You *can* have **perfect cadences** in jazz!)

Excerpt __B__
Two clarinets share a **syncopated** duet.

Excerpt __C__
The trumpet and the saxophone toss a short phrase back and forth. (Who's imitating whom?)

Syncopation

In syncopated rhythms, the accent is shifted from a strong beat to a weak beat. The normal pulse of the music is displaced. Many of the accents in *Play It Again* are "off" the beat. These rhythms are syncopated.

For example, in m. 1, the note on the __third__ beat is tied. This shifts the accent back to __the second half of beat 2__.

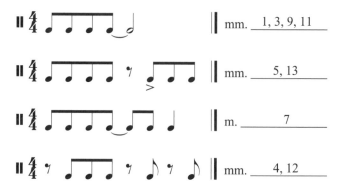

What do these rhythms have in common?
__They are all syncopated; beat 3 is either a rest or tied over.__

A Blues Scale

Many pieces written in jazz styles imitate the singing and playing of blues musicians. A voice can sing pitches in between the notes on a piano keyboard. Blues singers often slide from note to note and "bend" pitches up or down a little.

What is the key of this piece? __F major__

There are several accidentals in the music. These accidentals introduce notes that are not found in the major scale.

Put together a scale starting on F that includes all the notes used in this piece.

A Winter Melody

Yoshinao Nakada (1923–2000)
Student Workbook 4, p. 47

Melody

The key of the piece at the beginning is _A minor_.

Nakada uses the melody several times, in different ways.

At m. 9, which hand has the melody? _LH_

Is this the same melody as the beginning? _no_

Is the key the same? _no_ What would you say is similar? _the rhythm, at first_

How many measures does it go on? _8_

The melody next appears in m. _17_ in which hand? _LH_

Is it the same as the beginning? _almost_ Is it the same length? _no_

The final appearance of the melody is somewhat hidden, as if behind the clouds. Can you find it? mm. _21–25_

What is the name of the pattern in the melody at m. 24? _chromatic_ This is the last shift in the clouds before the sun breaks through. Nakada indicates the change in the sky in two musical ways:
1. _crescendo to forte_
2. _major chord in m. 25_

Harmonic Structure

First, write out the scale of A minor, one octave ascending only, in triads on the staff below. Don't forget the accidental!

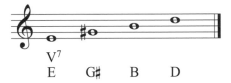

Add numbers in Roman numerals under each degree of the scale going up. The triad on V (the dominant) sometimes has a seventh note added to it like this (the chord has been moved down an octave so it is easier to look at):

As you can see, this is a four-note chord, called a **dominant 7th**. Name the notes from the bottom up on the diagram.

Now let's look further at the music of *A Winter Melody*.
What is the name of the first triad on the page? _A minor_

Now look at m. 5. What do you notice in the LH? _broken A minor triad_

Now look at m. 8. What do you notice in the LH? _broken A minor triad_

Because this stretches out to include an octave, we call this a four-note chord in the key of _A minor_. Are the notes the same as in the first triad? _yes_

At m. 9, play the RH. Has there been a change of key? _yes_ How do you know this? (There are two reasons—look ahead!)
1. _no G sharp_
2. _a dominant 7th on G, moving to C major triads in m. 12_

As you did in the exercise above, write out the scale of C major in triads on the staff below. Add Roman numerals under each degree of the scale ascending.

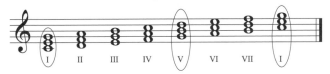

Write the triad on V again, and build a dominant 7th in C major.

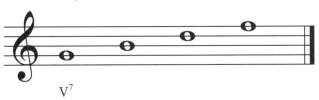

V^7

You already know that tonic means _I_ (Roman numeral) in the key; and **dominant** means _V_ (Roman numeral) in the key. Circle each of these triads on your triad scale diagram.

Checking your triad scale diagrams, answer the following questions:

In the key of A minor:
Find examples of I, root position in m. _1_; second inversion in m. _23_.

Find one example of V in m. _16_.

Find one example of V^7 (one note may be left out) in m. _4, 20_.

Find one example of VI in m. _2_.

In the key of C major:
Find examples of I, root position in m. _10_; first inversion (you may include the LH) in m. _12_.

Find one example of V^7 (one note may be left out) in m. _9_.

Find one example of IV in m. _13_.

Compare the chord of VI in A minor, with the chord of IV in C major.
What do you notice? _They are the same._

And now for the sunny ending!
What is the type of chord in m. 25? _major_ Is there any connection between the chord in the beginning and the chord at the end? _yes_

Which note of the triad has been changed at the end? _3rd (mediant)_

What is the sign added? _sharp_

Does this create a happy sound? _yes_

Children's Game

Béla Bartók (1881–1945)
Student Workbook 4, p. 50

Musical Shape
The *Allegretto* sections of the music are separated by short passages that present sudden changes of atmosphere.

Write the measure numbers of these passages.
 mm. _22_ to _26_
 mm. _48_ to _52_
 mm. _70_ to _73_

What does the Italian marking *adagio* mean? _very slow_

Which word would you use to describe this new atmosphere?

 laughter (stillness) stamping feet

Children's Game has _six_ sections: the _Allegretto_ (what tempo?) _not as fast as allegro_ sections alternate with the _Adagio_ (what tempo?) _slow_ sections.

Musical Building Blocks
Build a scale (or part of a scale) using the notes played by the RH in mm. 1–8:

Place your fingers over the notes you have written. This is the (how many?) _five_-finger pattern of _D_ minor.

Playing Tag
Let's see how Bartók uses this building block to play musical games.
Can you find places where your two hands play tag using this building block? mm. _9–12, 33–34, 37–38_

Label these measures "tag" in your music.
Are all these games of tag the same? _no_

Playing Ball
A new game begins in m. 13.

The LH plays a broken triad figure that sounds like a bouncing ball. Where does this figure first appear? m. _14_

Write the triad in solid (blocked) form and name it.

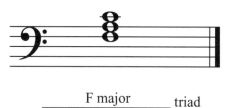

_____F major_____ triad

How does this triad relate to the triad from mm. 1–8? _relative major_

Find all the places where Bartók uses the bouncing ball building block and label them "bouncing ball" in your music.

Are all the repetitions of the bouncing ball exactly the same? _no_

How is the one in verse 2 different? _The triad is in G major._

What does the marking **smorzando** in m. 19 mean? _dying away._

How does Bartók use this marking to create surprise? _It leads to m. 47, which is unexpectedly silent._

How is the bouncing ball in verse 3 different? _LH triads change on beat 2_

How does the meaning of the sign in m. 23 differ from the meaning of the sign at the end of m. 36? _In m. 23, the chord is held; at the end of m. 36, silence is held before the a tempo in m. 37._

Staccatos, Slurs, Portatos, and Tenutos
As a composer, Bartók was very particular about articulation. Look through *Children's Game*.

Which notes do not have any articulation markings? _the half notes in Adagio sections_

Mélodie

Alexandre Tansman (1897–1986)
Student Workbook 4, p. 53

A Melody
The first step is to isolate the melody notes so that you can highlight them with greater depth of tone than the accompaniment.

What note values does Tansman use for the melody? _half notes_

Is the melody above or below the accompaniment?
above

Harmony

What is the home key of *Mélodie*? _A minor_
Does the music begin and end in this key? _yes_

The accompaniment is made up of broken chords. These chords create a rich and beautiful harmonic progression.

Write the chords of mm. 1–3 in solid (blocked) form:

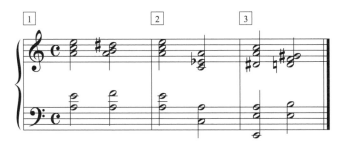

There is a "surprise" chord in the second half of m. 12.
Name the notes in this chord. _B D♯ F♯ A_

Write these notes as a chord in root position:

Play the chord as written in the piece, but in solid (blocked) form, then play the chord in root position.
How would you describe this sound? _like a question_

Do you feel the need to return to the opening section after this chord? _yes_

How would you describe what happens at m. 13?
Material from the beginning returns.

Melody Plus Accompaniment

What is the Italian term that means *smoothly*?
legato

Pedaling

What does *simile* mean? _play the same way throughout_

The Rooster Crows

Lajos Papp (b. 1935)
Student Workbook 4, p. 55

Program Music

There are three accompaniment patterns in the LH. Solid (blocked) 3rds moving stepwise; there's an example at m. _2_.

Broken 5ths on different pitch levels; there's an example at m. _7_.

Broken 5ths and octaves alternating; there's an example at m. _19_.

The Rooster's Song

Now observe what the RH does while (or in some cases, just before) the LH plays the patterns described above.

How do you think the RH part fits with the title of the piece? _It illustrates the rooster's crow._

As this motive recurs throughout the piece, it changes a little. At which measure does the following version occur? m. _7_

Rewrite these notes:

1. A 5th higher

2. A 4th higher

Both versions you have written appear in various places in the piece. Which one is a little different in the actual music, compared to what you have written? no. _1_

Rewrite it as it does in fact appear in the music:

This version appears in mm. _1_ and _4_.

It Suddenly Gets Quiet in the Barnyard

The rooster's music is <u>bright, cheerful</u>. Once in a while, the rooster stops crowing, and we hear a different sort of music.

How would you describe this music? <u>smoother, slower</u>

It occurs at mm. <u>12</u>, <u>17</u>, and <u>22 (coda)</u>. At the very end, we hear faint echoes of the rooster crowing.

Are these in the LH or RH? <u>LH</u>

Rooster Rhythm

What time signature is shown at the start of *The Rooster Crows*? <u>2/4</u>

In most of the pieces you have played, the time signature remains the same throughout; what is different here? <u>The time signature changes.</u>

What other time signature appears? <u>3/4</u>

How many times does the time signature change during the piece? <u>12</u>

Have you ever seen a rooster strutting about in the barnyard? His movements are certainly not graceful; in fact, they are rather jerky and unpredictable! How does Papp's unusual use of time signatures help describe this rooster's movements? <u>They are also unpredictable; they occur at irregular times.</u>

Monkeys in the Tree

Boris Berlin (1907–2001)
Student Workbook 4, p. 57

The Monkey Motive

Label mm. 1–19 section A on your music.

In this section, the monkeys play "Follow the Leader."
Write the RH rhythms of the short motive they toss back and forth:

What is the difference between mm. 1–2 and mm. 3–4? In mm. 3–4, Berlin repeats the music of mm. 1–2 (in what way?) <u>one octave lower</u>

This technique is called octave **transposition**.

Where does Berlin use octave transposition going in the other direction? <u>mm. 7–10</u>

How does this octave transposition imitate monkeys chattering in the tree?
<u>The monkeys climb and jump through the trees.</u>

This short motive has a lot packed into it!

Where do the monkeys echo each other? <u>mm. 3–4</u>

What musical marking helps create an echo effect? <u>p</u>

Where do the monkeys jump higher in the tree? m. <u>7</u>

Monkey Markings

Locate all the following markings in mm. 1–2, write the signs, and describe what they mean.

accent	<u>></u>	<u>play with emphasis</u>
tenuto mark	<u>—</u>	<u>hold for full value</u>
staccato dot	<u>•</u>	<u>detached</u>
slur	<u>⌒</u>	<u>smooth, connected (legato)</u>

Monkey Triads

Here are the broken triads in the monkey motive in mm. 1–2. Write the triads formed by the sixteenth notes beside each motive:

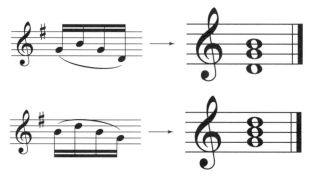

Which one of these triads is in root position? <u>the second one</u>
Can you name the inversion of the other one? <u>second inversion</u>
What is the key of this piece? <u>G major</u>
Are these **tonic** triads of that key? <u>yes</u>

The Big Baboon B Section!

In this section, Berlin tells us that a big baboon makes an appearance.

Where is this sudden change in the music? <u>m. 20</u>

Can you name the triad in the last chord before the baboon enters? <u>G major</u>

What else creates contrast in this section?
<u>The dynamics of the sixteenth-note sections are f and ff; there are longer note values (half notes); there are no chords.</u>

A Monkey Sequence

Both the monkeys and the baboon use another type of pattern in which a group set of notes is repeated at a higher or lower level.

What is this type of repetition called? <u>sequence</u>
Find the sequences in this piece using the clues below:

Find this clue in measure(s):	Write out the full pattern as played the second time:

A Ternary Form

Compare the closing section to the A section.
Is it exactly the same? _no_

Happy Meeting, op. 119, no. 15

Alexandr T. Grechaninov (1864–1956)
Student Workbook 4, p. 60

Skipping Rhythm

This consistent rhythmic figure (short, dotted rhythm) serves as a foundation for the structure of the piece, except in two places: mm. _12_ and _16_.

Articulation

Happy Meeting contains slurs everywhere! Do you see any detached notes? _no_

Grechaninov adds many _sixteenth_ rests to make sure the performer does not hold the LH down.

Phrasing

Play the melody through again.
How many phrases (sentences) do you hear in the first section? _2_

How many in the second section? _2_

Balance of Melody and Accompaniment

Do you think the piece sounds more graceful with the blocked LH intervals? _no_

Or do you think the piece moves more gracefully as written? _yes_

Fable, op. 21, no. 3

Robert Muczynski (b. 1929)
Student Workbook 4, p. 63

A Fable Told in Keys

As you will see, the composer's choice of keys is a part of how he tells his musical story.

What two clues can help you discover the key at the beginning of the piece?
key signature   _first notes_

On the staff below, write a solid (blocked) triad in root position using the notes of m. 1:

The key at the start of the piece is _C major_.

In m. 8, a new key signature appears. On the staff below, write the new key signature and the notes of that measure, as a solid (blocked) triad in root position:

The key signature and triad tell you that this may be the key of _E flat major_.

Check this by writing on the staff below all the notes that appear between mm. 8 and 14 as an ascending scale. (You will have to change the octave of some of the notes to make them fit into your scale.)

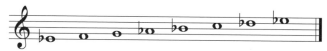

What one difference is there between the scale you have written and a traditional major scale starting on the same note? _The D is flat._

This is actually a very ancient scale that resembles the major scale of today. It is called the Mixolydian mode. Listen to the effect as you play it; it has a faraway, old-fashioned quality to it. How does it help convey the title of the piece?
makes it seem like an old story is being told

Are there any other key changes? _yes_

If so, name the measure _24_ and the key _C major_.

You will find that keys create a form. Choose the set of letters below that you feel best shows the form.
☑ A B A₁ (A slightly modified)

A Rhymic Left Hand

The LH accompaniment is full of rhythmic variety. Here are descriptions of four different rhythmic figures. Write out each exactly as described. The first has been done as an example:

eighth rest at the start of the measure

   m. _7_

80

rest for the second beat of the measure

m. _20_

eighth rest at the start of the second beat

m. _8_

play only on the "and" of each beat

m. _1_

Changing Bars

István Szelényi (1904–1972)
Student Workbook 4, p. 65

An Eighth-Note Beat

The title of this piece is Changing Bars.
What is the first thing you notice about the time signatures in this score? _They keep changing._

Which measures (bars), if any, do not begin with a change of time signature? mm. _19, 21, 36, 39_

What is the bottom number in each of the time signatures? _8_

This means that the _eighth_ -note beat remains the same throughout the piece.

Rhythmic Patterns

Now let's take a closer look.
How many times does Szelényi use each of these time signatures?

$\frac{2}{8}$ _7_ times $\frac{3}{8}$ _17_ times $\frac{4}{8}$ _11_ times

Are these time signature changes just random, or is Szelényi following particular patterns? _He is following patterns._

Which pattern does he use most often? _$\frac{4}{8}$ to $\frac{3}{8}$_

The $\frac{2}{8}$ measures on the second page seem to interrupt the main pattern.

What new pattern do these measures introduce?
$\frac{2}{8}$-$\frac{3}{8}$-$\frac{4}{8}$-$\frac{3}{8}$

Where does Szelényi use two $\frac{2}{8}$ measures in a row?
mm. _20–21_ mm. _35–36_ mm. _38–39_

A Left-Hand Drone

The LH part supports the rhythm by emphasizing the downbeat of each measure.

What is the interval between the two LH notes in mm. 1–5? _5th_

Are the two LH notes always this distance apart?
yes

Write all the different pairs of notes on the staff:

Which one does Szelényi use most often?
the first one

Accents

Szelényi uses accents to increase the energy and drive of the rhythm. Circle all the notes that have accents.

How many of these accents fall on the downbeat?
_4_
How many accents are on a weak beat? _7_

Barcarole

David Duke (b. 1950)
Student Workbook 4, p. 67

A Rhythm on the Water

The LH chords establish the barcarole rhythm before the melody enters. Play the LH alone from mm. 1–6.
What do you feel as you hear this rhythm?
gentle rocking

What does it make you think of? _a boat_

Can you find a pattern in these chords? _yes_

How long is the pattern? _2 measures_

How many times is it repeated? _3 times_

In $\frac{6}{8}$ time, the _eighth_ note gets the beat. There are _2_ pulses per measure, and each pulse can be divided into _3_ eighth notes. In mm. 9–10, there is a syncopated effect. The listener hears _3_ pulses of _2_ eighth notes (instead of _2_ pulses of _3_ eighth notes).

Pedaling

Duke has written pedal marks in the score.
How often do you change the pedal in mm. 1–6?
on each group of 3

How often do you change the pedal in mm. 9–10?
on each group of 2

Did you notice that the notes in m. 11 aren't tied to anything? What do you do with the pedal in mm. 11–12? _hold it to the end_

On a Boat in the Evening

Play *Barcarole* all the way through, then play each section separately. Listen to the different colors of sound in each one. Then connect the measure numbers on the bridge to the gondola below that contains the most appropriate description.

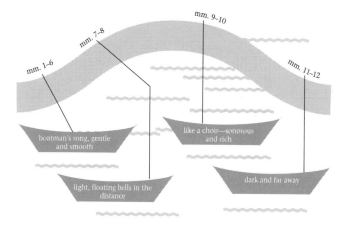

Thinguma Jig

Dale Reubart (b. 1926)
Student Workbook 4, p. 70

Rhythm

Music: If you have played a jig before, you will remember that "jig time" is __6/8__ (time signature).

The time signature is often divided into _2_ groups per measure, with _3_ eighth notes in each group. Look at all the note values in mm. 1–4 and write out the rhythm below on a single line.

Intervals

Look at mm. 1–4 again with intervals in mind. Play this section hands separately, naming the two intervals that Reubart uses in the LH: _perfect 5th_ and _perfect 4th_ .

Are these intervals harmonic or melodic? _harmonic_

The LH interval in m. 1 kicks off the piece. What is it? _perfect 5th_ What sign indicates the kick? _accent (<)_

Interval Quiz

Look through the entire piece to spot intervals.

1. Where do you see a pattern of descending perfect 4ths (blocked)? _m. 1 RH_

2. Which interval contains a surprising change of harmony to flats? _m. 9 LH_

3. How many intervals of a 6th do you see? _two_

4. Can you find any intervals of a 7th? _no_

5. Which interval contains both a sharp and a flat? m. _30 LH_

What is the interval distance? _3rd_

What does the interval sound like when played on the piano? _4th_

Is the sound the same as that of the pattern you identified in no. 1? _yes_

Technique Tricks

How far does your LH jump from m. 1 to m. 2? _one octave_ Try the jump with your eyes closed.

At m. 13, the RH thumb plays the same note just after the LH thumb has played it. Which hand needs to get out of the way of the other? _LH needs to get out of the way_

Articulation

If you were to use one word to describe the articulation in *Thinguma Jig* it might be "bouncy." How does the composer achieve this effect throughout the piece?
1. _two-note slurs_
2. _staccatos_

When both signs are used, does the sound become even more bouncy or is it the same? _more bouncy_

Do you think that Reubart is describing the thingumajig, or illustrating the dancing of the jig? _yes_

Or both, perhaps? _yes_

Chastushka, op. 89, no. 25

Dmitri Kabalevsky (1904–1987)
Student Workbook 4, p. 73

Jumping around the Keyboard

Kabalevsky shows the character of the piece in the first measure.

Which hand jumps over? _LH_ Which hand stays the same? _RH_

What is the name of the triad? _F major_ In which inversion? _1st inversion_

In m. 2, is the jumping pattern repeated? _yes_

What is the name of this triad? _C major_ In which inversion? _2nd inversion_

What is the interval leap in LH m. 1? _10th_

Is it the same distance in m. 2? _no_

Repetition, then Memory

There are basically two different sections, and the first is repeated (slightly decorated) at the end. Write the letter A in your score over the first-theme section, and B over the second.

Where does A return? m. _17_ What is the name of the form ABA? _ternary_

The repetition of the first four measures contains one different measure, m. _8_ .

Does the repetition of the second theme contain any changes? _m. 12 and m. 16 are slightly different_

When A is repeated at the end, is it exactly the same as the first A? _no_

Name two differences:
1. _The crossover in the LH has two notes._
2. _The last measure's repeated C's are broken up by octave leaps._

Is there any similarity between that one different measure that appeared in A the first time, and the one in the last section? Explain.
The composer uses all C's.

Contrast in Texture and Touch

Kabalevsky provides contrast as early as the first four-measure theme. After leaping around the keyboard in mm. 1–2, what do the hands do in mm. 3–4? _play the same notes in octaves_

What is the pattern called in m. 3? _scale pattern_
In m. 4? _broken chord_

Make a special note of the accents in this piece, and when you see notes that have staccatos combined with accents (sometimes known as accented staccatos), play them with a firmer, stronger touch, keeping the fingers rounded.

Where does Kabalevsky write these three times in a row on the same note? _m. 8_

Snickering 2nds

The laughter increases as the piece moves forward. Where does the composer introduce the interval of a 2nd? m. _9_ Once this interval has been introduced, it is used for the rest of the piece.

Seconds are often used for special effects. Listen to the dissonant sound of the 2nds by playing them by themselves. There are really only _three_ different 2nds played by the LH.

If you hold all the notes of the RH and LH down in each measure, the effect sounds like a _minor_ chord.

Student Workbook 5 Answers

Gigue in D Major

Johann Philipp Kirnberger (1721–1783)
Student Workbook 5, p. 4

A Leaping Melody

Unlike a minuet, waltz, march, or gavotte, this dance has a rollicking rhythm based on a time signature of $\frac{6}{8}$.

Play the RH melody of mm. 1–4, leaving out the ornaments for now. Be sure to include the first note of the melody that comes *before* m. 1.

What is that note called rhythmically? <u>upbeat</u>
The melody leaps upward in the first two notes by an interval of a <u>perfect 4th</u> .

There is another significant leap upward in the RH of m. 3.

Name the interval. <u>minor 7th</u>

A Leaping Melody that also Climbs!

Listen to the "climb" in the following diagram and find the hidden scale fragment. One accidental, <u>G sharp</u>, confirms the key of <u>A major</u> .

What is the scale degree (tonic or dominant) of the first RH note in the above example? <u>dominant</u>
What is the scale degree of the last note? <u>tonic</u>
What is the key relationship of this scale to the key of the piece? <u>dominant</u>

Name the intervals marked with brackets in the example. Write the intervals into your score. More interval leaps occur in the second section. Name the interval of the leap in m. 10 <u>octave</u> and m. 11: <u>minor 7th</u>

Imitation of the Melody

The LH begins as a canon.
Where does the canon begin? <u>m. 1</u>

How far apart are the two voices? <u>one octave</u>

How far does the canon go? m. <u>4</u>

Compare the imitation in the second section. The LH enters much sooner than in the first section. How far apart (in beats) are the two hands at first? <u>1 beat</u>

How far does the canon continue? <u>2 measures</u>

Play the LH melody from the middle of m. 10

Is the melody climbing? <u>yes</u>

Does the music make a small detour? <u>yes</u>

What scale is implied here? <u>G major</u>

The first and last notes of this melody are the same scale degree: <u>2 (supertonic)</u> .

A Summary of Kirnberger's Gigue Style

All gigues have some things in common. Write in the specific characteristics of Kirnberger's *Gigue* on the lines below:

Time signature: either $\frac{6}{8}$, $\frac{9}{8}$, or $\frac{12}{8}$.

Strong tone (dynamics) <u>forte</u>

Binary form (yes or no) <u>yes</u>

Allemande in G Minor, BWV 836

Johann Sebastian Bach (1685–1750)
Student Workbook 5, p. 6

Finding Chords and Keys in a Sequence

Bach often reinforces the shape of his phrases through the use of **sequences**. Sequences are often so short that you can hardly find them. In this piece, however, you can see an obvious sequence in mm. 6–8. The following steps will help you discover how Bach has built this sequence.

1. How long is the **motive** (the musical fragment that gets repeated) in this sequence? <u>one measure</u>

2. Is it repeated higher or lower? <u>higher</u>

3. In the music example below, the circled notes in m. 6 form two basic chords in G minor––the **dominant 7th** chord (V^7) followed by the **tonic** triad (I). These have been written out on the staff under the musical example. This pair of chords suggests a **perfect cadence** in G minor.

Since this is a sequence, you should be able to find similar pairs of chords in each of mm. 7 and 8. Circle the relevant notes in the music, and write them out as solid (blocked) chords on the empty staff. Name a key for each pair of chords.

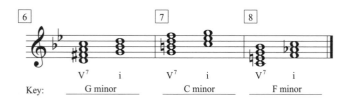

Key: _____G minor_____ _____C minor_____ _____F minor_____

As you can see, Bach travels easily from one key to another by using sequences. As you play the entire passage in mm. 6–10, observe how the first half / (second half) of the sequence is extended through m. 9.

A Rounded Binary Form

Describe what happens in the music after the short pause in m. 10.

<u>The opening material returns in the original key.</u>

Passepied in D Major

Charles Dieupart (ca 1667–ca 1740)
Student Workbook 5, p. 9

Make Music with a Piece of a Scale

On the staff below, write out the first note of the LH in each of the first four measures:

This is the (upper) / lower group of four notes of the scale (home key) of <u>D major</u>.

Are the notes ascending or descending? <u>descending</u>

Any scale can be divided into two halves, known as the lower and upper tetrachords.
Which tetrachord is this? <u>upper</u>

Triple Meter . . . and some Hidden Duple Meter

Although *Passepied* is written in triple meter, it is interesting to discover a few passages with a slightly different rhythmic feeling.

Add bar lines as though the passage were written in $\frac{2}{4}$ rather than $\frac{3}{4}$ time. In each of these new $\frac{2}{4}$ measures, an <u>F sharp</u> (name the note) is sounded on beat <u>1</u> in the LH.

Play this passage, imagining it as three measures of $\frac{2}{4}$ time, rather than two measures of $\frac{3}{4}$ time, as it appeared originally. This effect, known as **hemiola**, is quite common in dances in triple meter. A similar

effect may be felt at mm. 22 and 23. Add bar lines to these as you did in the previous example:

Perfect Cadences

Fill in the blanks under the LH of mm. 23 and 24:

Note name: ____A____ ____D____

Degree of
the scale: ____dominant____ ____tonic____

These notes suggest a <u>perfect</u> **cadence**.

As m. 15 crosses into m. 16, the LH moves from F sharp to B; these are the <u>dominant</u> and **tonic**, respectively, in the key of <u>B</u> minor. Once again, the preceding *hemiola* leads into a <u>perfect</u> cadence.

Verso in E Minor

Domenico Zipoli (1688–1726)
Student Workbook 5, p. 11

A Symmetrical Subject

1. The rhythm of m. 3 is a <u>mirror</u> image of m. 1. This technique is called rhythmic **inversion**.

2. Draw the shape (direction) of the melody.

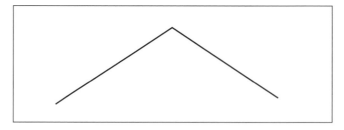

First it <u>rises</u>, then it <u>falls</u>.

A Musical Calendar

The "calendar" below has a square for each measure of *Verso*. As you answer the questions, add the details about the structure of the music to the appropriate squares.

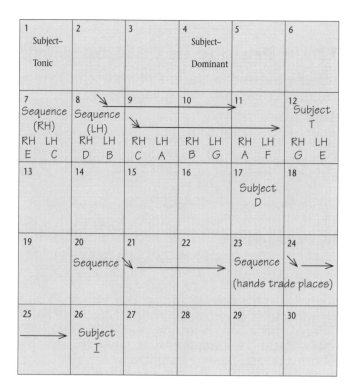

Introducing the Subject

Look at mm. 1–6.

Where is the subject introduced? m. __1__

Does it start on the **tonic**? __yes__

Where does the second voice enter? m. __4__

Does it start on the tonic or the **dominant**? __dominant__

What compositional technique is Zipoli using here? __imitation__

A Cartwheel

Look at mm. 7–11.

What is it about this passage that resembles the subject?
__the rhythm and the melodic shape of the LH figures in mm. 8–10__

From mm. 7–12, write the name of the first notes of every measure (both hands) in the calendar squares.

Do these notes form a pattern? __yes__

Is the pattern ascending or descending? __descending__

These measures form a short descending __scale__.

Fill in the Rest of the Squares

Mark **subject** or **sequence** in the appropriate squares for mm. 1–11. Now look for other statements of the subject and sequence patterns in the rest of the music. Indicate whether the subject starts on the tonic (T) or the dominant (D). Use up or down arrows to indicate rising or falling sequences.

Near the end of this piece, the hands exchange their motives. Look for the place where the hands seem to trade places and mark it on your calendar.

Fantasia in C Major, TWV 33:14
Georg Philipp Telemann (1681–1767)
Student Workbook 5, p. 14

Fill in the Phrase Map

Mark the cadences on the map, along with their keys, in the first half of each measure that has a dotted line. Then mark the beginning of each new phrase with its own letter (such as A, B, etc.). Remember, your phrase letters will always go into the *second half* of the appropriate measures. When a phrase is repeated in sequence, mark the same letter again but add Seq (for example, A, then A Seq). When a phrase is repeated with some other type of change, mark the same letter again with a subscript (for example, A, then A_1).

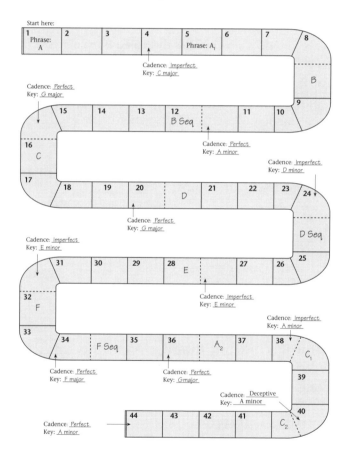

85

Bourrée in G Minor

Gottfried Heinrich Stölzel (1690–1749)
Student Workbook 5, p. 17

A Typical Bourrée

Examine this bourrée to discover some of the features of this dance:

Is it in duple or triple meter? <u>duple</u>

Does it start on the first beat or on an upbeat?
<u>upbeat</u>

A Baroque Sequence . . .

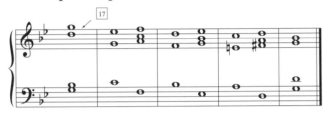

<u>F major</u>   <u>E flat major</u>   <u>D major</u>   <u>G major</u>

Write the note on the line indicated by the arrow. Which triad have you now created? <u>G minor</u>

The note you have added is the ☑ fifth of the chord.

Add the "missing fifths" to the other chords that need them, and identify those chords.

. . . that Copies Perfect Cadences

Fill in the bass notes in the following examples of a perfect cadence in G minor.

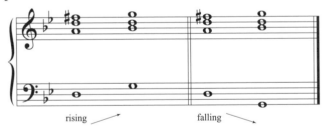

rising   falling

In the first instance, the bass rises a perfect <u>4th</u> ; in the second, it falls a perfect <u>5th</u> .

Compare this to the motion of the bass in the sequence you examined.

What do you observe?
<u>The bass alternates between 5ths and 4ths.</u>

One Last Question

Look at the fragment of music that comes right after the end of the sequence (beats 2 and 3 of m. 20).

Where did you hear it earlier in the piece?
mm. <u>3–4</u>

This passage actually makes the overall form a little clearer. Check the definitions of **binary** and **rounded binary form** in the Glossary at the back of this book.

Which one best fits Stölzel's *Bourrée?* <u>rounded binary</u>

Little Prelude in C Major, BWV 939

Johann Sebastian Bach (1685–1750)
Student Workbook 5, p. 19

Tonics and 7ths

Play m. 1 as a solid (blocked) chord and listen.

Can you identify this chord by its sound?
<u>dominant 7th</u>

If you answered a dominant 7th you are correct, but what key is it?

Here's the solution:
Name the triad formed by the notes in m. 2 and circle the root of the triad in your music. <u>F major</u>

Bach added the B flat in m. 1 to create the dominant 7th chord of <u>F</u> major. This dominant 7th **resolves** to an <u>F</u> major chord. Because the <u>F</u> major chord is the **subdominant** chord in the key of C major, and because there are no more accidentals, we hear the B flat as added harmonic color rather than a key change. Also notice that the bass note does not change; this is another indication that the key has not changed.

In other words, Bach has merely suggested the idea of a new key, rather than actually moving there.

What other measures have a similar-sounding dominant 7th chord? mm. <u>3, 5, 8, 9, 12, 13</u>

Exploring the Direction of the Phrase

The broken chords give this prelude a definite feeling of forward motion.

Do the chords in mm. 1–3 seem to be unwinding upward? <u>yes</u>

Another feature that moves the phrase forward is the addition of the added <u>7th</u> in the chord, as we noticed in the section, *Tonics and 7ths*.

Play mm. 1–4 and compare this long climb to that in mm. 8–12.

What is the name of the arrival chord in m. 4?
<u>C major</u>

What is the name of the arrival chord in m. 12?
<u>G major</u>

Pedals and Mordents

This prelude opens with a pair of bass notes that are held for three measures.

Can you find a place where Bach achieves the same pedal effect by repeating LH notes with shorter note values? mm. <u>9, 10, 11</u>

A Chord or a Scale

Preludes often have a flourish of scale passages and arpeggios near the end. These mini-*cadenzas* were often improvised by the performer. Those that were written out present a clear contrast in rhythm and they retain the quality of an improvisation.

Where is the flourish in this prelude? m. __14__

How might you play this final flourish to make it sound like an improvisation?
freely, rubato — with slightly varying speed

Allegretto in F Major

Johann Christoph Friedrich Bach (1732–1795)
Student Workbook 5, p. 21

Style

This elegant *Allegretto* is typical of J.C.F. Bach's style. It features a fluid stream of melody in the __right__ hand supported by an accompaniment in the __left__ hand.

Master the Accompaniment

On the staff below, write the chords in solid (blocked) form that are created by the Alberti bass pattern in mm. 5 and 6:

In m. 5, which note remains stationary? ☑ middle

The other notes move ☑ further apart and they move by ☑ half step.

In m. 6, how many notes remain the same between the two chords? __2__

How many change? __1__

In the case of the notes that change, the motion is ☑ down and the notes move by ☑ whole step.

Parallel Motion

In other places, the melody and accompaniment move together in **parallel** lines. Measures 3–4 are shown below; look at the notes in the box:

Three of these four notes form a triad; find it and write it in root position:

In which position is this triad actually played in the music? ☑ first inversion

Circle the other sets of notes that form similar triads in this passage, and then write out the entire sequence of triads on the staff below. Write them in the inversion in which they appear, but place the notes in close position.

Here is an example. The following chord:

written in close position becomes:

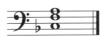

In both cases, this is the triad of __F major__ in __2nd__ inversion.

Write the triad chain from mm. 3 and 4 on the staff below:

As you can see, these chords form a chain moving in ascending / descending (circle one) parallel motion. Play this chain and listen for its special effect. Find two other places where Bach has created similar sets of chords in parallel motion:
mm. __11__ – __12__ ; mm. __31__ – __32__

Divertimento in G Major, Hob. XVI:8

Franz Joseph Haydn (1732–1809)
Student Workbook 5, p. 23

Third Movement: *Andante*
Gliding on a Smooth Surface

When you practice short motives for rhythmic accuracy, there is a tendency to forget that all the motives are contained within an elegant, gracefully shaped melody line. To play the RH melody smoothly on the piano, use a __legato__ touch.

For the LH accompaniment, remember the walking eighth notes, and decide whether you want them to glide smoothly like the RH, or to be detached lightly like dance steps. What instrument might the LH imitate? _bassoon, cello, double bass_

Finding the Phrases

In your score, draw long slurs over the melody to represent the phrases. Think about the upbeat, and remember to include it. Look through the entire piece.

Does every phrase begin with an upbeat? _yes_

How long are the questions and the answers?
1 measure

How long (in measures) are your phrases?
2 measures

There are _9_ measures in this piece. How many phrases in total? _4_

Most of the phrases in this movement of *Divertimento in G Major* are the same length, but at the end Haydn does something different. Then look at the measure just before it.

Are the two measures similar? _yes_

Composers sometimes repeat material just for emphasis. Haydn has created an emphatic answer! Look backward from the end.

Where does the last phrase begin?
m. _7 (with upbeat)_

Adding the Ornaments

How many ornaments do you see in the music? _6_

The trill in m. 4 is shorter /(longer) than the trill in m. 7. That is because the principal note in m. 4 is a _quarter_ note and the principal note in m. 7 is an _eighth_ note.

The double grace notes shown in footnote (d) are played quickly *on* the beat, and lead to the principal note. Find the two places where there are double grace notes: m. _7_ and m. _8_. Compare the note values of the principal notes. In which place is the figure played more quickly? _m. 8_

Fourth Movement: *Allegro*

This movement of *Divertimento in G Major* seems to be a complete contrast to the third movement in several ways. What do you notice on the page right away?

RH note values _eighth notes_

LH note values _sixteenth notes_

Where do the note values switch hands?
mm. _6_ and _9_

This movement clearly consists of a melody with accompaniment, but not always in the same hand!

Melody Based on Harmony

Is this movement in the same key as movement III?
yes

Name the notes of the **tonic** triad of the key. _G B D_

Looking at mm. 1–2, name all the RH notes in order _D G B D_.

What chord do you see? _G major_

Play the RH of mm. 1–4. Does this sound like one phrase? _yes_

Can you name the chord (triad) implied in the melody of m. 3? _C major_

The melody seems to disappear after m. 5, but it is actually hidden.

Where is the melody in mm. 6–8?
inside the sixteenth notes

Where is the melody in mm. 13–16?
inside the sixteenth notes

Have you heard that before? _yes_ Where? _m. 9_

Accompaniment Based on Harmony

In the first section, can you find a LH scale fragment? mm. _6–7_

(Don't be fooled by a change of clef.)

In the second section, can you find another one? mm. _13–15_

What makes this partial scale more tricky to play?
The LH scale is in octaves.

Comparing the Two Movements

When you have filled in this chart, you will have a useful summary of what you have learned about these movements of Haydn's *Divertimento in G Major*.

Divertimento in G Major, Hob. XVI:8	Movement III	Movement IV
Key	_G major_	_G major_
Time signature	**c** ($\frac{4}{4}$)	$\frac{3}{8}$
Tempo marking	_Andante_	_Allegro_
Ornaments	_yes_	_no_
Melody style	_built on scales_	_built on chords_
Accompaniment style	_walking eighth notes_	_modified Alberti bass_

Sonatina in F Major

Ludwig van Beethoven (1770–1827)
Student Workbook 5, p. 28

First Movement: *Allegro assai*

The Exposition: mm. 1–18

How would you describe the overall character of this theme?
☑ lighthearted and buoyant

Which accompaniment does the LH provide?
☑ The LH plays a simple accompaniment pattern based on harmony.

From mm. 13–18, Beethoven outlines **cadences** in the LH to indicate a brief passage through the key of _C major_ .

What are the two accidentals in m. 13?
B natural   _C sharp_

One of these accidentals merely provides a little **chromatic** interest in the melody.

Which accidental indicates the key change?
B natural

At the end of the exposition, does the music stay in this new key or does it return to the home key?
it returns to the home key.

How does it get back to the home key?
with a chromatic scale

The Development: mm. 19–50

Play through mm. 19–26. At the beginning, this development sounds like a continuation of the exposition.

Which measure signals a new section of the music?
m. _21_

What note in that measure seems intended to make the listener sit up and take notice? _E flat_

Now play mm. 27–39. There is an interesting interaction between the hands in this passage.

Is one hand asking a question and the other hand answering? Find a two-measure pattern where the LH **imitates** the RH: mm. _35–38_

How far behind is the LH? _1 measure_

What is this pattern of imitation called? _sequence_

Look at the final measures of the development (mm. 43–50).

What key does the music visit in these measures?
C major

Name the notes of the **tonic** triad in that key.
_C E G_

Name the notes of the **dominant** triad in the home key. _C E G_

The LH part reaches the dominant of the home key in m. _43_ .

How long does it stay there?
until he downbeat of m. 50

The Recapitulation: mm. 51–60

Compare the recapitulation to the exposition. Describe two differences between the two sections:

1. _The recapitulation is shorter (the first section from the exposition is missing)._

2. _The recapitulation stays in F major._

Which measures of the exposition are missing from the recapitulation? mm. _1–8_

The Coda: mm. 61–71

What is the meaning of the Italian word *coda*?
a concluding section added to the basic form

Often a *coda* is simply a larger and perhaps more elaborate version of the ending of the exposition. *Codas* are usually added to give the music an emphatic ending.

Is this the case here? _yes_

Which measures give you the impression that Beethoven is creating interest by briefly continuing his development of the theme? mm. _60–64_

Creating Momentum

What generates the forward motion and energy of Beethoven's theme in particular and the movement in general? Look at:
1. the increase in note values in the RH:

2. the almost constant two-measure sixteenth-note patterns, often tossed from hand to hand
3. the joviality of the short slurs from m. 8

What other musical elements generate energy and forward motion? _rising sequences, grace notes_

Second Movement: *Rondo*

The Rondo Theme: mm. 1–16

Play the opening section of this rondo (mm. 1–16). Does this theme have a similar character to the theme of the first movement, or does it present a contrasting character?
It is a contrast — rythmically it is mostly eighth notes in both hands; the accompaniment and touch are different.

How would you describe the accompaniment pattern? Does the LH part interact melodically with the RH melody? _yes_

Before you answer that question, you might want to take a closer look at the first few measures:

Play this excerpt as written, then play it again, but leave out all the F's. The accompaniment, at least in these measures, is actually a hidden second melody supporting the top melody.

Do these two voices move by half steps or by whole steps? _half steps_

Why do you think Beethoven added these accidentals?
It makes the harmony more colorful and interesting.

What is the interval between the two voices, i.e., RH and LH? _10th_

What would this interval be if the lower note were raised by an octave? _3rd_

Look through the music for each occurrence of this theme, and mark it A in your score.

Does this theme always appear in the same key? _yes_

The B Theme: mm. 17–28

List two similarities between the A theme and the B theme.
Both themes have similar dynamic shapes.
Both themes use accidentals that do not affect their home keys.
Both themes are in major keys.

List two contrasts between the A theme and the B theme.
The B theme has no ornaments.
The RH of the B theme is mostly legato.
The LH of the B theme is staccato.

The C Theme: mm. 37–66

What are the main contrasts between the A theme and the C theme?
The C theme is in a minor key; the A theme is in a major key. In the C theme, the same motive is repeated three times.

Can you find any similarities between them?
the LH rhythm; the dynamic shaping; the use of imitative repetitions and sequences; the use of short phrases; the bouncy eighth-note figures; the return of the first theme at the end of the sections

A Bridge: mm. 67–74

This short section builds first toward a *fermata* and then toward the F major chord that signals the return of the A theme.

What does the *fermata* tell you to do? _pause_

Name the LH chord under the *fermata*. _C major_

What is this chord in the key of F major? _dominant_

What is the name of the RH note? _B flat_

What is the name of the chord under the *fermata*? _dominant 7th_

The RH uses this chord as a launching pad for a tiny, but expressive *cadenza*.

What does *ad libitum* mean?
freely; the performer can improvise or vary the tempo

What could you do to add expression to this short passage? _Hold the fermata for a long time; play slowly toward the return of A._

The Final A Section

What has Beethoven added to make this last statement really final?
He added a codetta, confirming the home key of F major. (This can also be called a cadential extension.)

Setting out the Form

You've made your way through this movement. Now you can summarize the form. Fill in the measure numbers in the chart below, then add details such as key, length in measures, and the presence of repeat signs. When you finish, play the rondo all the way through, with all the repeats.

A	mm.	_1_	– _16_	key:	_F major_
B	mm.	_17_	– _28_	key:	_C major_
A	mm.	_29_	– _36_	key:	_F major_
C	mm.	_37_	– _66_	key:	_D minor_
bridge	mm.	_67_	– _74_	key:	_F major_
A	mm.	_75_	– _94_	key:	_F major_

Sonatina in A Minor, op. 214, no. 4

Cornelius Gurlitt (1820–1901)
Student Workbook 5, p. 32

First Movement: *Moderato*

Getting to Know the Themes

Match each of the following descriptions to the thematic fragment that you feel fits it best. Add measure numbers to each fragment.

Dance-like: theme _B (part 2)_

Theme A: mm. _1–2_
Simple, singing melody (also, very different from the other fragments): theme _B (part 1)_

A cheery motive that closes the exposition: theme _B (part 3)_

A set of notes that seems to curl around itself: theme _A_

Theme group B (part 1): mm. _23–26_

Theme group B (part 2): mm. <u>35–38</u>

Theme group B (part 3): mm. <u>45–46</u>

Fitting the Themes Together

Now let's discover how a composer creates an entire movement out of small musical fragments like these. Follow the outline, looking for clues and questions along the way.

Exposition

Theme A (mm. 1–16): At m. 3, the opening motive is repeated a <u>4th</u> (name the interval) higher. Find two other places in the movement where a similarly short motive is heard, then repeated at a different pitch level:

mm. <u>17–20</u>; mm. <u>45–48</u>.

Bridge (mm. 17–22): How is this section related to theme A?
<u>Theme A appears in the LH.</u>

As the name suggests, this section leads out of theme A into theme group B.

Theme group B (part 1):
Find the start of this theme in the examples above. In its first measure, circle three notes that form a triad in root position. This triad reveals the key of theme B, which is <u>C major</u>.

How is this key related to the opening key of the movement? <u>It is the relative major.</u>

Observe how Gurlitt prepares this key toward the end of the previous section (the bridge). The chord in the LH at m. 21:

is the <u>dominant 7th</u> chord of the key of theme group B. It announces the arrival of this new key.

As you observed earlier, several new ideas appear in the theme B section. This is why the B section is described as a theme group.

Development

The development is from mm. 47 to <u>61</u>.
Two of the thematic fragments shown earlier are explored a little further. Identify these two fragments: mm. <u>1–2</u> and mm. <u>45–46</u>.

Recapitulation

This section begins with the return of theme A in the ⟨home key⟩/ another key at m. <u>70</u>.

Look for the return of theme group B (part 1). Circle the three notes in the first measure of this theme that form a triad in root position:

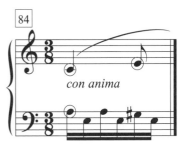

This time, these notes form the triad of <u>A minor</u>.

As you can see, keys are used differently in the exposition and recapitulation, even though the music itself is largely the same. Describe this difference by filling in the blanks.

In the <u>Exposition</u>, the music establishes a home key and then leaves it.

In the <u>Recapitulation</u>, the music establishes the <u>home</u> key again and then stays there.

Second Movement: *Andantino* (*Intermezzo*)

This gentle *Intermezzo* acts as an interlude between the more extensive first and third movements of the sonatina. Which keys does Gurlitt use to create contrast between the middle movement and those on either side of it?
<u>The second movement is in A major, whereas the first and third movements are in A minor.</u>

The composer uses short and simple ideas to charming effect here. Call the opening phrase A. How long is the A phrase? <u>4</u> measures

Using letters to represent each of the phrases, you can easily discover the form of this movement (you will need to use one of the symbols more than once):
A   B   *Coda*

The form is <u>A A B A coda</u>.

Which phrase is longer than the other ones? <u>coda</u>
This phrase is <u>5</u> measures long. Considering where this phrase lies within the movement, how does its added length actually help make the form even clearer?
<u>Since this is the last phrase, its greater length gives the music a feeling of finality.</u>

Third Movement: *Allegro capriccioso*

Creating Form out of Contrast

Which of the following best describes the character of the opening (A) section of this third movement:
☑ rapid rhythmic gestures

At m. _17_, a contrasting B section begins. What two aspects of the music create an obvious contrast with what came before?
1. _change from a minor key to a major key_
2. _longer rhythmic values_

Observe the overall layout of the movement. Which of the following letter schemes represents it best?
☑ A B A B₁

Which section—A or B—features melody in one hand and accompaniment in the other? _A_

In which section is the music shared equally between the hands? _B_

The Hands Become Equal Partners

Let's examine the interaction between the layers (or voices) in the B section. On the systems below, write out the notes of the highest and lowest voices in the following excerpts from this movement (refer to your *Piano Repertoire 5*, p. 25):

Excerpt no. 1
mm. 17–18

Excerpt no. 2
mm. 25–26

Match each of the excerpts to the appropriate descriptions below:

Outer voices move in contrary motion: Excerpt no.
_2_
Outer voices move in a mix of parallel and contrary motion: Excerpt no. _1_

In a major key: Excerpt no. _1_

In the relative minor key (the minor key that has the same key signature as the major key): Excerpt no. _2_

The Lake, op. 42, no. 9

Alec Rowley (1892–1958)
Student Workbook 5, p. 37

Rhythmic Spacing

What is the key of the piece? _E major_

Do you think this key lends a bright /(subdued) color?

Searching for Melody

If you look at the score away from the piano, it doesn't seem as if there is a melody at all. With your RH, play m. 1 and only the top notes of all the double notes in mm. 2–8.

Which measure is exactly like m. 1? _m. 5_

What happens to the top notes in mm. 9–15?
They repeat C sharp.

Rowley writes in a different style in the middle section (mm. 17–34). The RH consists of *staccato* broken octaves with one essential middle note. This middle note combines with the octaves and the LH to create chords. The melody is more exposed now. You should be able to find it if you remember what you did in mm. 1–8.

Where are the melody notes?
the top note in each RH measure

Have you seen them before?
yes, at the beginning (mm. 1–8)

Listening for Harmony

The first surprise is found at m. 6. What is the chord? _G major_

Does this chord belong in the key of E major? _no_

At m. 7, play the chord hands together. What do you hear? _a dominant 7th_ in the key of _G major_.

At m. 8, what is the chord? _G major_ The chord in m. 7 **resolves** (leads) to the chord in m. 8, and the result is a _perfect_ cadence.

Do you remember the top notes in mm. 9–16? Beneath those top notes the composer has created some movement in the harmony. Play the first beat of each of these measures and listen carefully. How many different chords do you hear? _4_
Which chords sound like dominant 7ths? m. _10_ and m. _12_

Play mm. 14 and 15. Another surprise!

Which chord is major? m. _14_

Which chord is minor? m. _15_

That is because the composer wants to return to the **tonic** key of E major. To do that he prepares in m. 15, then at m. 16 he uses the dominant 7th of what key? _E major_

There is one broken dominant 7th chord spread out between two measures on the first line of the second page.
Can you find it? mm. _27–28_

Play it blocked. Now write it out on the staff below, using only the treble clef.

Where have you seen the same dominant 7th before (in blocked form between the hands)? m. _10_

Cha-Cha

Siegfried Merath (b. 1923)
Student Workbook 5, p. 40

Cha-Cha

Within mm. 1–8, find two measures where nothing is played on one of the strong beats in the RH: m. _2_ and m. _4_.

The empty spot occurs at the start of the first / (third) beat.

Parallel Voices

Another feature in popular and jazz arrangements of all kinds is having the sounds move in **parallel motion**. In the following example, indicate the interval by which each note within the box moves (write your answer over or under each of the arrows). The first interval on top has been done for you.

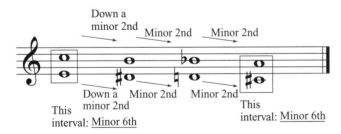

Also, indicate the interval between the upper and lower notes at the very beginning and at the end.

What do you notice? _They are the same._

This passage is in parallel _6ths_ (the interval you just observed).

Look for two examples of parallel motion in *Cha-Cha*. One involves the LH only, the other both hands, but neither lasts very long.

On the staves below, write the last set of sounds heard together in each passage you found. Then try extending each passage a little by adding further sets of notes, using the same parallel motion. (The first chord is done for to get you started.)

Ex. 1: mm. _9–10, 13–14_

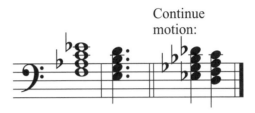

Ex. 2: m. _24_

Grandmother's Song, op. 27, no. 10
Friedrich Robert Volkmann (1815–1883)
Student Workbook 5, p. 42

Texture: A Way of Describing Sound
Which of the following is likely to produce sound of a smoother texture:
☑ a church choir

Which of the following music fragments has the thicker texture? ☑ b

How many notes are sounding at the very beginning of m. 2, including any note or notes that may be tied over from the previous measure? _4_

How many notes are sounding halfway through m. 2, including any note or notes that may be tied over from the previous beat? _4_

At the start of m. 4? _4_ At the start of m. 5? _3_

Do your answers suggest a texture that remains even and similar throughout, or that changes a lot? _even and similar throughout_

Now find the measure that has the fewest notes sounding at one time. m. _9_

There are _3_ notes sounding at any time in this measure.

What's a Double Sharp?
Volkmann uses an accidental (a double sharp) that might be unfamiliar: ✗

This accidental is used in mm. _6_ and _8_.

It does exactly what its name suggests: it raises a note not one half step but two.

Play the following notes:

D up a half step to / D♯ up a half step to / D✗ = _E_

Rewrite D✗ enharmonically without an accidental.

This note is the enharmonic equivalent of D✗. In other words, it sounds the same but looks different because it is written with a different letter name.

A Piece of Romantic Music
Grandmother's Song offers an example of one of the best-known types of piano music of the Romantic period, the **character piece**. (Volkmann's dates place him within the Romantic period.) Can you name two famous composers from this period? _Brahms, Schubert, Schumann, Chopin_

Waltz, op. 12, no. 2
Edvard Grieg (1843–1907)
Student Workbook 5, p. 44

Waltz Rhythm
The waltz is an elegant dance in which couples glide smoothly around the dance floor.

Play the LH part in mm. 1–10.
Which beat suggests a longer step? _beat 1_

What two markings emphasize this longer step and the gliding motion of the dancers? _pedal_ _slur_

Do you associate either of these markings with a minuet? _no_

A Norwegian Waltz
What marking does Grieg use to highlight the energetic attack of the bow on these triplet figures? _> (accent)_

Find several places where Grieg introduces a drone: _the dotted half notes in mm. 12–16_

An Offbeat Accent
Play the melody of mm. 3–6. Pay extra attention to the articulation markings.

What does the *tenuto* marking tell you to do? _stress; hold for full value_

Where are the accented beats in mm. 3–4? _beat 1_

Where is the accented beat in mm. 5–6? _moves it to beat 2_

Is it on a strong beat? _no_

In mm. 1–4, Grieg first establishes a rhythmic pulse. Then, in mm. 5–6, he upsets it with an offbeat accent, so that the hands are accenting different beats of the measure. This rhythmic ambiguity adds a little extra spice to the music.

Find other places where Grieg shifts the accent away from the first beat of the measure: mm. _38, 40, 44, 46, 48, 50, 51, 52_

Melody in the Left Hand
In mm. 37–50, the LH has the melody. Play the RH accompaniment lightly detached.

What is the key of this section? _A major_

The harmonies alternate back and forth between two chords. Can you name their function in the key of A major? _tonic_ _dominant_

Filming in the Ballroom
In movies, you have probably watched scenes where there is dancing. The camera follows one couple for a while, shifts to another couple to catch their conversation, and then returns to the first couple.

Suppose you were a director using this waltz in a film. Where would you shift the camera to the second couple? _m. 37_

Jig
Violet Archer (1913–2000)
Student Workbook 5, p. 46

Tap Your Feet! Clap Your Hands!
The LH of *Jig* seems to bounce along—like dancers and spectators clapping their hands in time to the music. It's hard to keep your hands or your feet still when you hear a good, strong, lively rhythm. What is the interval between the two LH notes in m. 1? _a 5th_

Does Archer use the same interval for all the LH double notes? <u>yes</u>

What instrument do you think these 5ths sound like? <u>violin</u>

Now look at the LH part through the rest of the piece.

How many different LH rhythmic patterns can you find? Write each one here.

Archer has used different LH note values because she wanted different types of sound. Give each note and rest the correct value, to capture these differences.

What is the marking on the first eighth note in m. 9? <u>tenuto and staccato</u>

How will you make that note different from the *staccato* eighth note that follows?
<u>by playing it only slightly detached</u>

Where else does Archer use this marking? m. <u>13</u>

A Lively Dance

This tune has a lively $\frac{6}{8}$ swing that keeps going measure after measure without stopping for a rest. How does Archer create this feeling of perpetual motion?
<u>There is movement on most beats.</u>

How long are most of the phrases in this tune?
<u>four measures</u>

What happens in mm. 29–33? <u>The composer adds a measure, making a five-measure phrase.</u>

Imagine this tune played on a country fiddle. Listen for the bow strokes and accents as the bow bounces on the strings.

What articulation mark indicates the notes that are played together in one bow stroke? <u>slur</u>

How does the fiddler play the chords in mm. 25 and 29? <u>accented on beat 1 and slurred</u>

What is happening in mm. 9–10 and 13–14? Are the dancers clapping to keep time while the fiddler takes a short break? <u>yes</u>

Form and Mode

Jig is in **rondo form**. The repeat sign indicates the A section. Can you fill in the other sections on the chart?

A mm. 1–8   :|| <u>B</u> mm. 9– <u>16</u> |A₁ mm. <u>17</u> – <u>24</u> |

C mm. <u>25</u> – <u>33</u> | <u>A</u> mm. 34–41 | <u>coda</u> mm. 42–47 ||

What is the key signature of this piece?
<u>no sharps or flats</u>

With this key signature, it is reasonable to assume the key is either <u>C major</u> or <u>A minor</u>. However, the melody begins and ends on <u>D</u>, and A seems to function as the <u>dominant</u> rather than the <u>tonic</u>.

The answer is that *Jig* is in the **Dorian mode**.

Little March

Talivaldis Kenins (1919–2008)
Student Workbook 5, p. 48

Here Comes the Marching Band!

We've all experienced a band marching down the street, so you will already have an idea of the sounds to listen for in this piece. Here are a few typical ones. Match the motive to the description that is most appropriate.

Wind instrument fanfare: Rhythm <u>2</u>

Beating of drums: Rhythm <u>1</u>

Find two pairs of measures where rhythm 1 appears in the LH only:
mm. <u>5–6</u> mm. <u>21–22</u>

Where is rhythm 1 used to lead back into the same music heard at the opening? m. <u>16</u>

Find the measure where the triplet figure of rhythm 1 is passed from one hand to the other, almost as though from one drummer to another: m. <u>23</u>

Listen for the effect as you play this rhythmic transfer.

An Interesting "Pop" Chord

Write a C major triad on the staff above. Next to it, write the chord played at the start of *Little March*. (Note: in the music, this chord is shared between the hands.)

The "strange" chord is widely used in contemporary music, especially in popular styles. In order to build this chord in its basic form, write a bass note and then add the triad whose root is a major 2nd (whole step) lower than that bass note. This is often called a *suspended* chord. For instance, a C suspended chord could be written as follows:

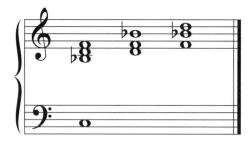

Triad of B♭
B♭ is a major 2nd lower
than the bass C note

Write out the inversions of the triad of B flat next to the root position on the staff above. Play all three forms—each has its own particular sound.

Now write a sus chord for each of the following bass notes:

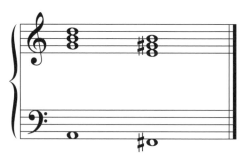

Postlude (à la Shostakovich),
op. 7, no. 6

George Fiala (b. 1922)
Student Workbook 5, p. 50

Flats!! (Don't Panic)
What is the key of Fiala's *Postlude*? <u>E flat minor</u>

All the notes are flat except the note <u>F</u>.

Layers of Sound
What are the two rhythmic elements that make up the LH accompaniment figure? Which carries the bass line and which provides the harmony?

1. <u>The half notes carry the bass line.</u>

2. <u>The eighth notes provide the harmony.</u>

Fiala combines these two elements to create a gentle, throbbing accompaniment. Play the eighth notes a little more softly than the half-note bass line.

Fiala has given the LH notes three different markings. What are they?
1. <u>tenuto</u>
2. <u>pedal</u>
3. <u>portato</u>

Play the melody alone and listen to the phrase structure.

How many phrases are there? <u>7</u>

Is each phrase the same length? <u>no</u>

Does each phrase have the same shape? <u>similar</u>

Expressive Markings
The music is marked *adagietto* and *malinconico*. What do these two Italian words mean?
adagietto <u>slightly faster than adagio</u>
malinconico <u>melancholy</u>

This piece has only one dynamic marking: <u>mp</u>.

A Rhythm in Five
Where does the time signature change?
mm. <u>20</u> and <u>22</u>

What is the effect of these changes on the melody?
<u>It lengthens the phrase (rhythmic augmentation).</u>

Why do you think Fiala chose to lengthen some of the measures at this point in the piece?
<u>to slow it down because it is coming to an end</u>

When composers use frequently changing time signatures, it is often useful to look for patterns by grouping several measures together.
What two time signatures does Fiala use here? <u>2/4 3/4</u>

If you "add" these time signatures together, what do you get? <u>5/4</u>

À La Shostakovich
Postlude is a tribute to Dmitri Shostakovich. In it, Fiala imitates characteristics of Shostakovich's style.

One of these characteristics is sudden **modulations**. In m. 7, the music moves quickly from the opening key of E flat natural minor to G natural minor. Write the **tonic** triads of these two keys.

E♭ minor triad   G minor triad

What note do these triads have in common? <u>B flat</u>

Fiala seems to use this note as a "bridge" to cross from one key into the next.

Another characteristic of Shostakovich's style is the use of **parallel motion**. Find three passages where Fiala uses parallel motion, and name the interval.

1. <u>mm. 1–6, 15–20 (parallel 3rds)</u>
2. <u>mm. 7–8 (parallel 4ths)</u>
3. <u>mm. 9–14 (parallel 5ths)</u>

Shostakovich often approached **cadences** in a surprising way. Let's see what Fiala does with the final cadence in this piece. Play the last two chords hands separately and listen to the sound.

Do the RH and LH notes approach the tonic in a more-or-less normal way? _no (the LH is closer to what would be expected than the RH)_

Can you hear any **dissonance**? _yes_

Now play these chords hands together. Both parts seemed fine on their own, but together they clash!

Do you think the tension created by this final dissonance strengthens the feeling of rest and the release of tension we hear in the final tonic chord? _yes_

Star Gazing

Jean Coulthard (1908–2000)
Student Workbook 5, p. 53

Star Points

In m. 2, Coulthard uses delicate, *staccato* notes to suggest tiny points of light twinkling in the dark sky. Imagine looking at individual stars in the sky, one after another, as you let your fingers wander from note to note.

This measure is marked "freely."

Does the $\frac{4}{4}$ time signature apply to this measure? _no_

Do the quarter notes have to be played at a specific speed? _no_

Coulthard has indicated that the pedal should be held down through the measure.

How would you describe the effect this creates? _It connects the stars together, like constellations._

Look through the rest of the piece.

Where are the other "star point" measures? _m. 7   m. 12   m. 17_

Contrast in Character

List five differences between m. 2 and mm. 4–5 in the following chart:

	measure 2	measures 4–5
Tempo	free	moderate
Touch	staccato	legato
Note values	quarter notes only	varied; eighth, quarter, half notes
Rests	rests appear	no rests
Ties	no ties	ties appear

Does the music in these measures seem to be in any particular key? _no_

What is the reason for your answer? _there is no pull toward a tonic or home key_

Transition Measures

Now look at m. 1.

What is the marking above the second chord, and what does it tell you to do? _It is a fermata; it means "pause."_

Where are the notes in this measure repeated? _in m. 3_

How many lines of music begin in the same way? _six_

Twelve-Tone Stars

Let's see what Coulthard does with her tone row. Here is the pattern of notes in m. 2:

Here are the notes in the three other star-point measures. Write your explanation of how Coulthard changes the row under each example.

The pattern is backward.

Each pair of notes is inverted and the order is rearranged.

Most of the intervals are inverted and the order of the notes in the intervals is reversed.

Sounding the Accordion

Jenő Takács (1902–2005)
Student Workbook 5, p. 56

Dancing the Polka

Remembering the definition, and looking at the opening rhythm, can you tell where the hop would be? m. _1, 2nd half of beat 2_. The piece does begin with a hop!

Two other words fit into the picture: the tempo marking _vivace_ meaning _lively_ and a word for touch in m. 1 _pesante_ meaning _heavily_ .

20th-Century Sound

The piece begins in the key of _C major_ , and if you play the RH from mm. 1–8 you will hear a melody in two-part harmony that is as conventional as a folk song. But Takács adds sharp **dissonances** in certain places in the LH accompaniment, creating a humorous quality. It sounds as if he's having fun!

What is the interval between the two voices in the RH? _3rd_

Now look at the following example, and play the two circled notes in each measure together.

What interval do you hear? _minor 2nd_

Contrasting Key and Form

The key changes in m. _9_ to the key of _E flat major_ . So that it will not come as a complete surprise, the composer prepares the dancers for what is coming.

Where is the new key signature first displayed? _the end of line 2_

Where does it change back? _after m. 16_

A contrasting key helps us to assess the form of the piece. On your score, label the first section A. Label the second (new key) section B.

How many measures are in A? _8_

How many are in B? _8_

Are they equal in length? _yes_

What happens next? _a return to A_

Is there a second contrasting section? _yes_

What is its key? _G major_ Label this C.

What does the composer indicate at the end? _D. C. al Fine_

Your score should look like this: ABACA Therefore, the dance is in _rondo_ form.

Playing Repeated 3rds

Play these measures slowly, beginning with the fingering given.

Your hand lies over the triad of _C major_ .

Now isolate the repeated 3rds in m. 2 and work on them separately.

Which fingers have you landed on? $\frac{5}{3}$

Articulation and Accents

Name all the types of articulation that you see in section A. (You should have five.)
staccato
portato
slur
accented staccato
tenuto

When Rivers Flowed on Mars

Nancy Telfer (b. 1950)
Student Workbook 5, p. 59

Flowing Eighth Notes

Apart from the very last measure, are there any measures without eighth notes? _m. 27_

Making Waves

Using the free-flowing eighth notes first, Telfer sets the pattern in the beginning. There is a _two_ -measure introduction before anything begins to happen.

What is the interval between the first two notes? _perfect 5th_

Is this interval consistent throughout the piece? _yes_

Melody Floating Downstream

Where does the melody enter? m. _3_

What are the note values? _half notes_

What is the direction of the first three notes?
☑ descending

Already the musical texture becomes more complex. How many parts does the RH play? _two_

The melodies and partial melodies throughout the piece appear in different forms. At m. 5, the eighth-note pattern remains the same, but there is something added. What indicates the presence of melody? _quarter note stems going up_

The fluidity of water is portrayed in m. 6. The melody ends on the half-note _D_ , with the flowing eighths coming in on beat 2. Would you play the half-note D and the eighth-note D at the same dynamic level? _no_

At m. 13, how is the melody different? _It is in 3rds._

What is the dynamic level? _f_

Two markings on the score are significant in these measures:
1. _mp (quick drop in dynamics) in m. 16_
2. _rit. in m. 17_

Arabesque, op. 6, no. 2

Génari Karganov (1858–1890)
Student Workbook 5, p. 62

Stitching the Fabric

Play the RH in mm. 1–2.
If you count 1 and 2 and 3 and, what part of the count are you playing on? _and_

What is the name of this offbeat rhythmic pattern? _syncopation_

To play the RH alone successfully, tap the beats with your LH and play with the RH.

Listen again to the opening 3rds. (Don't look at the key signature.)

What key do you hear? _G major_

Interestingly, it sounds like G major, but when the LH is added, the key is clearly _B major_.

Following the Melodic Thread

What do you see above and below the staff in m. 1? _pp above, mf below_

Where does the melody transfer to the RH? m. _3_

Do the same dynamics apply? _yes_

How many measures of melody are played before the hands alternate? _two_

Is this number always the same? _yes_

Which hand plays the melody at the end? _RH_

Coloring the Texture

There are many ways of adding color to a musical composition. The two most often used are varying dynamics and varying harmonic progressions.

Dynamics are easy to _see_ on the page, and for this reason are the most obvious. The term _espressivo_, meaning _expressively_, indicates that there will be flexibility in the tempo and shading in the quantity of sound. This _Arabesque_ is an elaborate design, intricate in its detail.

Notice the long "hairpin" marking underneath the first LH melody. What is it called? _diminuendo_ But this melody is rising. Do you associate this type of dynamic suggestion with a rising melody? _no_ Why is it there?
The LH becomes the accompaniment in m. 3.

Play m. 13. Is the _più forte_ meant for the LH? _yes_

Possibly the most intricate place in variety of color is at mm. 15–16. Describe the effect in sound. (Translate all the markings in order.)

loud – getting softer – moderately quiet – getting louder – slowing down a bit

Where in the first line do you see the dominant 7th resolving to the tonic? _mm. 3–4_

In m. 7, there is a **modulation**, begun by another dominant. What is the key at m. 8? _D major_ The color becomes more and more vivid by using a sequence of cadences, arriving at a musical climax in mm. _15–16_. To find the climax, look and listen for dramatic dynamics and harmonic intensity.

Two Parts in One Hand

Two places indicate melody and accompaniment to be played in one hand, mm. _11–12_ and mm. _15–16_. These passages need special practice.

Dimensions of the Tapestry

This piece is _24_ measures long. The phrases appear in a pattern of alternating hands, but they may not be as short as they look. If you play as suggested above, following the "thread" of the melody, you will hear a longer line. If you think of the phrase line as being horizontal, what is the length of the phrases? _two measures_

A Slow Waltz, op. 39, no. 23

Dmitri Kabalevsky (1904–1987)
Student Workbook 5, p. 65

Find the Form

Does the music of the opening return?
If so, where? mm. _25_ to _32_

Between the two repeating sections, look for a section that is obviously different. There is an Italian indication, _un poco più mosso_, which means _a little more motion_.

The LH accompaniment changes. It is now written exclusively in harmonic _3rds_. (Name the interval.)

Look for a change of key. It is often easy to discover the key of a passage simply by finding the **tonic** triad. Write out the notes contained in m. 1 as a triad in root position:

triad of _A minor_

Look at the measure where you spotted the Italian marking earlier. Write out the notes from this measure as a triad in root position:

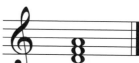

m. _9_ ; triad of _D minor_

Finally, choose the set of letters below that best represents the overall form of _A Slow Waltz_.
☑ A B A _Coda_

Interval Identification

There is an interesting relationship between the intervals used in this waltz. In the A section, the RH uses which harmonic interval exclusively?
☑ 6th

Write this interval above the following note:

Rewrite it, by moving the lower note up an octave. Leave the other note where you wrote it:

What is the new interval? 3rd

In *A Slow Waltz*, this interval is used only in the LH.

This creates a hidden connection between various sections of the piece.

When you took the original interval and turned it upside down, you **inverted** it. The intervals above are each other's inversion. As you can see from this example, an interval plus its inversion always add up to the number 9.

A 7th inverted becomes a 2nd.

A 4th inverted becomes a 5th.

The Left Hand: It Makes a Difference!

Much of the graceful charm of this *Waltz* derives from the way in which Kabalevsky varies the rhythm of the accompaniment in the LH.

In which group of measures is the rhythm of the LH very repetitive?
mm. 9–24

In other sections, the LH has slightly more intricate patterns. The *low* notes (for part of the time, at least) suggest one of the following rhythmic patterns:

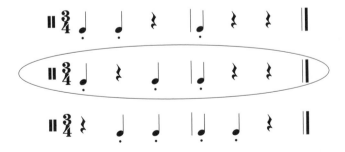

Circle the pattern that you feel is most appropriate.

Jest

Béla Bartók (1881–1945)
Student Workbook 5, p. 67

A Joke . . . and A Dance

A jest is a witty or bantering remark—like a joke. The *giocoso* marking at m. 5 sums up the mood of this jest perfectly.

What is the meaning of this Italian word? joyfully

Look at the rhythmic style of this piece.

Would you describe it as simple or complex? simple

Is it in duple or triple meter? duple

Find the Structure

Measures 5–16: The LH accompaniment up to m. 11 is centered around the triad of D major. But look out for those clever changing notes in these chords; Bartók may already be playing a little joke on the performer! The note that changes is the ☑ middle of the chords.

The melody is repeated from mm. 21 to 31.

Describe the change in the LH accompaniment. It becomes a broken-chord pattern instead of solid chords

The melody is repeated yet again from mm. 35 to 49. This time, the LH is really full of surprises. Its patterns suggest three distinct triad shapes.

Write these out in solid (blocked) form on the staff below, and indicate the measure where each appears.

m. 35   m. 36   m. 39

The first of these is the triad of B minor. What is the relationship between this key and the one that you identified in the first statement of the melody at m. 5? relative minor This is one of the reasons that this new accompaniment sounds so convincing.

A Musical Interruption

Play mm. 5–16 through. Play them again, but this time, leave out mm. 12–13 to better appreciate the effect of these two measures.

How might you describe this effect? mm. 12–13 interrupt the music

Write in the measure numbers of the places where this effect occurs in the other statements of the melody.

mm. 12–13

mm. <u>28–29</u>

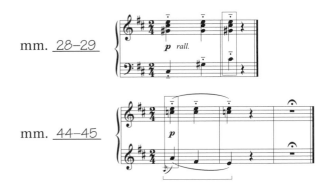

mm. <u>44–45</u>

Bartók has added something to the last excerpt to make the musical point even stronger. What is it? <u>pedal</u>

Look at the boxed chords in the excerpts above. Each contains the notes of a triad; write these triads in root position below.

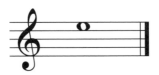

Triad of <u>C major</u>   Triad of <u>C sharp minor</u>   Triad of <u>A minor</u>

Which of the first two triads is somewhat similar to the third triad? <u>the triad of C major</u>

In all three versions, one note is heard constantly. Write it here:

The indication *rall.* appears with (or near) all three excerpts shown above. This term is an abbreviation for the Italian word <u>rallentando</u>, which means <u>slow down gradually</u>.

Play the three "interruptions" above, one after the other, and listen for the way in which they sound so similar yet so different. Each one can grab the listener's attention in its own particular way.

The Last Laugh

At the very end, what happens to your RH? Where does it play? <u>under the LH</u>

Does the sound of this ending contribute to the humor of the piece, and if so, how? <u>It sounds like deep laughter.</u>

Romance

Larysa Kuzmenko (b. 1956)
Student Workbook 5, p. 70

Sound and Color

Romance is a character piece. This means that its music conveys a mood or atmosphere to the listener. As you learn it, listen for the atmosphere suggested by the music. One of the ways to help

this along may be to compare it to other pieces in your *Piano Repertoire 5*. For instance, take a look at *Scamp* or *Little March*. Each of these has a definite mood that you will easily identify.

Is Romance similar to or different from those pieces? <u>different</u>

From the following list of words, circle two that you feel apply to the sound of this piece:

(delicate)

(the atmosphere of a late autumn day)

A Subtle Key

Three of the notes of m. 1 can fit together as a triad in root position.
Write it here:

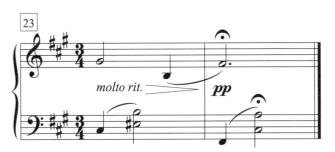

This shows the key of the piece, which is <u>F sharp minor</u>. Check the notes of the last measure. If they match this triad, you have the correct key.

bass note: tonic or dominant?   bass note: tonic or dominant?

<u>dominant</u>   <u>tonic</u>

This is a <u>perfect</u> **cadence.**

When you play this piece, can you hear a strong pull toward the **tonic** note? <u>no</u>

Although the music ends with a definite cadence, the tonic note seems to be absent a great deal of the time.

A Subtle Melody

The rhythm of the melody contributes to the waltz rhythm, but the notes don't follow an equally predictable pattern. Play the melody alone (leave out the middle voice in mm. 7–12), and listen to the tune.

Do the notes in mm. 17 and 18 go where you expect them to? <u>no</u>

Countermelodies

You have seen that the RH and LH work together to create the rhythm of this music. The LH also provides a countermelody. Much of the time, this melody is easy to see and hear, as in mm. 1–4.

However, Kuzmenko has also chosen to use some of the lower bass notes both as a foundation for the harmony and as a melodic line. There are two places where the bass line descends step by step down a scale. Once you know what to look for, these scales are easy to spot! Circle the scale notes in these two excerpts.

Espressivo and *Rubato*

The music is marked *tempo rubato*.
What does this mean?
A flexible tempo using slight variations in tempo to enhance musical expression

Melancholy Reflections

Mike Schoenmehl (b. 1957)
Student Workbook 5, p. 73

Mournful Melody

Begin by playing the opening phrase. The composer has marked slurs to indicate phrases _2_ measures in length. There is a distinct shape to the notes of the melody.

What does the shape of the sound make you think of? _breathing or sighing_

Most of the notes make up a scale-like pattern.

What scale? _D minor_

However, two significant notes that we would recognize from classical music are missing. Which ones? _B flat and C sharp_ Schoenmehl chooses this note pattern for the phrase in three places: mm. _1–2_, mm. _5–6_, and mm. _13–14_.

Which melody shows a slight **variation**? _mm. 5–6_

Variations on a Walking Bass

Notice how the composer uses the walking bass even in a conventional accompaniment pattern. What types of scale fragments are shown in the circled notes? _chromatic_

Look at the next example:

There's a slight variation to the pattern of the lowest notes. The last eighth note of the pattern helps push the walking bass downward. A slight change of direction occurs in m. 10. Can you describe it?
Instead of continuing downward, the notes turn around in m. 10.

Blocking the Chords

Play the LH in solid (blocked) form:

At least two of the chords will be familiar to you from your classical pieces. On the example above, circle the two chords you recognize.

At m. 4, play the LH together with the lower voice of the RH. Now you can hear complete chords.

How do the chords move? ☑ by step
If your hand will stretch, try blocking the LH patterns at m. 9.

Which one results in the same triad as used in the RH of m. 9:
(the first)/ the second?

Classical Harmony with a Jazz Twist

Mixed into the sound of Melancholy Reflections are several chords leading to harmonic progressions you have seen and heard before. Play these examples, RH only.

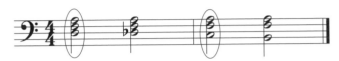

In examples 1 and 3, even without the LH part, you can hear _perfect_ **cadences**.

In example 2, you will hear **dominant 7ths** even though one note is missing from each chord. To find the missing notes, invert each chord until the notes are a 3rd apart (in root position).

The missing note in the first chord is _G_, and in the second chord, _F sharp_.

Play the LH of the last two measures alone.

What are all these intervals? <u>5ths</u>

These notes act as the foundation of the RH chords above. Play the RH alone. Circle two triads you recognize.

In the RH, where do the chords start to sound jazzy? <u>m. 15, beat 2</u>

Scamp

Christopher Norton (b. 1953)
Student Workbook 5, p. 76

Ragtime with Swing

Syncopation occurs when notes are played *between* rather than *on* the beats. This creates an offbeat effect.

There are many examples of this effect in *Scamp*. Match each of the following musical excerpts to the sentence that best describes it:

RH is held through beats 2 and 4 while the LH plays on each beat:
Excerpt no. <u>4</u>

Both hands are held through beat 3:
Excerpt no. <u>2</u>

RH is held through beat 3, while the LH plays on beat 3:
Excerpt no. <u>1</u>

The start of beat 3 is completely silent, but there is playing on either side of it (on the *and* of both beats 2 and 3):
Excerpt no. <u>3</u>

Seventh-Chord Hunt

Not to worry, you don't have to learn all of the different 7th chords in order to play *Scamp*. You may, however, enjoy doing another match-up. Start by playing each of the 7th chords written on the following page, and listen for the particular sound of each. Each of the musical examples contains the notes of one of these chords (although, in some cases, only three of the four notes of the chord may be present). Draw a line from each chord to the music to which it corresponds.

Student Workbook 6 Answers

Les Carillons

Johann Philipp Kirnberger (1721–1783)
Student Workbook 6, p. 4

Exploring the Form

One way to identify the form of a piece is to look for double-bar divisions and changes of key, either through **modulation** or change of key signature.

A great deal of the music written during the Baroque period features two main forms, **binary** (or **rounded binary**) and **ternary**.

Binary form means: <u>two-section form</u>

Ternary form means: <u>three-section form</u>

On the second page of *Les Carillons*, look at the marking, *Alternativement*. This is a term often used in 18th-century dance music (for example, in the *bourrées* of the Bach suites). It denotes a contrasting middle section that later became known as a Trio.

What instructions appear above m. 40? <u>D.C. al Fine</u>

What do they mean?
<u>Go back to the beginning and play to the "Fine" sign.</u>

In your music, label the first section (up to the key signature change) A and the second section B. Count the number of measures in each of these sections.

How many in A? <u>20</u>   How many in B? <u>20</u>

Are the two sections of equal length? <u>yes</u>

Taking into consideration the directive at m. 40, what is the overall form of the piece? <u>ternary</u>

We can look further at the form *within* each of these larger sections.

Do the double bar lines suggest binary or ternary form? <u>binary</u>

Which of the two larger sections ends with a return of its opening melody? <u>the second</u>

What term describes a two-part form with this feature? <u>rounded binary</u>

First Section
Key: <u>A major</u>
Melody: There is one main melody, with an active bass line that supports and occasionally imitates it. Play mm. 1–4, first RH, then LH.

Upbeat: What is its direction? <u>up</u>

By what interval does it move? <u>2nds</u>

What is the direction at m. 9? <u>down</u>

By what interval? <u>2nds</u>

How would you describe the articulation?
<u>slurred upbeats</u>

Imitation: In the LH, you will hear imitation of the opening upbeat motive, then the bass continues with bouncy quarter notes and running passages. Identify two other places in the first section where you hear LH imitation: mm. <u>4–5</u> and <u>10–12</u>. Mark these on your score.

Modulation: Where does the composer signal the first modulation? (HINT: Look for the first accidental.) m. <u>6</u>

Name the **cadence** in the example below, and name the key and its relationship to A major.
<u>perfect cadence in E major (dominant of A major)</u>

This type of short modulation is typical of Bach dances, and of the historical period in general.

Two more brief modulations occur in **sequence** in mm. 9–12. (HINT: The sequence is shared by the hands.) The first is to the key of <u>D major</u>. The second is to the key of <u>E major</u>.

Leaping pattern: Kirnberger illustrates the carillon effect with wide RH leaps at mm. <u>12–16</u>. The lower notes form a partial scale of <u>A major</u>, which always leaps up to the same upper note of <u>A</u>. Lean with your thumb on the lower notes of the leaping pattern to give them more sound.

In mm. 17–20, Kirnberger creates a variation of the leaping pattern. Describe the variation. <u>The bottom note of the pattern is displaced up an octave and the pattern is filled in with eighth notes.</u> In the example below, continue circling the "skeleton" notes in the variation and then circle them in your score. Emphasize these notes slightly when you play this passage.

Second Section

Key: <u>A minor</u>

Melody: There is a main melody supported by a dance-like LH, featuring mainly quarter notes. How is this melody similar to the melody of the first section?
<u>begins with an upward-moving upbeat; includes scale</u>
<u>patterns; ends on the dominant</u>

Upbeat: What is its direction? <u>up</u>

By what interval does it move? <u>3rds</u>

How would you describe the articulation?
<u>not slurred, except for m. 36</u>

Imitation: Where do you see imitation in this section? <u>mm. 33–34</u>

Is it *exact* or *free* imitation? <u>free</u>

Modulation: What is the chord in m. 28? <u>E major</u>

What is its relationship to the tonic key of this section? <u>dominant</u>

Play the RH from mm. 29–32 (with the upbeat). Is this a **transposition** of mm. 21–24? <u>yes</u>

The last line of this section brings back the melody from mm. 21–23.

How has the LH changed?
<u>Notes are played on beat 1 of mm. 37 and 38,</u>
<u>creating octave leaps.</u>

Burlesca in D Major

Johann Ludwig Krebs (1713–1780)
Student Workbook 6, p. 7

Finding a Sound

Just as actors must find the right tone of voice for the characters they are portraying, musical performers must find the right sound to project the character of the music they are playing. Below are three possible descriptions of the sound for *Burlesca*. Which would you most like to hear as you play this piece?
Sparkling and electric ☑

A New Broken Chord Pattern . . .

Begin by writing out the inversions of the D major triad in broken form on the staff below. The root position chord has been written for you. (Leave some space between each inversion.)

Now add a fourth note to the end of each chord inversion by taking the first note and writing it again one octave higher. This will turn each triad position into a four-note chord. The RH part of *Burlesca* features a descending pattern of four-note broken chords.

. . . and Several Other Patterns

Of course, it would be difficult to create an interesting composition with only one pattern, so Krebs uses other patterns as well. These are described below and shown in the musical examples. In the spaces provided, write the number of the musical example that matches each description. There will be a few questions to answer along the way!

Excerpt no. 1

Excerpt no. 2

Excerpt no. 3

Excerpt no. 4

Excerpt no. <u>3</u>
An accompaniment figure that features a combination of leaps and half steps. Every other note is played by the (thumb)/ fifth finger.

Excerpt no. _4_
Broken triads expanded into four-note chords.
In _Burlesca,_ these broken chords are ascending / (descending).

Excerpt no. _2_
Sharp-sounding repeated-note figure. This could be played by a pair of trumpets.

Excerpt no. _1_
A rising / (falling) **sequence** featuring descending scale motion and a pair of rising leaps.

Tonic vs. Dominant

The **tonic** and **dominant** notes are among the most important in any given key. You may also recall that it is possible to build a triad using any note of the scale as a root.

Reminder: the tonic is the (identify the scale degree) _first_ note of the scale.

The dominant is the _fifth_ note of the scale. Write the triad of D major in root position on the staff below:

This is the (tonic) / dominant triad of D major.

On the staff below, write the triad whose name you did _not_ circle in the previous question:

Return now to the descending patterns of four-note broken chords discussed earlier.
Where does this pattern use the notes of the tonic triad? m. _1_

Where does this pattern use the notes of the dominant triad? m. _3_

By using the notes from both triads with the opening pattern, Krebs strongly establishes the home key.

As its title suggests, _Burlesca_ opens in D major. Does the first section end in D major, or in a new key? If it's a new key, what key is it? _A major_

What relationship exists between the key at the end of the first section and the opening key of D major?

☑ The new key is the dominant key of D major.

Compare the relationship between the two keys with the relationship between the two triads discussed earlier. What do you observe? _they both feature tonic then dominant_

Here is one last question. Find another statement of the descending pattern of four-note broken chords in the second half of Burlesca, this one using the notes of a new triad. Write out the triad in root position on the staff below:

To which of the keys discussed earlier is this new triad related? _It is the dominant of A major._

Interestingly, Krebs uses this chord to draw the music back toward the closing key of _D major_, bringing the piece to a strong and satisfying conclusion.

Aria

Georg Philipp Telemann (1681–1767)
Student Workbook 6, p. 10

Keeping the Pace
What is the note value most frequently used by the left hand? _quarter notes_

Rhythmic Diversity
Telemann uses many distinct rhythmic patterns in the melody, sometimes in **sequence**.

Where do you see the following pattern used?

 mm. _1_ and _7_

Where do you see a sequence using this pattern?

 mm. _2–3_

Where does this pattern appear?

 m. _4_

The four sixteenth notes at the end of this measure look unusual. Draw the notes the way you are used to seeing them notated:

Why did Telemann group these differently?
The first sixteenth ends the phrase.

Where does this rhythm occur? mm. 9, 12

 mm. 9, 12

How does this pattern feel compared to the second beat of m. 1? To the fourth beat of m. 4?
It feels less melodic.

Find at least one instance of each of the following patterns in *Aria*:

 or or

mm. 3, 4, 5–6, 8–9, 10, 11, 12, 13–14

What is occurring at each of these instances?
a cadence

Melody and Balance
What dynamic level is shown at the beginning? mf

What Italian term is used to indicate the type of tone the composer wants? cantabile

What does it mean? in a singing style

Play the RH (treble clef) separately to the end of the first section. The melody divides into two voices in two places: m. 1 and m. 5.

Does the lower part function melodically or harmonically at these points? harmonically

When the RH has two voices, the lower voice should be softer than the upper voice.

Tone Matching
When a melody contains a tie, as it does in m. 1 and m. 7, you need to play the note just after the tie carefully to avoid creating a bump in the melody.

Minuet in G Minor
Gottfried Heinrich Stölzel (1690–1749)
Student Workbook 6, p. 13

Find the Musical Characters
Stölzel manages to blend several musical characters in this *Minuet.* The motives associated with each character are shown below. These motives reappear with slight variations as the music unfolds. Match each motive to the description that fits it best:

Motive a

Motive b

Motive c

Motive b :
Group of dancers all stepping in the same direction

Motive c :
A flowing phrase played by an instrument such as the flute or the violin

Motive a :
Bouncy melodic fragments punctuated by bold chords

Articulation
How can you emphasize the chords in mm. 1–2 without overpowering the lighter eighth notes in these measures?
by not accenting them too strongly and by releasing the LH chords right on beat 2

How can you highlight the contrast between the eighth notes in m. 1 and the eighth notes in m. 5?
by using a different dynamic and touch

Travel the Minuet Map
Stölzel has created something of a musical collage with these three motives. As you travel along the Minuet Map below, insert the appropriate letter (a, b, or c) in the measures where one of these motives appears. As you learn the piece, listen for the clear change of character created every time a new motive is heard.

As is typical of dance pieces from this period, Stölzel uses these motives to travel through a few different keys along the way. Each new key is always clearly established with a cadence. In this case, each important cadence is a **perfect cadence.** We have placed signposts for them along the way, but it will be up to you to identify the keys at these cadences. Have a good journey!

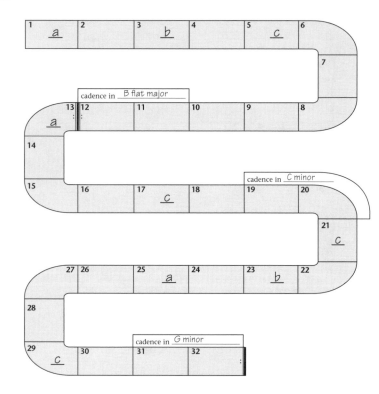

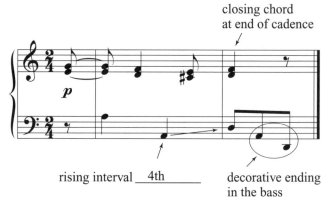

closing chord
at end of cadence

rising interval ___4th___   decorative ending
                                   in the bass

What key is suggested by this cadence? _D minor_

Find two other such cadences before the first double bar:
mm. _7_ – _8_ ; mm. _11_ – _12_

Based on the location of these cadences, how long is each phrase in the first half of this piece? _4_ measures. In fact, that's the length of every phrase in the entire piece!

Answering Phrases

Observe the beginning of the first phrase after the double bar:

Rewrite this phrase, with each pitch a whole step *higher.*

Now write it again, this time with each pitch a whole step *lower.*

Find a place where Bach has done one of the above **transpositions.** mm. _17–18_

The return of motive _a_ in m. 25 is a clue that the form of this *Minuet* is **binary**, **rounded binary**, or **ternary** (choose one). _rounded binary_

Scherzo in C Major

Johann Christoph Friedrich Bach (1732–1795)
Student Workbook 6, p. 16

Perfect Cadences

Let's review the **perfect cadence**. A cadence occurs at the end of a phrase, much as a period closes a written sentence. In a perfect cadence, the music moves from harmony built on the **dominant** of the key to harmony built on the **tonic**.

Write the dominant note *rising* to the tonic in C major:

What interval does this create? A rising _4th_

Now write the dominant *falling* to the tonic in the same key:

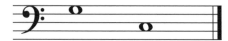

What interval does this create? A falling _5th_

The perfect cadence at the end of the first phrase shows this characteristic bass line. Notice the decorative use of the dominant note between the two tonics at the end.

Is the transposed phrase a step (higher) or a step lower than the original one?

How many measures altogether are repeated at this new pitch level? _4_

Are there perfect cadences at the ends of each of these two phrases? If there are, you will find them by locating the telltale rising 4th or falling 5th (from dominant to tonic) in the bass at each phrase ending. (HINT: Neither of these phrases is in the original key of C major.)

The phrases end at m. _16_ and at m. _20_. The bass notes indicating the end of the first phrase are _C_ and _F_.

The bass notes indicating the end of the second phrase are _D_ and _G_.

Toccata in C Minor

José António Carlos de Seixas (1704–1742)
Student Workbook 6, p. 19

Movement in Music

Match each musical fragment to the description that fits it best. For each gesture, identify the measure where it first appears in the piece, then find other measures where it appears in a varied and/or extended form.

Fragment _C_:
A strongly **syncopated**, offbeat gesture, usually with an upward leap:
First appears in m. _7_, thereafter in mm. _12–13, 30–31_.

Fragment _B_:
Vigorous bowing on a violin, changing rapidly from one string to another:
First appears in mm. _5–6_, thereafter in mm. _9–10, 24–27_.

Fragment _A_:
A strong, leaping gesture made from bouncy eighth notes:
First appears in mm. _1–2_, thereafter in mm. _20–21_.

Fragment _D_:
A sweeping, melodic gesture made up of mostly stepwise sixteenths and eighths:
First appears in mm. _3–4_, thereafter (varied) in mm. _22–23_.

A Few Key Notes

Let's return to the opening motive. Circle the two notes of the home key of C minor that its notes emphasize:
(tonic and dominant)

Now, head for the end of the first section. The last two notes of this section, in both hands, are _B flat_ and _E flat_.

Do these two notes fit into the pair of terms that you chose as your answer to the previous question? _yes_ If so, in what key? _E flat major_
How is this key related to the home key?
relative major

Now, turn your attention to the next section. Find a pair of measures whose notes match those of the *ending* of the first section: mm. _20–21_.

Find a pair of measures whose notes match those of the *beginning* of the first section: mm. _36–37_.

As your answers suggest, Seixas has used a simple pair of notes to construct the overall form of the piece. Based on your answers, the first section started in the key of C minor and finished in the key of _E flat major_; the second section started in the key of _E flat major_ and finished, as you might expect, in the key of _C minor_.

Which basic form does this plan suggest? ☑ binary

Little Prelude in E Minor, BWV 941

Johann Sebastian Bach (1685–1750)
Student Workbook 6, p. 21

Imitation

Because we see remarkable **imitation** in two voices immediately in the opening four measures, it is easy to miss the fact that there are more than two voices for many measures at a time.

How many voices are present at first? _three_

Where do you see a change? m. _11_

Where does the extra voice return? m. _19_

The extra voice supports the **counterpoint** by providing harmony.

Play the RH opening motive as illustrated:

Then play the LH of mm. 3–5:

When Bach uses imitation, it usually consists of two types: exact and free. Even in exact imitation there can be slight alterations of notes. In the second example above, look at the LH part carefully. What two things do you see that are different from the RH?
1. _It ends with eighth notes instead of quarter notes._
2. _The last two notes move up instead of down._

What type of imitation occurs here? _exact_

At m. 5, the LH gets "carried away" and begins a long extension based on the original motive, winding its way to a **cadence** at mm. 10–11. What is the key of the cadence? <u>G major</u>

Although there is no marking, it looks like a new section begins at m. 11.

Do you see any imitation here? <u>yes</u>

What type? <u>free</u>

Practicing for Flexibility and Fluency
Has Bach used scales or broken chords for most of the piece? <u>broken chords</u>

Chord Hunt
Name the chord found in each of the following examples, and identify the measure number where it appears in *Little Prelude in E Minor*.

Playing them first in solid (blocked) form will help you identify them right away.

	Name of Chord	Measure Number

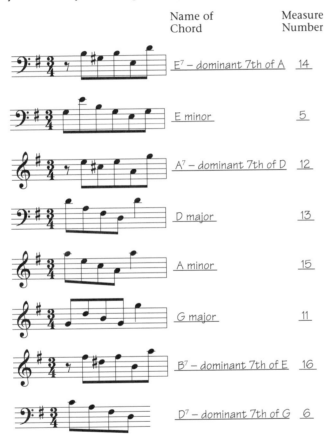

	E⁷ – dominant 7th of A	14
	E minor	5
	A⁷ – dominant 7th of D	12
	D major	13
	A minor	15
	G major	11
	B⁷ – dominant 7th of E	16
	D⁷ – dominant 7th of G	6

Sonatina in G Major, op. 214, no. 3
First Movement

Cornelius Gurlitt (1820–1901)
Student Workbook 6, p. 24

Exposition
The First Theme
Look at the first two measures. What triad do the circled notes form? <u>G major</u>

In which inversion? <u>second</u>

Now go to mm. 3–4. Circle the notes that you see at the same points in the music as those circled in the example above. Describe what triad and inversion these notes form. <u>G major in first inversion</u>

As these examples show, the opening theme establishes the tonic key of the movement very clearly.

The Second Theme
Here are two passages that follow the statement of the opening theme. Find them in the score and identify the measures.

mm. <u>5–6</u>

mm. <u>11–14</u>

Which of these passages clearly shows a root position triad in its melody or accompaniment? mm. 11–14

What key does this triad suggest? D major

This same excerpt contains all the notes of what scale? D major

Does this scale match the key of the triad you identified? yes

In relation to the opening key, this key is the:
☑ dominant

There are Italian terms in the score that suggest a contrast of character between these two themes. What are they and what do they mean?
risoluto—resolute, decisive, energetic
cantabile—in a singing style

Return for a moment to mm. 5–10. What description best fits this passage?

☑ a series of short, similar phrases

Development

As is typical of a sonata-form movement, the development section begins after the double bar line. The development is the least predictable of the three sections—anything goes! In this movement, the development does start in a somewhat unusual manner. It borrows the rhythm of one of the musical elements discussed earlier. Check which one below:
☑ bridge

Look for more thematic links between the development and the exposition.

This fragment (mm. 35–36) appeared in mm. 27–28 in the exposition.

This fragment (mm. 37–38) appeared in mm. 19–20 in the exposition.

Recapitulation

The recapitulation begins at m. 41 . This time the bridge passage is: ☑ shorter

The second theme now appears in the: ☑ tonic

Sonata in A Minor

Domenico Cimarosa (1749–1801)
Student Workbook 6, p. 27

Rhythm and Melody

What is the time signature in the piece? $\frac{6}{8}$ In order to move forward even at a slow tempo, this time signature is often counted in 2 beats. There is a steady pacing established in the opening, almost a "processional" feeling. In the first four measures, which hand establishes the beat? LH

The rhythm of the melody is active and ever changing. How would you describe the rhythm of the RH in m. 1? dotted

We often see this rhythm pattern in lively pieces. But three things suggest that the character of this melody is different:
The key of the piece is A minor .

The tempo marking is Largo , which means slow, broad .

The Italian word in m. 1 is cantabile , which means in a singing style .

How would you shape the melody expressively? lilting, following the grace notes and dotted rhythms

Interval Intelligence

In the delicate texture of this piece, Cimarosa uses 3rds and 6ths rather than complete four-note chords. Look for them everywhere in the melody, in the accompaniment, and even in the harmony between the two hands. What interval is created if you turn a 3rd upside down? 6th

When the two notes are played by the same hand, the interval is easy to see and easy to hear. In looking at mm. 1–3, one specific interval jumps off the page. Which one? _3rds_ Is it in the melody or the (accompaniment)?

Do you see the same interval anywhere in the other part? (Look carefully at both pages.) _no_

In mm. 15–16, what is the RH interval? _6th_

On the staff below, **invert** the intervals, that is, turn the intervals upside down. In your technique practice, you're used to working on triads and their inversions.

Play what you've written. Does it sound the same as or similar to the original in mm. 15–16?
yes — similar

This is one of the ways composers experiment with intervals and chords when they create pieces.

The texture becomes thinner at mm. 17–20. Do you see any harmonic intervals played in either hand? _no_ Play the following excerpt and listen closely.

Can you hear a "hidden" interval between the hands that is similar to the one in the opening? _yes_ If you transposed the treble clef part down an octave, the interval would immediately become clear. What would it be? _a 3rd_

Harmony Landmarks

Playing any piece from beginning to end is like traveling on a journey. You start in the home key and begin to travel through other keys (**modulating**), passing some familiar territory on the way, and some that is unfamiliar. **Cadences** serve as landmarks, or signs of key change, and often bring phrases to a close. Look for cadences at the following points, identify the key, and mark them in your music:

	Type of Cadence	Key
mm. 5–6	perfect cadence	A minor
mm. 9–10	half cadence	C major
mm. 15–16	perfect cadence	C major
mm. 17–18	perfect cadence	D minor
mm. 19–20	perfect cadence	C major
mm. 29–30	perfect cadence	C major
mm. 33–34	perfect cadence	A minor

Look at the chord in mm. 11–12.

Play it hands together. Listen to the sound. Remember that Cimarosa liked to keep the texture light and clear, so he often didn't write complete four-note chords. One note is missing; identify the missing note. _G_ When it is added, what is the type of chord here? _dim. 7th_

Now look on the second page. Can you find an example of the same chord turned upside down (in another inversion)? m. _28_

Which note that was on top is now on the bottom?
C sharp

This note is the leading note of which minor scale (key)? _D minor_

Home at Last!
Take another look at the cadence in mm. 33–34. Are we in the home key? _yes_

Sonatina in G Major, op. 20, no. 1
First Movement

Jan Ladislav Dussek (1760–1812)
Student Workbook 6, p. 30

Harmony and Accompaniment
The harmonic patterns of this piece are largely built on three chords. Write the **tonic** (I), **subdominant** (IV), and **dominant** (V) chords in G major on the staff below. (Double the bottom note to create four-note chords.)

G major   tonic   subdominant   dominant

What term describes the sixteenth-note accompaniment pattern in the LH of this piece? <u>Alberti bass</u>

Two other dominant 7th chords are used. One is built on A: A–C sharp–E–G. What tonic note would this chord resolve to? <u>D</u> Where in the piece is this chord used for two whole measures? mm. <u>21–22</u>

The other dominant 7th is built on E: E–G sharp–B–D. What tonic note would this chord resolve to? <u>A</u> In what measure does this chord appear? m. <u>17</u>

The LH part in mm. 1–3 contains a repeated G. What do you call a note that is held or repeated underneath a moving melody? <u>pedal point</u>

Imagine a cello playing the repeated G's in mm. 1–3. Give these notes a smooth line and try not to "bump" your thumb. Think of each group of four as one movement of the cellist's bow. These single notes actually imply the chord of <u>G major</u>.

Melody

The melody voices in mm. 1–4 are separated first by the interval of a <u>6th</u> and then by a <u>3rd</u>.

Technical Challenges

3. Think about voicing the 3rds and 6ths: make sure the upper notes sing out clearly. How can you make this happen?
<u>give more weight to the top fingers</u>

4. Remember that the LH **Alberti bass** pattern can easily overpower the melody. In which measures does Dussek use an Alberti bass?
<u>mm. 5–7, 13–15, and 29–33</u>

How will you project the melody in these measures?
<u>be sure to play the LH lightly and connect the melody notes with slurs</u>

Now have some fun with a musical road map of Dussek's *Sonatina*. Mark the keys and sections on the signposts as well as each dominant and subdominant harmony along the way.

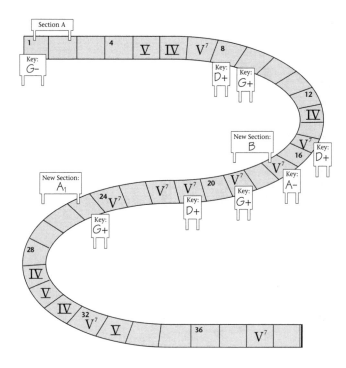

Big question—is this movement in **sonata form**? Explain your answer.
<u>No. The B section has a new theme.</u>

Sonatina in E flat Major, op. 4, no. 7

Samuel Wesley (1766–1837)
Student Workbook 6, p. 33

A Three-Part Form

As the title indicates, the opening section (the A section) starts in E flat major.

Look now for a new section: this will be a place where the music obviously changes. mm. <u>25–27</u>

This is section B. In the opening measure, all of the notes, in both hands, belong to the tonic triad of <u>C minor</u> (key). What is the relationship between this key and the opening key? <u>relative minor</u>

What does the marking in m. 37 (*D.C. al Fine*) mean? <u>Return to the beginning and play to Fine.</u>

From your observations, would you describe this movement as being in **binary form** or **ternary form**? <u>ternary</u>

Making Melody Richer

Now, complete the following fragments in the same way, first naming the opening interval:

Interval 3rd

Interval 4th

Interval 9th

Interval 6th

All of these fragments offer examples of **parallel motion.** Play them on the piano. Do some sound more or less **dissonant** than others? Go through the music of the *Sonatina,* and find examples of parallel motion that uses two of the four intervals you wrote above.

Interval: 3rd mm. 1 – 3 ; mm. 15 – 16 .

Interval: 6th mm. 33 – 34 .

What does the indication *maestoso* tell you about the how the piece should sound? majestic

An Alberti Bass

A common accompaniment pattern in Classical music appears in which section, A or (B)? This pattern, called an **Alberti bass,** is created out of chords. It supplies a harmonic background under the melody, and also helps create a feeling of motion.

Look for and identify one example of each of the following in Wesley's Alberti bass patterns. Write each chord in root position.

A triad in first inversion: m. 27
Triad of G major

A triad in second inversion: m. 30
Triad of D major

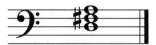

A triad in root position: m. 25
Triad of C minor

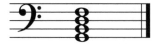

A dominant 7th chord in root position: m. 25
Dominant 7th of C minor

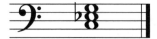

Sonatina in D Major, op. 12, no. 1
First Movement

James Hook (1746–1827)
Student Workbook 6, p. 36

Character

This sonatina is full of speed and energy. Which words on your music tell you that?
Allegro con spirito

Repetition

Where do you see the first example of repetition? m. 1 It seems as though Hook likes to say everything twice! In mm. 1–7, you will notice three different types of repetition. The first type is of individual notes; the second and third types are repeated phrases and motives.

Where is the phrase beginning at m. 2 repeated? mm. 4–5

Where is the motive in m. 6 repeated? m. 7

What do you call the effect when repetition occurs at a softer dynamic level? echo

Exposition

Theme 1 is in the home (**tonic**) key. Hook uses two *forte* chords in quarter notes to announce the tonic key. What effect does this have on the listener?
It gets the listener's attention and establishes the tonic key.

The RH has a triad in _first_ inversion, but when you include the bass octave in the LH, the chord is a four-note chord in root position.

After the key is announced, the first theme proceeds toward a bridge (mm. 8–11) that links it to the second theme. The bridge contains an important accidental in m. _10_. This accidental indicates a key change to the key of _A major_.

Theme 2 (upbeat to m. 12) is usually in the **dominant** key. Is that true here? ☑ yes

The second theme is usually a contrasting type of theme. In this case, the rhythmic patterns in theme 2 are different, and it appears to have two distinct parts: mm. 12–15 and mm. 16–20. After the cadence at mm. 19–20, what happens to the rhythmic pattern? _It uses the pattern from the beginning._

This little ending section is called a _codetta_, and it uses the rhythmic pattern from m. _2_.

Look at m. 24. Why does this ending seem emphatic? _The A major chord is played three times._

Development and Recapitulation
Look carefully at mm. 25–30. Why does this section seem familiar?
It is the same as Theme 1 but in a different key.

What is the name for this compositional technique? _transposition_

What happens at m. 32? _Material from m. 6 returns in the original key._

What key is implied by the C naturals in mm. 34–35? _G major_

What key is implied by the G sharps in mm. 36–37? _A major_

In many Classical sonatas, the recapitulation brings back both the first and second themes in the tonic key. There is often a noticeable buildup and a feeling of having "arrived" at theme 2 and the tonic key.

This recapitulation is a little different. Do you ever hear theme 1 presented in D major in the second section? _no_

Is the melody in mm. 38–43 a repetition of something that was presented earlier, or is it new? _It is new._ What key is this passage in? _D major_

Which part of the second theme reappears in m. 44? _the part at m. 16_

Is it in D major? _yes_ How did the melody and harmony of m. 43 prepare for this "arrival"? _a descending D major scale from dominant to tonic_

The last line, which now can be called a _coda_, uses more repetition. Is this an exact replica of the _codetta_, transposed to the tonic? _yes_

Sonata in G Major
Second Movement: Romance
Antonio Rosetti (_ca_ 1750–1792)
Student Workbook 6, p. 39

Melodic Movement
The melody is full of beauty and tenderness. Can you think of any other words to describe this melody?
sweet, peaceful, thoughtful

In m. 1, the word _cantabile_, meaning _in a singing style_, indicates that the tone should be as full as the human voice.

When the melody rises dramatically to an octave, how would you shape the dynamics? _slight crescendo_

The movement is marked _larghetto_, meaning _slightly less slow than largo_. Play with a definite pulse and an almost dance-like stepping movement at the beginning.

The time signature of ¢ insures that the piece will move forward, even at a slow tempo. How many beats will you count in each measure? _two_

The priority is an expressive, flowing melody line. The challenge for the performer of this _Romance_ is to keep the melody moving forward despite visual obstacles such as articulation markings. Sing as you play, aloud or in your mind, and allow some flexibility in the tempo to accommodate your expressive feelings. What is the Italian musical term for flexibility of tempo? _rubato_

Articulation
To review the articulation that Rosetti uses, find the following examples in the music, then fill in the answers.

m. <u>17</u> Name <u>portato</u>
How played <u>with a slight lift</u>

m. <u>7</u> Name <u>slur</u>
How played <u>smoothly and connected</u>

m. <u>3</u> Name <u>two-note slurs</u> How played <u>down–up,</u>
<u>lifting slightly on each group of two</u>

Musical Material

Compare the following measures with m. 1.

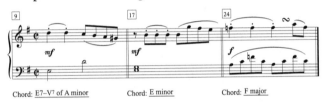

Chord: <u>E7–V⁷ of A minor</u>   Chord: <u>E minor</u>   Chord: <u>F major</u>

Which melodic feature of m. 1 is used in each of
these measures? <u>repeated notes</u>

Rosetti uses a similar pattern, but each of these
measures implies a different harmony. Name the
chord for each one.

In the section from mm. 17–23, the melody seems
to move more quickly.

Why? <u>The melody is made up entirely of eighth notes.</u>

What is the key here? <u>E minor</u>

We know that intervals of 3rds and 6ths are
considered as pleasing or **consonant**. How would
you describe the relationship between the 3rds in
m. 30 and the 6ths in m. 31?
<u>They are the same notes but inverted.</u>

Notice that the 3rds and 6ths rise and fall just like
the melody does elsewhere.

The example below is from m. 8. Where do you see
this measure repeated? m. <u>45</u>

Where do you see it borrowed? mm. <u>46–49</u> It seems
as though Rosetti liked the effect of this little pattern
so much that he improvised on it in **sequence**,
building toward a dynamic climax in m. <u>51</u>.

In the last four measures, he ends quietly with the
same thematic material as the opening. Are the
notes exactly the same as the opening? <u>no</u>
Which ones are different? <u>RH bottom voice on beat</u>
<u>2 of m. 53; ending moves to I instead of V</u>

Sonatina in C Major, op. 20, no. 1
First Movement

Friedrich Kuhlau (1786–1832)
Student Workbook 6, p. 42

Exposition

First Theme

The opening theme is laid out with the melody in
the <u>right</u> hand and an accompaniment in the
<u>left hand</u>. The opening key is confirmed at the
outset by the accompaniment notes. These notes
form the triad of <u>C major</u>.

At which measure do melody and accompaniment
switch hands? m. <u>9</u>

As you progress through the music, you will sense
an increase of energy at m. 13. This is the
beginning of the bridge (transition) toward the
second theme. Describe two ways in which Kuhlau
creates excitement within this bridge section.
1. <u>strong octaves in the LH</u>
2. <u>RH speeds up from eighth notes to eighth-note</u>
   <u>triplets</u>

Second Theme

In a sonata-form exposition, a change of key often
coincides with a new theme, as is the case here.
Look for a place where the accompaniment suggests
a new key as clearly as it suggested the home key at
the beginning. m. <u>17</u> What is the new key and
how does it relate to the key of C major?
<u>G major—dominant of C major</u>

Codetta

Expositions often end with a type of closing section referred to as a *codetta*. The goal of such a section is to confirm the new key established by theme 2, and, more importantly perhaps, to convey the message that an important section of the music is coming to an end. Composers often use repetitive scale and chord patterns in a *codetta*, which is a practice that makes sense: the end of a discussion or speech is not the place to introduce fresh new ideas, and the same is true of music. How well do these characteristics apply to this *codetta*? Starting at m. 24, the music is made up of scales and repetitive figures.

Development

Look at the first note of each measure of the LH in this section. Notice that one pitch, G , occurs more than any other. This note is obviously related to the two keys found in the exposition. It functions as the **tonic** of G major , but the **dominant** of C major .

To find out exactly how long the development section is, look for the return of the opening theme (theme 1). Where does that occur? m. 50

Recapitulation

Compare the statements of the first theme in the exposition and in the recapitulation. Are they the same or different? the same

Now compare the bridge sections (mm. 13–16 and 62–65). What is different in the recapitulation? It does not move to the dominant (it stays in C major at m. 64).

Now compare the statements of the second theme in the exposition and recapitulation. What is different in the recapitulation? Theme 2 is in C major and not G major.

Finally, compare the *codetta* (at the end of the exposition) with the *coda* (at the end of the recapitulation), paying special attention to how they end. What is different at the end of the recapitulation? It ends in the tonic and with a sense of finality.

Mixing Major and Minor

If you noticed a few places in this movement that sounded unexpectedly minor, chances are that you were right. Classical composers often enjoyed the contrast created by slipping from major to minor (or vice versa). Find two places where the patterns you expect to be in major are presented in minor instead. (One of these patterns occurs twice: once in the exposition and once in the recapitulation. The other occurs in the development.)

Type of Pattern	Appearance in Exposition	Appearance in Recapitulation
triad (in octaves)	mm. 13–14	mm. 62–63

Type of Pattern	Appearance in Development
scale	mm. 42, 44, 45

Divertimento in G Major,
Hob. XVI:GI
First Movement

Franz Joseph Haydn (1732–1809)
Student Workbook 6, p. 45

Getting Acquainted with the Form

The first movement of Haydn's *Divertimento in G Major* is in **sonata form**. Complete the following sonata form chart by adding measure numbers and keys in the spaces. (You may want to work through some of the exercises before filling in all the spaces.)

Exposition	mm. 1 – 28	
theme 1	mm. 1 – 12	Key: G major
bridge	mm. 13 – 16	
theme 2	mm. 17 – 21	Key: D major
closing theme	mm. 22 – 28	
Development	mm. 29 – 57	
	starting key: D major	
	key at m. 35: C major	
	key at m. 40: D major	
	key at m. 44: E minor	
Recapitulation	mm. 58 – 80	
theme 1	mm. 58 – 64	Key: G major
bridge	mm. 65 – 68	
theme 2	mm. 69 – 73	Key: G major
closing theme	mm. 74 – 80	

Getting Acquainted with the Themes

In mm. 10–11, the scale is <u>D major</u> and the run starts on the <u>4th</u> note of the scale. (CLUE: The leading note of this key has appeared.)

In mm. 12–13, the scale is <u>D major</u> and the run starts on the <u>5th</u> note of the scale.

This new key is the: ☑ dominant key

At m. 13, the music is in the new key, and the musical texture changes. Play mm. 13–14 hands together, starting with the upbeat in m. 13, then playing just the circled notes.

Does this motive sound familiar? <u>yes—like the opening motive</u>

What is the interval between your hands? <u>10th</u>

What is the relationship between this interval and the parallel 3rds in m. 1? <u>If one note is displaced by an octave, a 10th becomes a 3rd.</u>

Conclusion: the theme at m. 13 is:
☑ a variation of the first theme

Now describe the accompaniment in mm. 17–21. <u>broken-chord pattern</u>

Does the more lyrical RH in these measures suggest a new theme? <u>yes</u>

Just before you leave the exposition, take a quick look at mm. 22–28 (the closing theme).

Which feature of this musical material is also found in the first theme?
(triplets)

Developing the Themes

Play through the development section, then take a good look at the music in your score to see what Haydn does with the themes he presented in the exposition.

Haydn chooses to develop: ☑ both themes

Find the place where Haydn uses part of the first theme in a **sequence** pattern. <u>mm. 53–57</u>

Find two places where Haydn repeats a two-measure figure like an echo.
1. <u>mm. 36–39</u>
2. <u>mm. 40–43, mm. 44–47</u>

Revisiting the Themes

Why do you think Haydn's restatement of this area is only eleven measures in the recapitulation? <u>In the recapitulation, the theme stays in G major and does not modulate.</u>

Winter Scene

William L. Gillock (1917–1993)
Student Workbook 6, p. 48

Minor Scale Theory

Winter Scene is a good place to review some minor scale theory. As you know, each key signature is shared by a major and a minor key. These keys are each other's relative major and minor. The major key with three sharps is <u>A</u> major; its relative minor is <u>F sharp</u> minor.

Look at the beginning and end of *Winter Scene*. Is the piece in the major or the minor mode? <u>minor</u>

Composers use several forms of the minor scale. The natural minor stays in the key signature; none of its notes are altered. In the <u>harmonic</u> minor, the seventh note (**leading note**) is raised a half step. In the <u>melodic</u> minor, the sixth and seventh notes are raised in the ascending form of the scale. When this scale descends, these same notes are usually as designated in the key signature. So in fact, the descending scale is once again the natural minor.

There are three clear examples where Gillock has used the ascending form of the melodic minor scale in *Winter Scene,* occurring at mm. <u>3</u>, <u>7</u>, and <u>17</u>.

A Hidden Scale

Gillock also uses a scale other than the minor. Look at the passage from m. 15 to the first beat of m. 17, where the RH seems to split into upper and lower voices:

Write out these two voices on the grand staff below, starting with the given notes.

The voices move in: ☑ contrary motion

Each voice moves by: ☑ half steps

What type of scale is Gillock using here? <u>chromatic</u>

An Unusual Seventh Chord

You have probably learned the **dominant 7th** chord. This chord consists of a triad whose root is the <u>fifth</u> note of the key, with another 3rd added on top to create the interval of the 7th.

There are, however, numerous types of 7th chords. To find one, go to mm. 25–26 and make a list of all the different letter names of the notes in these two measures. Don't forget the accidentals. <u>F sharp, A, C sharp, E sharp</u>

Three of the notes can be stacked to form a minor triad in root position. Write the triad here:

Place the remaining note above the top note of the triad, and play the resulting four-note chord. This can be called a minor-major 7th chord, a minor triad with an added major seventh (counting up from the root). This exotic sounding chord is very common in jazz and popular music.

Bright Orange

Robert Starer (1924–2001)
Student Workbook 6, p. 50

A Jazzy Orange Rhythm

This **syncopated** rhythm is a lot of fun to play, but it can be tricky to learn. First tap the RH rhythm against a steady quarter-note beat:

Write the beat numbers (1, 2) below the rhythm.

Now look at mm. 10–15. Write the beat numbers below the rhythm:

There are many examples of syncopation in the rhythms shown above. Circle four places in your score where syncopation appears. What kind of expression marks do you see over the syncopated notes in the RH? <u>accents, tenuto</u>

In these measures, the LH chords:
☑ usually match the offbeat rhythm of the RH

Jazzy Phrases

How long are the first two phrases? <u>three measures</u>

Are all the phrases this length, or are some a little longer? <u>some are longer</u>

Jazzy Sounds from Traditional Harmonies

In *Bright Orange*, Starer uses traditional chords in a non-traditional way so that they produce an entirely different sound. Here are the first two triads that appear in the LH:

Each of the top, middle, and bottom notes moves in the same manner from the first to the second triad. They move: ☑ up

☑ by step

There is a term that describes this type of motion: <u>parallel</u> motion. Popular music often moves from one chord to the next this way.

Almost all the LH chords are:
☑ triads in root position

Where is the one exception to the answer you checked above? mm. <u>8–15</u> This is a <u>C major triad</u> in <u>2nd inversion</u> (which position or inversion?).

Color and Mood

Are there different shades of orange in Starer's piece or is the mood equally bright throughout? <u>different shades</u>

A Tale, op. 62, no. 3

Xaver Scharwenka (1850–1924)
Student Workbook 6, p. 52

The Beginning

We already know a little bit. The Italian word *mesto* means sad or mournful.
Composers of this period often chose keys (major or minor) to indicate emotion. Based on the key signature alone, the key of the piece could be either _F_ major or _D_ minor. What is the key of the piece? _D minor_

What was the clue to your answer? _C sharp in m. 1_

Beginning with an upbeat could mean that the story has been going on before we hear about it. On what degree of the scale is the upbeat? _5_

To put the story in context, write the scale of the key on the staves below. Write both the harmonic and melodic forms of the scale, ascending and descending.

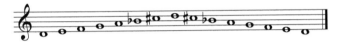

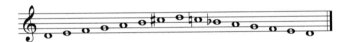

Phrases and Cadences

In mm. 1–16, identify where the phrases end. Some are four measures long, while others are much shorter:
m. _4_
m. _8_
m. _10_
m. _12_
m. _14_
m. _16_

Let's take a closer look at the two phrases in mm. 1–8. Are the rhythms the same or different?
almost the same

Now look at the **cadence** in m. 4. Does it end on a **tonic** or **dominant** chord? _dominant_ What type of cadence is it? _half cadence_

Now look at the cadence at m. 8. What is the key? _D minor_ Does this cadence end on the tonic or the dominant of that key? _tonic_
What type of cadence is it? _perfect cadence_

What term is normally used to describe the "conversation" between these two phrases?
question–answer or antecedent–consequent

A Colorful Chord

The first *sf* sign occurs in m. _12_. Write the chord (as printed in the score) on the staff below. Can you identify the sound of the chord? _diminished 7th_

Composers use this type of chord to show something dramatic. Now rewrite the chord, arranging it into a stack of 3rds, and use the top note as the root of the chord. This now becomes the diminished 7th chord of _G_ minor.

But look at the first chord in m. 13. Is it what you expect? _no_ Scharwenka surprises us. What is the chord? _E flat major_ in _first_ inversion. This is definitely the expressive high point of the piece.

The End of the Story

The main part of the story seems to be over at m. 16. Do you see a cadence in the home key at mm. 15–16? _yes_

The last two lines tie together the various patterns of the piece. Play the LH in mm. 16–18. Where did you see the dotted rhythmic pattern before?
m. _1, RH_

Name the descending scale in the LH beginning in m. 17. _D minor melodic_
(It is one of the scales that you wrote out.)

The scale is interrupted by a surprise. Where have you heard the chord at the beginning of m. 18?
m. _12_ Does the dynamic marking match the mood? _yes_

Suddenly the dynamics become softer. Think about why, and listen carefully to the sound of the chord formed on beat 1 of m. 21. Is that the same type of sound you heard in mm. 12 and 18? _yes_ Why do you think the composer chose not to add a *sf* marking?
The LH accent is a less-intense stress, which helps show that the piece is nearing its end.

Notice how the composer used an eighth note followed by an eighth rest at the phrase endings in mm. 18 and 21. What effect do you suppose he was after?
a sense of breath before continuing in pp

Name these last three chords:

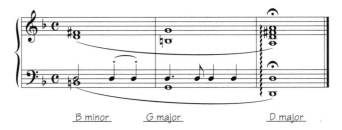

B minor   G major   D major

Waltz in A Minor, op. 124, no. 4

Robert Schumann (1810–1856)
Student Workbook 6, p. 55

Harmonic Surprises

This impulsive waltz shows the impact of daring and imaginative harmony. It seems to burst into the room by surprise. The angular melody leaps downward with abandon to an unexpected accidental, _D sharp_, but the real surprise is in the harmony.

Schumann uses the same unexpected note to create a wonderful harmonic progression in the LH. The surprise is that the listener expects to hear the tonic chord but instead hears a different one.

Where do you first see the **tonic** chord? m. _2_

It's easy to see because it appears as a triad in _root_ position.

However, if a lower bass note exists, you need to include it to identify the position of a chord. What position is this? _2nd inversion_

After rushing in, where does the waltz arrive with stability at a root position? m. _3_

Although the melody begins on A, Schumann doesn't really establish a strong tonal center in the opening measures. Instead, he introduces a different chord in the first measure. This chord is a type of augmented 6th chord called a German 6th. Let's put one together so you can see how this chord is built.

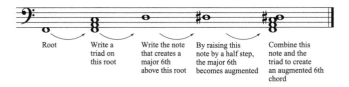

| Root | Write a triad on this root | Write the note that creates a major 6th above this root | By raising this note by a half step, the major 6th becomes augmented | Combine this note and the triad to create an augmented 6th chord |

Play the chord you have written. Does it sound familiar? _yes_ Do you know a chord with a similar sound? _dominant 7th of B flat major_ (CLUE: Change the D sharp to an E flat.) Sometimes it's a small world when it comes to chords!

What do mm. 1–2 add to the atmosphere of Schumann's *Waltz*: intensity or calm? _intensity_

A Contrasting Middle Section

The double bars and repeat signs divide this waltz into three sections. Write in the measure numbers and the letter names of the sections. (Then mark the letters of the sections in your score.)
_A_ mm. _1–16_
_B_ mm. _17–28_
_A_ mm. _29–44_

The middle section is also set off by a change in key.

What is the new key? _F major_

What is the relationship between A minor and this new key? (submediant)

This key relationship is somewhat unusual. How does it highlight the change of atmosphere in this section?
The key sounds less intense.

Schumann seems to prepare the listener for this key by using the tonic chord once in the first section. Where did he first use the tonic of this new key? _m. 14_

Does this measure contain the entire tonic triad of this new key? _yes_

A Rhythmic Sequence

Can you find a **sequence** in the middle section? mm. _21–26_

Now look at the rhythm of these measures. Schumann has used ties to create **syncopation**.

Does the LH play a downbeat in each measure? _yes_

How often does the RH play a downbeat?
every 2nd measure

What beat of the measure does Schumann accent with the tied notes? _3_

Song of the Cavalry, op. 27, no. 29

Dmitri Kabalevsky (1904–1987)
Student Workbook 6, p. 57

An Energetic Accompaniment

Kabalevsky's accompaniment helps to create the driving, rhythmic character of this music. In the first section of the piece, the accompaniment is in the _right_ hand. Later on, there's a switch. In m. _26_, the _right_ hand has the melody and the _left_ hand has the accompaniment. Finally, where do melody and accompaniment return to the hands they started with? m. _43_

In the outer sections of the piece, the accompaniment is played in one of these two rhythms; circle the correct one:

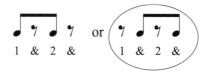

Does this rhythm fall *on* or *off* the beats? _off_

Play mm. 3–11 as written. Then play them again but shift the accompaniment to the *other* part of the beat. How would you compare the effect of these two ways of playing? _As written; it is more exciting, energetic, and driving._

Dotted Rhythms

You will need to listen very carefully to the coordination between the hands whenever the  rhythmic figure appears in the melody.

How many times does this figure appear in the section from mm. 1–20? _seven_

Which of the following patterns represents the combined rhythm of both hands in these measures (in other words, the overall rhythm that the listener actually hears)?

☑ ♩ ♫♫ ♫

A Closer Look at the Form

What is the key of *Song of the Cavalry*? (Check the opening triad in the RH.) _B flat minor_ Another triad reveals the new key at the start of the section where the melody switches to the other hand: _F minor_

What is the relationship of this key to the **tonic**?
☑ other

Key changes such as this, where both keys are in the minor mode, are fairly rare in tonal music.

Where do the hands play in **parallel motion**? mm. _21_ – _25_

This passage can be best described as a short bridge connecting the A and B sections. Based on your earlier observations of the accompaniments and how they defined the sections, fill in the measure numbers on the following chart:

A section: mm. _1–20_
Bridge: mm. _21–25_
B section: mm. _26–43_
A section: mm. _44–63_

The middle section presents a technical challenge. Observe the writing in the hand that carries the melody. What else is going on in that hand while the melody is being played?
Part of the offbeat accompaniment appears in the RH here beneath the melody.

For Susanna Kyle

Leonard Bernstein (1918–1990)
Student Workbook 6, p. 59

A Musical Birthday Card

When you listen to this piece, imagine the personality of young Susanna, who was no older than two when Bernstein wrote it.

Is she dreamy or agitated? What do you think?
dreamy

Did you hear a sensitive performance with flexible pacing? _yes_

Did the performer linger slightly in places to capture a floating quality? _yes_

Blurring the Edges of Keys

This music has no sharps or flats in the key signature. Is it in C major? _yes_

If you follow the old rule of looking at the first and last chords, you would say, "Yes, of course." But once you started to play the music, you would start to wonder. Play mm. 1–4.

Do these two phrases look as if they're in C major? _yes_

Are there any accidentals? _no_

Do these two phrases sound as if they're in C major? _no_

Look at the chords that end these phrases.

The chord in m. 2 could be a _dominant_ chord of C major, but the fifth of the chord is in the _RH_, and the root only lasts for half a beat.

The chord in m. 4 might have been a _tonic_ chord of C major, but the chord has no fifth. Bernstein writes a _7th_ instead!

Now for the big question: can music like this **modulate** to another key? _yes_

An Exotic Cadence

This is not to say that there is no chromatic movement in the music. Cross-relations add some beautiful harmonic colors. In mm. 13–14, the music comes to rest on an exotic-sounding cadence.

One note is circled in the example above. Look for another note bearing the same letter name and circle it. What two things are different about the note you have circled?
1. It is not flat.
2. It is played against two sharps.

Now find another note in the piece that changes pitch by a half step (semitone) while keeping its letter name. Circle both notes.

This is a **cross-relation** (also know as a false relation), created when notes repeat but in a different voice and with accidentals omitted or added. Which one of the following progressions contains a cross-relation?

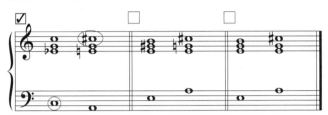

Blurring the Meter

Just as Bernstein has blurred the edges of the keys, he also blurs the edges of the time signatures. He does this first of all by changing time signatures. Name the three time signatures he uses:

$\frac{3}{4}$ $\frac{2}{4}$ $\frac{5}{4}$

However, even within these changing time signatures, he blurs the pulse. The example below shows the rhythms of the three separate voices in mm. 7–8.

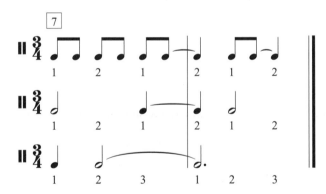

What is the first thing you notice about m. 8?
All three voices are tied into beat 1.

In addition to using **syncopation**, Bernstein uses another device called **hemiola** in these measures. Which two of the three voices illustrate this type of rhythmic shift? the top two voices

Can you find two other places where Bernstein uses the same rhythmic pattern?
mm. 3 – 4
mm. 17 – 18

Arietta, op. 12, no. 1
Edvard Grieg (1843–1907)
Student Workbook 6, p. 62

Hearing the Texture
Here is a fragment of each layer of the texture. Match the appropriate labels with each fragment:

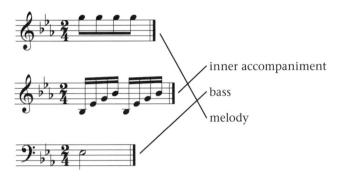

Harmonic and Non-Harmonic Notes
Play m. 2, then play the notes of the inner voice together with the melody note of the second beat as a solid (blocked) chord.

Can you identify this chord? diminished 7th In m. 10, Grieg creates harmonic tension. The first chord resolves into the second chord. Compare these two chords with the ones in m. 12.

Does Grieg use the same chords in both measures? If not, what is different?
No – in m. 12, the C is left out of the first chord and the bass holds a B instead.

You can highlight harmonic tension with expressive playing. What might you do in these measures to enhance the harmony? Emphasize the first chord and arrive on the second chord gently.

Form
The form of this piece is quite simple.
How many times does Grieg repeat the melody?
two times

Does he make any changes in the repetition? yes

An Ending or a Beginning?
The first time you heard (or played) this piece, what was your impression of the final measure? Did it sound like an ending, or a beginning, or a little of both? a little of both

Play m. 1 and then play m. 23:

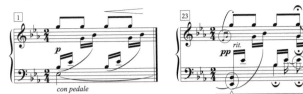

What differences of notes can you find between the two measures? Circle the "new" notes in m. 23 in the example above.

What differences in markings can you find between the two measures? List the "new" markings in m. 23.
staccato
rit.
fermata signs
_pp_
pedal bracket
tie in LH

Romantic character pieces often end with music that is similar to the beginning, which binds the composition into a whole.

Do you think the changes Grieg made in m. 23 create a definitive ending? Explain.
Grieg creates a definitive ending with the use of a
ritardardo, the addition of fermatas to sustain the
final chord, and a sudden drop in dynamic.

Prayer, op. 43, no. 2

Reinhold Glière (1875–1956)
Student Workbook 6, p. 65

Atmosphere

The tempo marking *Andante religioso* gives us a clue as to the character and mood of the piece. *Andante*, meaning _at a walking pace_ , might indicate that there is a procession.

By looking at the music and playing some of the chords, you can imagine that this is a chorale sung by a choir. The feeling is one of calm. What word on the music says that? _tranquillo_ Therefore, the tempo should be fairly steady. When you perform the piece, however, leave room for a little flexibility in the tempo because the prayer needs to be expressive.

Lush Harmonies

Visually, this score is rather daunting because of the thick texture and frequent accidentals. Start with some listening exercises. Use a simplification of the chords and play these progressions over and over until you get used to the sound. For example:

By playing the simplification, you will notice two **cadences**, one at the end of m. 3 moving to m. 4, and another at the end of m. 7 moving to m. 8. Is the first chord in both cadences the same? _yes_

The cadences resolve differently. Identify the resolution in m. 4 as (major) or minor. Do the same in m. 8: major or (minor)? What type of cadences are they?
☑ **perfect (authentic)**

Thick Texture

Look at the first five chords in the piece. How many "voices" do you see? _five_ Some choral music calls for one or more voice sections to divide into two parts, such as Soprano I and Soprano II. In *Prayer*, the number of notes or "voices" in each chord varies from 4 to as many as 6.

If you imagine the chorale orchestrated for a string group, which instruments might take the parts? _violin I and II, viola, cello, double bass_ You might also imagine this piece played on the organ, which is definitely an appropriate instrument for a piece with this title!

There is a middle section that looks and sounds different from the blocked chords in the outer sections. Where does it begin and end?
mm. _8_ to _12_

Articulation

One special articulation mark stands out in a striking way because it is used so much. Which one? _tenuto_ What is the usual meaning of the mark? _hold for full value_

An "Extra" Note

Look at mm. 10 and 12. Play these measures and focus on the dynamic markings:

The resolution of any non-chord note is usually played a little more softly; that is the reason for the *diminuendos*. What is the name of the resolution chord in m. 10? <u>E major</u> And the name of the resolution chord in m. 12? <u>B major</u>

Transposition

In the final section, Glière uses **transposition** in a clever way. At m. 13, directly following the middle section, he returns to the material from the opening, but in a different key. What is the first chord in m. 13? <u>E major</u> Is the second chord the same as the second chord in m. 1? <u>yes</u> Play this pair of chords back and forth, listening and comparing as you did in the listening exercise above.

Where else have you heard the phrase that begins on the fourth beat of m. 14? mm. <u>2–4</u>

Identify the two chords in m. 17:
<u>F sharp minor</u>   <u>D minor</u>

How does the phrase end in m. 8: major / (minor)?

Does the piece end on a major or a minor chord? <u>major</u>

Cancan

Douglas Finch (b. 1957)
Student Workbook 6, p. 68

Spot Those Dance Moves

Cancan has an almost perpetual, non-stop motion to it. How does Finch create this feeling of continuous activity?
<u>continuous eighth notes throughout the piece</u>

Within this activity, Finch creates many different dance moves and stage effects.
Take a look at the descriptions below, and match each musical excerpt with the description that suits it best. (HINT: Some of the examples may go with more than one description.) Along the way, watch for a few questions.

Excerpt <u>7</u> : The theme is short and simple—it's only two measures long. The <u>right</u> hand plays it first, in mm. <u>1–2</u> .

Excerpt(s) <u>2, 4, 7</u> : A kind of **Alberti bass** figure, appearing first in m. <u>1</u> in the <u>left</u> hand.

Excerpt <u>1</u> : The dancers vanish offstage as the music suddenly becomes louder/(softer).

What kind of scale is used? <u>chromatic</u>

The last chord is formed from the notes of the triad of <u>C major</u>.

Excerpt <u>5</u> : The theme is played a half step
☑ lower

Excerpt <u>6</u> : The theme is played in imitation. There is, however, one note that does not match up in the two hands. Circle the two versions of this note (one in each hand).

Excerpt <u>3</u> : The accompaniment becomes a series of dry, offbeat chords.

Excerpt <u>2</u> : The theme, transposed an octave
☑ up

Excerpt <u>5</u> : The theme played in parallel octaves.

Excerpt <u>4</u> : This excerpt portrays the high kicks of the dancers.

Choreography with a Form

As *Cancan* unfolds, you may be able to imagine changes in the lighting.

What color of lighting might go well with the opening? <u>yellow or orange</u>

Where might the lighting change noticeably? m. <u>5</u>

Where might the lighting return to what it was at the beginning? m. <u>14</u>

Using the above overview as a guide, which of the following best describes the musical form of *Cancan*?
☑ A B A₁ *Coda*

Fantasy

Nancy Telfer (b. 1950)
Student Workbook 6, p. 71

Rhythm and Tempo

Right away, you are faced with an unusual first measure. What does the Italian term *senza misura* mean? <u>without measure</u>

Play mm. 1 and 25 freely. The color of the note heads indicates relative durations—play the black notes more quickly than the white ones, but imagine that the notes are floating freely in space.

These measures establish the mood for the rest of the piece. On the empty staff below, rewrite the set of notes from m. 1 a perfect 5th lower:

The bottom staff is the same as m. _25_. The pattern of notes from m. 1 has been _transposed_ in m. 25.

Which musical element is "free" here?
☑ rhythmic values

Tempo
Measure _4_

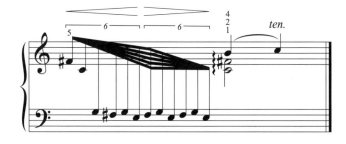

Again, the performer is in charge of how much the music:

(speeds up then slows down)

Telfer uses somewhat similar notation in m. _14_; this time, the player must _speed up_.

Visit the Composer's Workshop
Despite its contemporary sound and use of modern notation in places, this piece has a very traditional three-part structure:

A section:	mm. 1–9 (m. 1 is like an introduction)
B section:	mm. 10–15
A section:	mm. 16–25 (m. 25 is like a postlude)

What is the term for this form? _ternary_

Study the two A sections: Are they exactly the same? _no_

Compare mm. 2–5 with mm. 16–18. What do you notice? _Measures 16–18 are almost the same as mm. 2–5, but one measure is missing and the dynamics are louder._

Now compare mm. 6–7 with mm. 19–21. What do you notice? _Measures 19–21 are almost the same as mm. 6–7, but there are longer note values, the LH leaps into a different octave, and the dynamics are louder._

An Ancient Mode in a Modern Setting
Several measures in this piece are based on the following set of notes:

These notes can and do occur in different octaves. Find *all* of the measures that contain only notes taken from these pitches: mm. _2–7, 16–21_

Return to the set of notes written above. Add notes between the leaps, as shown by the arrows, so that the motion is stepwise throughout. Don't add any accidentals. Which major scale do these notes match? _G_ major

On which note (first, second, third, etc.) of the major scale does this set of notes start? _fourth_

On the Lake, op. 77, no. 12
Heinrich Hofmann (1842–1902)
Student Workbook 6, p. 74

Imagery
The melody is in long phrase lines, and you will hear a definite rhythmic flow, characteristic of the time signature of _6/8_. How many beats are in each measure, and what note gets the beat?
six beats per measure; eighth-note beat

Touch
Continue to practice the LH until you reach m. 21. What do you notice about the direction of the notes? _They go up and down._ It sounds as though there has been a shifting of the wind—small ripples perhaps. Follow the downward pattern from m. 22 to the end of m. 25, and then . . . what do you see? A leap to the _treble_ clef! It would have been much easier if Hofmann had written a low D in the bass, continuing the pattern. There is another leap on the same line. Where is it? m. _28_

Melody and Phrasing
Imagine someone is singing a beautiful melody as the boat is steered around the lake. The continuity of the phrase line is extremely important. How long are the RH slurs (in measures) in the first part of the piece? _four measures_

The texture is primarily melody with accompaniment. Where do you see additional notes supporting the melody? <u>m. 15</u> What happens at m. 36? <u>solid (blocked) chords</u> What marks are used to indicate articulation for this passage? <u>tenuto</u>

What does it mean to "voice" the melody, when there are chords directly underneath the melody? <u>play the melody notes slightly louder</u>

Valse miniature, op. 10, no. 10

Vladimir Ivanovich Rebikov (1866–1920)
Student Workbook 6, p. 77

A Ternary Form

Miniature Waltz has a simple **ternary form**. Fill in the measure numbers:
A mm. <u>1</u> – <u>9</u>
B mm. <u>10</u> – <u>25</u>
A mm. <u>26</u> – <u>33</u>

A Haunting Melody

If you play the first four measures of the RH melody, you will hear and see the contour (shape) of the melody. Play the melodic contour below:

Now play the RH melodic contour of mm. 1–4:

Perhaps the turning inward of this shape suggests the idea of longing or looking "inside."
What is the difference in shape between the two melodies?
<u>The first melody changes direction only once; the second one changes many times.</u>

Do they both have the same haunting quality? <u>no</u>

If not, why do you think this is?
<u>The haunting quality comes from the melody's twists and turns.</u>

Now play the melody in mm. 17–25. The melody is obviously different, but how does it contrast in character to the opening melody? Do you think it might be looking "outward" instead?
<u>There are more rising passages in this melody than in mm. 1–9, which does make it sound less introspective.</u>

A Subtle Accompaniment

As a general rule, the accompaniment is played one or two dynamic levels softer than the melody.
In m. 1, the melody is marked *mf*. What dynamic levels might you use for the accompaniment? <u>mf</u>

What is the meaning of the Italian word *sotto*?
<u>under/below</u>

What is the composer indicating by the use of this word in m. 2?
<u>He is indicating that the LH should be played more softly than the RH.</u>

In mm. 2, 4, 27, and 29, the melody is quite low in pitch. If the chords in these measures are played *pianissimo*, the melody notes will be heard clearly.

What is the meaning of *più mosso*? <u>more motion</u>

Where does it occur in the score? <u>m. 17</u>

Cantabile

You might think of this waltz as an elegant salon piece, written for a string trio made up of a violin, a viola, and a cello.

Which instrument plays the treble-clef portion of the melody? <u>violin</u>

Which instrument plays the bass-clef portion of the melody? <u>cello</u>

Which instruments play the chords in the accompaniment? <u>viola</u>

Childhood–Spring

Zdeněk Fibich (1850–1900)
Student Workbook 6, p. 79

Ternary Form

Like many **character pieces**, *Childhood–Spring* is in **ternary form**. Fill in the sections below:

Follow the Story

A mm. <u>1</u> – <u>8</u>
B mm. <u>9</u> – <u>14</u>
A₁ mm. <u>15</u> – <u>22</u>

This musical story is held together by simple musical elements put into an equally straightforward form. Consider the opening melodic motive:

Mark each of its appearances on the map that follows, using the letter "a." Does "a" appear only in the RH? <u>no</u>

On the map below, add LH inside those measures where motive "a" moves to the LH.

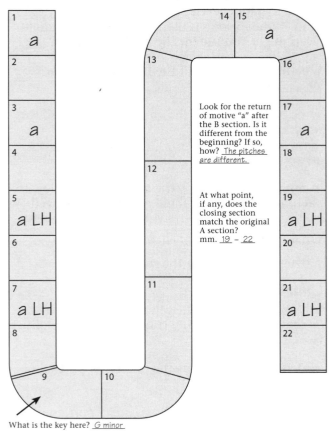

What is the key here? _G minor_

Does the section starting at m. 9 use motive "a" or a new motive? _a new motive_

If it is a new motive, label it "b" and write out its opening rhythmic figure here:

Accompanying Rhythms

Observe the rhythm of the accompaniment in the B section:

```
|| C  ⁷  ♩   ♪ ⁷  ♩    ♪  ||
   𝅗𝅥        𝅗𝅥
   1  & 2 &  3  & 4  &
```

Mark the divisions of the pulse below the rhythm (1 & 2 &, etc.). What term is used to describe this type of rhythm? _syncopation_

Listen for the character created in the B section by the combined effect of the rhythms in the RH and LH. If you hear a contrast with the A section, describe it here.
The B section sounds more agitated; there is more activity.

An Ancient Tale

Bohdana Filtz (b. 1932)
Student Workbook 6, p. 82

Folk-Song Style

1. **The falling 3rd.** The falling 3rd is one of the easiest intervals to sing. Track the interval of a 3rd throughout the piece. How does Filtz treat this interval in m. 17? _It is a rising 3rd._

2. **Vocal and speech patterns.** Notice the symmetry of the two-measure phrases and the gentle, rhythmic figures of the melody, reflecting poetry or words. Sing the melody, adding words if you like. Where do you naturally breathe?
every two measures

3. **Sequences.** Repetition of a phrase at different pitches is one way of extending a song. Mark the sequence pattern in the following excerpt.

This sequence is extended further in mm. _5–6_. Notice that one of the intervals is slightly changed.

Now look at the LH accompaniment. The open position of the LH chords creates a gentle sweep in the bass line. It has an almost improvised quality. In which direction does the LH almost always sweep? _upward_

Describe the mood or feeling this conveys.
an uplifting feeling

The High Point of the Story

For most of the piece, the atmosphere is subdued, but like all stories, it has a climax.
Where is the high point of *An Ancient Tale*?
_mm. 15–16_

Can you name two things Filtz does to reinforce this climax?
1. _The dynamic making is ff. A new rhythm is introduced_ .
2. _The melody is an octave higher. The notes in m. 16 are tenuto and the pedal is used to blur the sounds._

Write the notes of the chord on the second beat of m. 15 in close position. (Use the lowest note as the root.) Then play the chord you have written.

This chord consists of a _B minor_ triad plus a _3rd_. What is the interval if you count up from the root to the note added at the top? _7th_

Scales in 7ths

Now let's have some fun with 7th chords. Write triads above each note of the A major scale in the following example. Then play the scale and listen to the sound of the parallel triads.

Now add a 7th above each note of the scale to create a series of 7th chords.

Which one of these chords is the **dominant 7th** chord of A major? <u>E (the fifth chord)</u>

Write the 7th chords in mm. 1, 6, 11, 21, and 23 in solid (blocked) form:

Hungarian Dance

Lajos Papp (b. 1935)
Student Workbook 6, p. 84

Modal Melody

What is the key of the piece? <u>A minor</u> In the harmonic minor scale of a key, the seventh note, **the leading note**, is raised. Write the A harmonic minor scale on the first line below for one octave, ascending and descending.

Next, write the melodic minor scale.
(Quick review: Which scale degrees are raised in the ascending form? <u>6, 7</u> Lowered in the descending form? <u>6, 7</u>)

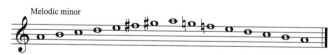

Finally, write the natural minor scale. What happened to the leading note? <u>It is lowered.</u>

The natural minor scale is also known as the **Aeolian mode.** Look through both pages of music. Do you see any leading note accidentals in the piece? <u>no</u>

The melody contains another mode (a composite mode) as well. If you look through the structure as a whole, you will see that there is a close tie to the relative major of A minor, which is <u>C major</u>.

Notice that the first four measures don't stay in A minor for very long. Look at the LH part. What is the chord in m. 2? <u>D⁷</u> This chord resolves to what chord in m. 3? <u>G⁷</u> This chord resolves to what chord in m. 4? <u>C major</u>

Papp sets up this same major key differently in mm. 17–18. Are these triads? <u>no</u> Which note is missing? <u>E</u>

Rhythm

What is the time signature? $\frac{2}{4}$ Name another lively dance in this meter: <u>polka</u> .

Articulation

Look at the last four measures. What does the word *marcato* mean? <u>well-marked</u>

A Round Dance, or a Square Dance?

The form can be assessed at a glance. All the sections (within the double bars) are the same length, and all are repeated, with the exception of mm. 17–18 and mm. 43–46.

At first glance it seems as if the first four measures are the same as the next four. Are they? <u>no</u> Look for these kinds of subtle changes throughout the piece.

The formula for *Hungarian Dance* is 4 + 4, then double bar line. The chart below has been started for you. Continue labeling the musical material (the phrases) with letters. Mark everything in your score so you will see it quickly as you play.

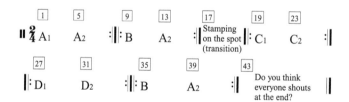

Roundup

André Previn (b. 1929)
Student Workbook 6, p. 87

Getting the Rhythm

In a western dance, there would be lots of foot stomping, finger snapping, and hand clapping. Here's a bouncy exercise to get you warmed up for the party!

The 5ths are meant to remind you of the sound of open strings on a violin.

Now play the LH part of mm. 1–2 as written, and tap steady eighth notes with your RH. When this is easy, stop tapping, and count beats instead.

This rhythm is **syncopated.** How does the syncopation change from m. 1 to m. 2?
In m. 2, beat 3 is the only syncopated beat.

The RH rhythm is just as interesting as the LH, and combining them will be even more interesting. Does the RH rhythm also have a two-measure pattern? yes

Are both measures syncopated? no

What markings does Previn use to highlight the syncopation? an accent

Fifths and Sevenths

Your two hands will feel different because they play in different positions.

What is the interval between the highest and lowest notes in the RH part in m. 1? 7th

Where else does the RH play this pattern of descending notes? mm. 2, 3, 4, 9, 10, 11, 12, 15, and 16

Does the LH play this pattern anywhere? yes, m. 15

What Scale Are You Playing?

In mm. 5–8, the RH and the LH play very close together. Each hand plays only a certain set of notes, but the hands have no notes in common. This certainly gives the music a distinctive sound! Write the notes of the LH as a scale:

This scale is called a **pentatonic scale.** It has five different notes, and there are no semitones. The RH scale has the same notes as the beginning of a major scale, but the melody is centered around D. The LH plays black keys. The melody goes up and down the scale, starting and ending on G flat.

When you play these measures, which hand will you put on top? LH

A Finale with Pizzazz

Play mm. 15–16, paying special attention to the dynamic and articulation markings.
Why is the *forte* such a contrast here?
Because it was *p* previously. It marks the return of the opening melody.

What are the two markings on the final chord, and what do they tell you to do?
The accent means to play the notes with emphasis. The sfz sign means to play strongly accented.

Student Workbook 7 Answers

Sonatina No. 4 in B flat Major
Third Movement: Vivace

Johann Ludwig Krebs (1713–1780)
Student Workbook 7, p. 4

Put It All Together

Take a trip through the movement, using the map laid out on the next two pages. Virtually all of the examples will involve some type of scale fragment or broken chord. By answering the various questions, you will discover some of the ways that Krebs uses the simple building blocks of music to create phrasing, form, and direction.

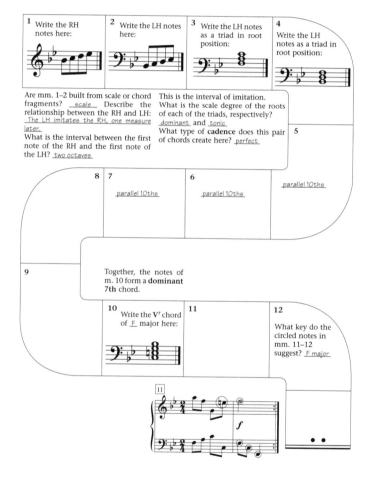

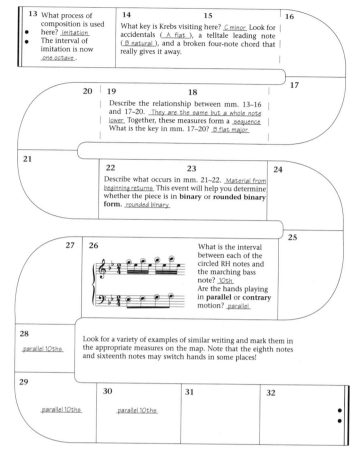

Suite No. 8 in G Major, HWV 441
First Movement: Aria

George Frideric Handel (1685–1759)
Student Workbook 7, p. 7

Form and a Motive

Play the RH part from the beginning to the third beat of m. 2. Label this motive "a" in your score.

Is this motive repeated in the A section? _yes_

If so, is it exactly the same? _no_

Is this motive repeated in the B section? _yes_

If so, is it exactly the same? _no_

Fill in the measure numbers, **cadences**, and keys in the form chart below, and label the sections in your score.

Section _A_	mm. _1–8_	Cadence at end _perfect_	Key _D major_
Section _B_	mm. _9–20_	Cadence at end _perfect_	Key _G major_

How is the key at the end of the A section related to the home key? _D is the dominant of G_

Is this music in **ternary**, **binary**, or **rounded binary form**? _rounded binary_

Sequences and Patterns between the Hands

Part of the brilliant clarity of this piece comes from Handel's use of patterns. Let's look at the sixteenth-note opening pattern in motive "a":

Where is this pattern used in **sequence** in the first half of the aria? mm. _3–4 (with upbeat)_

How long is the sequence pattern, and how many times is it repeated? _The pattern is two beats long, and is repeated three times._

What is the interval between each repetition? _a 2nd_

Does the sequence rise or fall? _it falls_

Rather then repeat the pattern in m. 4, Handel "spins it out."

Find other measures that contain any of these four patterns in sequence (or beginning on different notes).

1. _mm. 2 and 3_   3. _mm. 9 and 10_

2. _mm. 6 and 7_   4. _mm. 18–20_

In the parallel motion, what is the interval between the hands? _10th_

Look through the rest of the piece, and find other places where Handel has incorporated contrary or parallel motion.

contrary motion: mm. _1, 5, 9_

parallel motion: mm. _2, 4, 6, 7, 10, 11, 15, 16, 18, 19_

Suite in G Major, op. 1, no. 1
Eleventh Movement: Andante

Joseph-Hector Fiocco (1703–1741)
Student Workbook 7, p. 9

A Lilting Melody

What is the key of this movement? _E minor_

How is this key related to G major?
It is the relative minor.

Play mm. 1–8, and listen to the shape of the melody.

There are three phrases in these measures. Where does each one begin?

1. m. _1_

2. m. _5_

3. m. _7_

Where does the next phrase end? _m. 13_

What kind of **cadence** does Fiocco use to end this phrase, and what is the key?
Cadence: _perfect_ Key: _G major_

The longer phrase in mm. 14–23 rises gradually, and the changing harmonies create musical tension.

Where is the climax of this phrase, and what markings does Fiocco use to highlight it?

The climax of this phrase is on beat 1 of m. 18, and is highlighted by the mordent in the RH.

Harmonic Embellishment

In this piece, a regular motion in _eighth_ notes is set up in the LH. Find the pair of measures where another rhythmic value appears: mm. _10–11_.

In the upper staff, write the triad formed by the RH and LH notes in the first beat of the first of these measures:

On the lower staff, write the LH notes that are not part of the triad. One of these, the one played on the beat, is an *appoggiatura*, or "leaning note."

This note is:

☑ above the note belonging to the triad, and resolves downward

Solo in F Major, TWV 32:4
Second Movement: Bourrée

Georg Philipp Telemann (1681–1767)
Student Workbook 7, p. 12

Telemann's B*ourrée*

The bourrée is a fairly rapid, energetic dance, with a strong rhythmic feel. Most bourrées begin on an upbeat, as this one does.

How many beats in the measure are indicated by the time signature? <u>four</u>

How many beats do you *feel* per measure? <u>two</u>

How could you change the time signature to indicate this? <u>¢</u>

A Two-Part Form

The repeat signs divide the music into two sections. Fill in the measure numbers, **cadences**, and keys to determine more about the form.

Section A	mm. <u>1–18</u>	Cadence at end <u>perfect</u>	Key <u>C major</u>
Section B	mm. <u>19–44</u>	Cadence at end <u>perfect</u>	Key <u>F major</u>

What is the home key? <u>F major</u>

How is the key at the end of the A section related to the home key? <u>dominant</u>

Is this music in **ternary**, **binary**, or **rounded binary form**? <u>rounded binary</u>

Finding the Musical Ingredients

Play the RH of mm. 1–5. This theme consists of three motives that have different personalities:

Which motive moves by step? <u>b</u> by leap? <u>a and c</u>
In what other ways do the personalities contrast with each other? <u>phrasing, note values</u>

Write "a," "b," or "c" beside any colorful words you feel describes the character of each motive.

swinging <u>c</u>   rolling <u>b</u>

brilliant <u>b</u>   swaying <u>a</u>

skipping <u>a/c</u>   bouncing <u>a</u>

jumping <u>a</u>   singing <u>b</u>

The third motive, "c," is spun out in the RH of mm. 5–8 and its arpeggio pattern continues in the LH, mm. <u>9–12</u>.

Match each item in the box to the correct example below.

1. a form of motive "a" in the LH
2. fragment of motive "c" **inverted** (going in a direction opposite from that of the original)
3. blend of motives "a" and "b"
4. motive "c" extended by **sequences**
5. fragment of "c" in **imitation** between the hands

A Simple Framework

Identify the key of *Bourrée*. <u>F major</u>

In the tonic key, write the notes of the 1) tonic triad; 2) subdominant triad; 3) dominant triad; and 4) dominant 7th as specified below. Play the chords you have written and listen to the sound of each one.

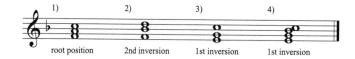

Sonata in E Minor, Wq 62 / 12, H 66
Third Movement: Sarabande

Carl Philipp Emanuel Bach (1714–1788)
Student Workbook 7, p. 15

Following the Melody

In the first example, the LH imitates the RH. Is the LH an exact **transposition** of the RH? <u>no</u>

What is the interval between the fourth and fifth RH notes in m. 1? <u>perfect 5th</u>

What is the interval between the fourth and fifth notes LH in m. 2? <u>diminished 5th</u>

Now look at Examples 2 and 3 above and ask yourself the same questions.

Which example shows an exact transposition in the imitation of the RH by the LH? <u>Ex. 2</u>

In the first section (mm. 1–8), the composer uses **imitation** and **sequences** to create a flowing texture in two voices. What sign changes the rhythm slightly in Examples 2 and 3? _eighth rest_

Some of these techniques carry over into the second section. In mm. 9–10, the motive looks similar to Examples 2 or 3. What is one difference? _downward direction_

Compare the motives in mm. 9 and 10. Is the LH an exact transposition? _yes_

Interweaving of Voices

At m. 16, you will hear the beginning of another compositional technique.
(This effect is used in many of J.S. Bach's *Inventions* and *Preludes and Fugues*.)

Play the LH only in mm. 16–17, then the RH. What do you hear? _a canon_

To which note does the pattern go before changing direction? _E flat_

The two hands (voices) continue with a wonderfully inventive harmonic blend, twisting and turning (rising and falling), finally opening out by the use of a partial _chromatic_ scale in contrary motion.

Where is the arrival point of the long phrase? m. _21_

Do you hear any dissonance between the hands along the way? _no_

Toward which key is the composer heading? _E minor_

Melodic Decoration

A composer can decorate a melody in many ways. Rhythm is one; ornaments are another. Both are used in the following excerpt:

The melodic skeleton is circled in the RH part of mm. 11–12 above. The rhythmic decoration consists of a series of sixteenth notes in a pattern, most falling one step below the essential melody notes. Circle the corresponding LH skeleton. What do you discover in the imitation? _It is an exact tranposition of the RH._

Another rhythmic decoration appears near the end, in m. 27. The melody that clearly lies behind the elaborate rhythm falls straight down from the high E to the E one octave below. What is the scale? _E minor melodic_ Play the RH of the entire measure without the dotted rhythm, ending on the last note in m. 28. Without the dotted rhythm, what are the note values of the scale? _sixteenth notes_

Shaping the Melody

The visual shape of a phrase on the page often indicates the dynamic shape. An ascending melody often has a built-in (crescendo). An arched melody implies ◁ ▷.

Listen to the sound of each phrase as you play it. Think about where it is going, and where it is coming from. Only two dynamic markings are provided by the editors: _mf_ and _mp_ . However, within these markings, you can use many shades of musical color. Vary the sound accordingly for the high points and low points. Where do you think the highest point of the piece is? m. _20_ By listening and experimenting, you will be able to give real meaning to the music and bring out its beauty.

Musical Evolution

J.S. Bach lived in the Baroque period (his dates) _1685–1750_ and his son C.P.E. Bach lived into the Classical period (his dates) _1714–1788_ .

Invention No. 1 in C Major,
BWV 772

Johann Sebastian Bach (1685–1750)
Student Workbook 7, p. 19

Introducing the Motive

Does the motive begin on the downbeat, or on a weak beat? _on a weak beat_

What replaces the sixteenth rest at the beginning of m. 2? _a sixteenth note_

Now play the complete motive. What are the two elements that make up this motive?
1. _sixteenth notes_   2. _eighth notes_

When the LH enters, which element does it imitate? _the sixteenth notes of the RH motive_

What is the interval between the RH and the LH entries? _one octave_

A Sequence

Play the two-beat figure in the RH m. 3 (start on the A):

How is this figure related to the motive in m. 1?
<u>They are in contrary motion.</u>

With a pencil, trace each note pattern shown below:

In mm. 3–5, Bach uses this figure in a **sequence**. How many times is the figure repeated? <u>three times</u>

Is it a rising or falling sequence? <u>falling</u>

What is the interval between each repetition? <u>a 3rd</u>

Bach uses this sequence to **modulate** to a new key. What is this key, and how is it related to the home key?
<u>G major—the dominant of C</u>

Climbing to a Cadence
In mm. 5–6, the RH climbs stepwise:

How is this climbing figure related to the motive?
<u>It is a rising sequence based on the notes of the second part of the figure in m. 3.</u>

The A section of the invention ends on the first RH eighth note in m. 7.

What is the key at this point? <u>G major</u> What type of **cadence** does Bach use to end the section? <u>perfect</u>

The A₁ Section
The second section opens with a restatement of the original figure with two important changes. What are they?
1. <u>The figure is in the LH.</u>   2. <u>It is in G major.</u>

In this section, Bach also uses sequences to pass through several keys. The section ends on the first eighth note of m. <u>15</u>.

What is the key at this point, and what type of cadence does Bach use to end the section? <u>A minor; perfect cadence</u>

The A₂ Section
How is the sequence figure related to the original motive? <u>It presents the original motive first in inversion, then in its original form.</u>

Notice that each statement of the motive begins on the weak beat and moves to the next downbeat through the long tied notes. What key does Bach visit on the way back to the home key of C major?
<u>F major</u>

Passepied in D Major

Johann Philipp Kirnberger (1721–1783)
Student Workbook 7, p. 22

Baroque Dance Style
Look through Kirnberger's *Passepied* to check for the typical style features described above. It is important to remember Kirnberger's dates, which span the end of the Baroque period and the beginning of the Classical period.

Tempo? <u>lively</u> How many metronome ticks per measure? <u>one</u>

Is the *look* of the music simple? <u>yes</u>

Time signature? <u>3/8</u>

Length of phrases? <u>four measures</u>

Is there an upbeat? <u>yes</u> Does every phrase have an upbeat? <u>yes</u>

What are the shortest note values that run through most of the piece? <u>sixteenth notes</u>

Texture
Find one place where Kirnberger uses **imitation**. m. <u>25</u>

Recognizing Patterns
Match the patterns to their descriptions and fill in the pattern numbers:

Pattern no. <u>6</u> : trill pattern

Pattern no. <u>4</u> : ascending scale in RH (key? <u>A major</u>)

Pattern no. <u>2</u> : ascending scale in LH (key? <u>D major</u>)

Pattern no. <u>7</u> : zigzag pattern

Pattern no. <u>3</u> : "back and forth combination" ending in three consecutive notes

Pattern no. <u>1</u> : descending scale in RH (key? <u>D major</u>)

Pattern no. <u>5</u> : leaping intervals followed by two-note slurs

Sonatina in C Major, op. 36, no. 3
First Movement

Muzio Clementi (1752–1832)
Student Workbook 7, p. 25

Sonatina Spirit
This work is known for its bright and cheerful personality. There are several factors that contribute to its lighthearted energy:

1. The tempo indication, which is <u>spiritoso</u>. What does this suggest to you? <u>spirited, energetic</u>

2. The brightness of the key, which is <u>C major</u>.

3. The energy of the constant eighth-note pattern in the LH.

4. The use of repeating notes. As an experiment, play the first four measures and hold the three or four repeating notes for their combined value:

Then play the repeated notes as written. What do you notice about the energy level now? It is higher.

5. The use of musical dialogue—tossing an idea back and forth between the hands, as in mm. 5 and 6. What image does this suggest to you? laughter

6. The contrast of musical character between ideas. How might you describe the difference of energy and personality in:

mm. 1–12 bright, full of life

mm. 13–17 charming, sweet

mm. 18–26 suspenseful

Chords and Scales

It has been said that all music is made up of scales and chords. Look at mm. 1–4 of this sonatina movement.

Which of these measures contain both scales and broken chords? m. 2

What inversion of a C major chord does the RH play in m. 1? 2nd inversion

Half an Alberti

Through most of the movement, the LH plays a modified **Alberti bass**, modified because the upper note of the chord figure is missing. Which string instrument might play this oscillating figure in the middle range? viola

Describing the Form

The movement is in **sonata form**. In the exposition, Clementi presents two themes: The first theme begins in m. 1 and is in the key of C major. The second theme begins in m. 13, and is in the key of G major. This key is the dominant of the home key.

Which theme moves by leaps? theme 1

Which theme moves by steps? theme 2

In mm. 5–6, Clementi extends the phrase using a **sequence** that also includes **imitation**.

Which hand leads the sequence? RH

Which hand leads the imitation? LH

This passage contains two **chromatic** notes that create a slight **dissonance**. These notes move or **resolve** upward (direction?) to a note that is part of the scale. The end of this section actually occurs with a **cadence** in mm. 23–24 in the key of G major. The next three measures create a *codetta* (a miniature *coda*).

The development section ends at m. 35. In mm. 34–35, the music pauses on a G major chord, creating a (scale degree) dominant **preparation** before the return of the first theme. This increases the listener's anticipation that something is around the corner; that "something" is the recapitulation section, which begins at m. 36.

In the recapitulation, how does the main theme differ from its first presentation in m. 1? It is an octave lower.

Where does the material in m. 42 come from? m. 10 Clementi obviously liked this material so much that he expanded it in the recapitulation. Where does the second theme begin? m. 49 What key is it in? C major

Does this section end with a *coda*? yes What key is it in? C major

Sonata in D Major, Hob. XVII: D1
Third Movement: Finale

Franz Joseph Haydn (1732–1809)
Student Workbook 7, p. 28

A Sparkling Musical Machine
This movement amply demonstrates many of the features of the Classical style of piano writing. You can explore some of these features by finding the musical excerpt that best matches the description provide

Excerpt no. 1

Excerpt no. 2

Excerpt no. 3

Excerpt no. 4

Excerpt no. 5

Play the melody as solid (blocked) chords from m. 2 to m. 11 so that you can hear the harmonic progression. Identify as many chords as you can, and write the names or chord symbols under the music. For example:

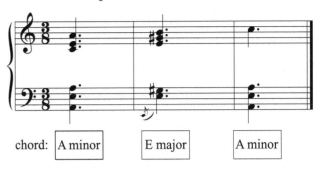

chord: A minor   E major   A minor

Excerpt no. 1: The writing here suggests the sound of a symphony orchestra. By juxtaposing a smaller group of instruments (or one single instrument) against a larger group of instruments, the composer creates vivid contrasts of dynamics and sound.

Excerpt no. 5: A strongly rhythmic rising motive made out of the **tonic** chord—this is sometimes referred to as a "rocket motive."

Excerpt no. 2: Here's an example of **sequence**. Draw a bracket over the initial portion of the sequence (the portion that is then repeated). Is the repetition higher or lower, and by what interval? _lower by a 2nd_

Excerpt no. 3: These descending scales reinforce the key that each of the two halves of the movement will end in, respectively. Label the scales as tonic key or **dominant** key. Which of these keys is reached at the end of the first section? _dominant_ At the end of the second section? _tonic_

Excerpt no. 4: Four-measure phrase with repeated halves.

Für Elise, WoO 59

Ludwig van Beethoven (1770–1827)
Student Workbook 7, p. 30

A Rondo Form

Look through the music to find these sections, and mark them in your score as well.

A   mm. _1_ – _22_
B   mm. _23_ – _29_
Bridge 1   mm. _30_ – _37_
A   mm. _38_ – _59_
C   mm. _60_ – _76_
Bridge 2   mm. _77_ – _81_
A   mm. _82_ – _103_

The Main Theme

What is the opening key? _A minor_

Beethoven touches briefly on a new key in this section.

What is the new key, and how is it related to the home key? _C major_

What is the key at the end of the first A section? _A minor_

The B Section

The B section presents several contrasting elements.

What is the opening key of this section? _F major_

How is it related to the home key? _submediant_

What is the new rhythmic note value introduced in this section? _thirty-second notes_

The C Section

4. Play this pair of chords once more. This time make the second chord softer.

    Which creates more of the feeling of mystery that makes this passage special? _playing the chords more softly_

The chord in m. 60 is a **diminished 7th** chord.

Find two other diminished 7th chords in this passage. (Look at the notes in both hands. One of these chords is incomplete; the third of the chord is missing.)

m. _62_

m. _65_

m. _74_

Sonatina in C Major, op. 55, no. 3

First Movement

Friedrich Kuhlau (1786–1832)
Student Workbook 7, p. 33

Two Themes

In the exposition, Kuhlau presents these two themes.

1. The first theme is packed with energy and optimism. The ideas are punctuated with emphatic **cadences**. Look at the RH. It begins with a motive in parallel intervals.

What is the interval in mm. 1–2? _6th_ Notice the bright, triumphant sound of this interval.

What is the interval in mm. 5–6? <u>3rd</u> How would you compare the sound of this interval with the first one? <u>Similar, but the 3rd is tighter, closer.</u>

What is the relationship between these two intervals? <u>They are inversions of each other.</u>

What is the key of this first theme? <u>C major</u>

Notice the repeated notes in the LH. How do they support the RH character?
<u>They give the melody energy and direction.</u>

There are two energetic cadences in the first theme, in mm. <u>4</u> and <u>8</u>.

What two triads form each cadence in C major?
<u>G major</u> and <u>C major</u>

What does Kuhlau do with the rhythm of each cadence to make it even more energetic?
<u>He repeats the cadence as an eighth-note figure.</u>

2. The second theme (beginning in m. 13) has a contrasting personality to the first theme. How would you describe it?
<u>more authoritative, driving, flowing</u>

Two elements that add to this difference are the **syncopated** rhythms and the slurred figures. This theme serves as a **bridge** between the two key areas. What is the key at the beginning of this theme? <u>A minor</u>

What is the key at the end? <u>G major</u>

How is the new key related to the home key?
<u>dominant</u>

Now that you've identified the two themes, you can see what Kuhlau does with them.

The first theme is used in a rising **sequence** from mm. <u>21</u> to <u>24</u>, bringing to a close the:
☑ Exposition

Where do you see the opening theme return?
m. <u>25</u> This is the start of the:
☑ Development

For a moment, the listener might imagine that you have really returned to the beginning. This is one of the techniques that a clever composer can use within sonata form. Whereas the first eight measures lead to a **perfect (authentic) cadence** in the key of <u>C major</u>, this version of the theme arrives at a perfect (authentic) cadence in <u>E minor</u> (look for a leading note, <u>D sharp</u>, going to a tonic, <u>E</u>), followed later by a cadence in <u>G major</u> (leading note <u>F sharp</u> to tonic <u>G</u>).

Which theme does Kuhlau use in his development section?
☑ theme 1

Dominant Preparation

What happens to the rhythm of the motion in 3rds in this fragment? <u>It slows down.</u>

Measure: 32	33	34	35
eighth notes; 3rds are heard twice per beat	How many 3rds per beat? <u>1</u>	How often do the 3rds sound here? <u>beats 1 and 3</u>	
The composer is			
(slowing down) the rate of the rhythmic activity ↓ creating rhythmic **augmentation**		speeding up the rate of the rhythmic activity ↓ creating rhythmic **diminution**	

During this passage, how would you describe the pitches in the LH?
☑ stationary

This is an example of **dominant preparation**. Why is it called dominant?
<u>The LH repeats the dominant of the home key.</u>

The dominant preparation is preparing us for music heard earlier in the:
☑ Exposition

This is the start of the recapitulation, the portion of sonata form that repeats the exposition but remains in the home key. One theme is missing in this recapitulation:
☑ theme 1

Sonata No. 5 in D Major
First Movement

Stephen Storace (1762–1796)

Student Workbook 7, p. 36

Sonata Sound

Which instruments of the orchestra might play the first two measures? <u>trumpets, horns</u>

Can you find another two measures in the first section that are similar in style? mm. <u>7–8</u> Just by looking at the dynamic markings, you can imagine the orchestral contrast. What instruments would be suitable for mm. 3–6, and mm. 8 (last beat)–12?
<u>strings, flutes</u>

This movement is not entirely orchestral though. There are two typical pianistic features, both in the LH. They are running sixteenth notes in mm. <u>13–16</u> and an **Alberti bass** in mm. <u>22–27</u>.

Sonata Form

Write down the measure numbers of the sections that you recognize.

Exposition

Theme 1 in the **tonic** key: mm. _3–12_

Is there a **bridge** to the second theme? _no_

Theme 2 is usually in the dominant key, which is confirmed by a perfect cadence.

Is that the case for this Theme 2, mm. 13–16? _no_

Development

Describe the opening of this development. _a fanfare similar to m. 1_

Is the composer using new material in the first two measures (mm. 17–18)? _no_

Is there new material at m. 19? _yes_

What happens in the RH at m. 22? _an F major scale_

Recapitulation

Do you see a fanfare? _no_
What happens instead? _repeated notes_ What is the musical name for the repeated notes leading to the return of theme 1? _pedal point_ How does this note relate to the home key? _It is the dominant of D major._

Theme 1 (return to tonic key): m. 32
Theme 2 is usually transposed to the tonic key. What happens in this sonata?
The LH accompaniment returns in the tonic.

Harmony and Cadences

Compare the following excerpts:

Ex. 1

Ex. 2

Cadence: _deceptive_

Key: _D major_

Ex. 3

The second and third examples on p. 37 each finish with a type of cadence. In Ex. 2, label the cadence and the key where indicated.

In the development section, the cadence in Ex. 3 is rather mysterious. By using an F natural, what key is the composer implying? _D minor_

What type of chord is the circled chord? _diminished 7th_

Mixing Sharps and Flats

In a piece from the Classical period, we don't usually see a composer moving from a sharp key to a flat key. But in the development section, beginning with the chord of _D minor_, Storace moves quickly to using flats in m. 19.

What key comes to the foreground by m. 22? _F major_

There must be some connection between this new key and the beginning of the development. What is it? _F major is the relative major of D minor._

Bagatelle, op. 119, no. 1

Ludwig van Beethoven (1770–1827)

Student Workbook 7, p. 39

A Ternary Form

Take a closer look at the form and the elements of contrast between the A and B sections. Look at the score, then add the measure numbers and short descriptions in the chart below.

	A section mm. _1–16_	B section mm. 17–_36_ (bridge mm. 33–36)	A₁ section mm. _37–51_	Coda mm. 52–_74_
Key	_G minor_	_E flat major_	_G minor_	_G minor_
Articulation (*legato, staccato, slurred, etc.*)	_staccato and legato_	_legato, slurred_	_staccato and legato_	_legato, some staccato_
Final **cadence**	_perfect_	_perfect_	_perfect_	_plagal_
Phrase length	_2–3 mm._	_4 mm._	_2–3 mm._	_2 mm._
Chordal or linear musical texture	_chordal and linear_	_chordal_	_chordal and linear_	_linear and chordal_
Thematic character	_dignified_	_graceful, lyrical_	_dignified_	_intense_
Use of pedal or type of pedaling	_sparingly, discreet_	_used with most chords, on each beat_	_none_	_on the final cadence_

Development and Variation

Although Beethoven uses **ternary form**, he extends the third section by means of a lengthy *coda* which is like a development of the primary material. What is the difference in length between A and A₁ + *coda*? _22 measures_

Beethoven starts by restating the A theme. In mm. 45–52, he presents a variation of the theme. Play the RH part of these measures. Can you hear the notes of the theme? _yes_ Circle these notes in the following example:

In the RH, Beethoven has created an ornamented version of the melody. How has Beethoven varied the LH part from the opening section—has he changed the harmony, or just the texture? just the texture

In mm. 52–65, Beethoven has written a miniature development section. In these measures, he also emphasizes the tonic key. There is a brief **modulation** in this passage. Where is it and what is the new key? mm. 52–60 key C minor How is this key related to the tonic key? subdominant

Look at the eighth-note figures in both hands from mm. 52–56 and 59–62. Notice how successive pairs of notes in the two hands create a pattern of consecutive chords. The first pattern is boxed in the example below.

Circle the beat that each pattern begins on:

m. 52:
1 2 ③ | 1 ② 3 | ① 2 ③ | 1 ② 3 |

How long is each pattern? two beats

This creates some rhythmic ambiguity, as the overall beat pattern of *Bagatelle* is three beats per measure. This rhythmic effect is sometimes referred to as **hemiola**.

The **C**oda
In the last line, Beethoven brings back the opening theme but in a different key. Write out the notes of mm. 65–69 in descending scale form:

These notes suggest the key of C minor. Beethoven uses this key to create an ending that doesn't really end! The last chord is not the **tonic** chord of the original home key of G minor; rather, it is the dominant chord (name the scale degree of the root of the chord) of the key you named above. How would you describe the effect of this ending? It slips away mysteriously rather than ending definitively.

Arietta, op. 43, no. 7
Reinhold Glière (1875–1956)
Student Workbook 7, p. 42

A Flowing Melody . . .
According to its key signature, *Arietta* begins in either F major or D minor.

Observe the motion of the melody at the start; you will notice that it forms a rising scale. However, the scale does not progress from tonic to tonic, but from dominant to the next higher dominant. Is this scale in the *harmonic* or *melodic* form of its key? melodic

. . . Shared between the Hands
As is often the case in piano music, the melody appears from the outset in the right hand. Is this the case throughout *Arietta*, however? Find two places where the hands trade places, so to speak—the LH carrying the melody while the RH offers a background of eighth notes (see the next paragraph): mm. 17–18 and mm. 49–50 .

A Graceful Accompaniment
On the staff below, write in the lowest and highest notes of each accompaniment figure in mm. 1–8. Identify the interval formed by each pair of notes. The first and last are done as examples.

| 6th | octave | 10th | 10th | octave | octave | 10th | 11th |

What conclusion can you draw from this? Is the span changing constantly, or do certain intervals recur? It changes, but octaves and 10ths recur.

Venetian Boat Song, op. 30, no. 6
Felix Mendelssohn (1809–1847)
Student Workbook 7, p. 44

The Gondolier's Oar
How does the LH part suggest the gentle gliding of the gondola, or the long strokes of the gondolier's oar? with the repetitive eighth-note rhythm

When does the gondolier move his oar? usually at the beginning of each measure

The Gondolier's Song
In mm. 3–4, the RH plays a dramatic pair of notes. This motive sets the mood for the entire piece. What is the interval between these two notes? minor 3rd

The interval of a rising 3rd seems to permeate the gondolier's song. Look through your score to find where Mendelssohn uses the following specific 3rds, and write the measure numbers here. Don't stop at these; look for other rising 3rds throughout the music.

1. Find a rising 3rd with a **passing note** between the two notes.
mm. <u>6–7, 11, 12, 14–15, 22–23, 24–25, 26–27, 36–37</u>

2. Find a two-measure fragment in the RH containing both a harmonic 3rd and a rising melodic 3rd. mm. <u>22–23, 24–25, 26–27, 27–29</u>

3. Find a place where the opening motive returns. mm. <u>13–14, 29–30</u>

4. Find a chain of parallel 3rds in the RH. mm. <u>23–30</u>

5. Find a chain of parallel 3rds in the LH. mm. <u>6, 14, and 32</u>

In mm. 32–34, there is a long, shimmering trill in the melody. What musical effect does this create? <u>suspense</u>

Write the notes of mm. 33–34 as a solid (blocked) close-position chord on the staff below. Then do the same for m. 35. Play the two chords and listen to the sound.

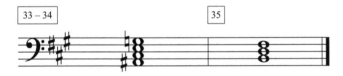

The chord formed by mm. 33–34 is a **diminished 7th chord**.

What do you think this harmony adds to the music? <u>mystery, intensity</u>

Name the triad to which the diminished 7th **resolves** in m. 35. <u>B minor</u>

Waltz

Vladimir Ivanovich Rebikov (1866–1920)

Student Workbook 7, p. 46

Waltz Style

If you were to arrange this waltz for string orchestra (first and second violins, violas, cellos, and double bass), how would you divide the parts?
Which instruments might play the parallel 3rds in the melody? <u>first and second violins</u>
Sometimes there is a third melody voice—which instrument might play this? <u>viola</u>

Ternary Form

Rebikov's *Waltz* has a simple three-part form. Add measure numbers to the form chart.

A   mm. <u>1</u> – <u>16</u>
B   mm. <u>17</u> – <u>32</u>
A   mm. <u>33</u> – <u>48</u>

Rhythm

Compare the LH rhythm in the A section of Rebikov's *Waltz* with the LH part in the excerpt above. How is Rebikov's bass obviously different? <u>It incorporates rests, creating a two-measure rhythmic pattern.</u>

Waltzing in Phrases

How long are the phrase marks in the A section? <u>two measures</u>

Expressive Dissonance

Rebikov also builds rich, dissonant chords using the dominant (C sharp) as the root, and stacking additional 3rds above it.

Here is the dominant triad of F sharp:

In the blank measures above, repeat the dominant triad, then write a minor 7th above one chord and a minor 9th above the other.

Look for a dominant 9th in the music. This occurs twice, in mm. <u>8</u> and <u>47</u>.

Go to Sleep!, op. 77, no. 9

Heinrich Hofmann (1842–1902)

Student Workbook 7, p. 48

Melody and Accompaniment

Both melody and accompaniment in the first eight measures should be learned together. The two are interdependent in the flow of the long phrase line. But it is the melody that displays a somewhat pleading quality right from the beginning. Which two aspects of the melody might indicate this emotion?

1. <u>the slurred falling 3rd</u>

2. <u>the diminuendo</u>

This LH is similar to the kind of accompaniment that Franz Schubert wrote for some of his songs when the poetry called for a flowing stream or babbling brook. In this case, what might the sixteenth notes represent? <u>a breeze ruffling bedroom curtains</u>

Take a closer look at the LH notes in mm. 1–5. In each measure, the sixteenths are arranged in <u>two</u> groups, with <u>six</u> notes in each group.

Where has the composer used double stems?
on the first and fifth note in the group

Does he use them in each measure? _no_

What is the pattern? _every other measure_

What do they mean, and why do you think he adds them? _for emphasis and direction_

Phrasing

The real length of the phrases must be decided by the performer, and there are two possibilities. Sometimes the length of a phrase depends upon the tempo.

At a slower tempo, what do you think is the length of the phrase? _two measures_

At a faster tempo, how many measures would there be in a phrase? _four measures_

The final decision could be made based on this question: Is the piece written for a singer or for the piano? _for the piano_

Dynamics and Balance

Where does the melody begin to divide into two voices? _m. 8_

Here's where balance is important. The dynamics must be relative, with degrees of loud and soft for each voice. When your hand plays two voices at the same time, how do you project the top voice?
by leaning into it and remaining light on the bottom voice

What intervals occur in the RH mm. 9–12?
3rds and 6ths

In the above example, the inner voice (the *lower* voice) moves in which direction? _down_
By what interval? _minor 2nd (starting on F)_

The two most harmonically complex sections (mm. 12–14 and mm. 21–23) are marked *pianissimo*. What would you do to make sure the listener can hear both voices distinctly?

Use the una corda pedal; project the moving melody notes by playing a little more loudly.

Harmony

Now block the main beats of mm. 21–22, RH and LH together, and the LH only of m. 23. They should sound like this:

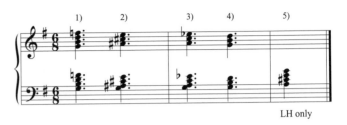

LH only

Play these chords, and listen to them carefully.

Which chords are dominant 7ths? _1, 5_

Which chord is a diminished 7th? _2_

Which is a tonic chord? _4_

Waltz

Viktor Kossenko (1896–1938)
Student Workbook 7, p. 51

Phrasing the Melody

Looking at the slurs, it appears that most phrases are two measures long. But, there are some exceptions. Trace the phrase structure by playing or singing the melody. Identify places where two or more shorter slurs form a longer phrase unit. Mark these on your score:

mm. _9_ – _12_

mm. _21_ – _23_

mm. _28_ – _29_

Romantic Harmony

Which two keys are suggested by the key signature? _D major and B minor_

Examine the two opening measures. In which of these two keys is *Waltz* written? _B minor_ What are the reasons for your answer? _A sharp (leading note), final chord (B minor)_

The notes of mm. 1–2 form a pair of chords. Write them in root position on the staff below:

Identify the first chord: ☑ dominant 7th

Identify the second chord: ☑ tonic

What common **cadence** does this progression remind you of? _perfect_

In this progression, the roots of the two chords move:

☑ up a perfect 4th (or down a perfect 5th)

There are several examples of this type of root movement in *Waltz*. Identify them below:

mm. __5__ – __6__ (bass moves from __E__ to __A__)

mm. __7__ – __8__ (bass moves from __D__ to __G__)

mm. __33__ – __34__ (bass moves from __F sharp__ to __B__)

Now look for examples of other bass progressions.

- From mm. __19__ – __23__, the bass ascends stepwise, without using any accidentals.

- From mm. __25__ – __29__, the bass ascends by half steps.

- From mm. __34__ – __43__, the bass remains stationary while the harmonies change above it. This is called a **pedal point**. Does your example contain a tonic or a dominant pedal? __tonic__

In mm. 30 and 32, a colorful-sounding chord is heard at the beginning of each two-measure phrase. What is the name of this chord? __C major__

Does the root of this chord belong in the key of this piece? __no__

A major triad built on a lowered second scale degree is called a **Neapolitan chord**. Neapolitan chords usually have a predominant function; that is, they precede a dominant or dominant 7th chord. Is that the case here? __yes__

Look at all the tonic chords in the section you identified as having the pedal point, including the final chord. How are these chords different from the expected tonic chord of the piece?
__They are B major triads.__

The mixing of major and minor tonalities in the same piece is another Romantic characteristic.

Left-Hand Technique

In what measures does the LH *not* have this pattern? mm. __11–12, 24–25, 30, 32, 43__

First Sorrow, op. 149, no. 6

Benjamin Godard (1849–1895)
Student Workbook 7, p. 53

Pacing of the Tempo

Because the piece is expressive, you might think of using a lot of *rubato*. But the composer gives us a clue about the tempo in the note values of the LH opening (which are? __half notes__).

There is another clue in the accompaniment pattern at m. 9. What note values are shown in the lower part of the accompaniment? __quarter notes__ This indicates a kind of steadiness, almost a walking

beat. The tempo marking at the top of your music is *Andante quasi Adagio*, which means: __at a walking pace, rather slowly__.

There are also some indications to slow down the tempo. What is the name of the Italian term used? __rallentando__ And where do you see it? __mm. 13, 15, 21__

Melody

What do the slurs indicate? __phrases__ Remember, the phrase line of the melody is often longer than any slurs contained within it. The most appropriate touch is __legato__.

The opening two measures of melody are based on the scale of __E flat major__.

Draw this scale, ascending and descending on the staff below. Is this the **tonic** scale of the key? __yes__

Now compare the scale with the melody. How would you describe the movement of the melody? __winding around the scale__

Now look at mm. 3–4. Is this based on the same scale? __yes__

Describe the movement. __more intricate__

What is happening in the music at mm. 13–15? __It is building to a climax.__

What sentiment might Godard be expressing? __the pain of loss__

Cadences

Sometimes a **cadence** can be an indication of the ending of a phrase. Main sections usually end with cadences.

Name the cadence (and key) in m. 8. __perfect in B flat major__

Name the cadence (and key) in m. 16. __perfect in E flat major__

In the ending (m. 22), what is the cadence? __perfect in E flat major__

Chromatic Harmony

There are many **chromatic** chords in the piece but only one real **modulation**. Where does the composer change key? __m. 8__

Trace the path of each voice of the three-note chords above. Play each voice separately. Then with the LH, play them solid (blocked) as written. Play them also with the RH one octave higher. Do they

144

have a similar sound? <u>yes</u> Do they feel the same under your hand? <u>no</u>

Now look at the next example:

The LH intervals are mostly <u>6ths</u>. Each voice moves chromatically downward, arriving where? <u>m. 22, beat 1</u>

Prelude in E Minor, op. 28, no. 4

Frédéric Chopin (1810–1849)
Student Workbook 7, p. 55

Tempo *Rubato*

The melody is marked espressivo, meaning <u>expressively</u>, which suggests sensitive dynamic shaping and use of rubato.

A Joke

Pierre Gallant (b. 1950)
Student Workbook 7, p. 57

A Dynamic Joke?

What is the softest marking used in the piece? <u>pp</u>

Where is it used?
m. <u>13</u> and m. <u>37</u>

What are the two loudest markings used? <u>ff</u> in m. <u>19</u>; and <u>sff</u> in m. <u>38</u>

Exaggerate these contrasts. The *subito* in mm. 14 and 19 indicates <u>a sudden change</u>.

A Musical Laugh

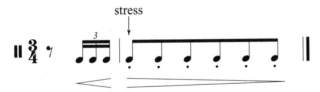

The third appearance of this motive in the RH is in mm. <u>6–7</u>. What is different about this statement?
<u>It is one octave higher, grows to a louder dynamic (f), and is on a different beat.</u>

How do these changes contribute to the humor?
<u>The rhythmic shift is an unexpected surprise; the louder dynamic and higher octave could indicate a more hearty laugh.</u>

Form

Based on the descriptions below, fill in the measure numbers for each section:

A: (mm. <u>1</u> – <u>13</u>) Based mainly on the "laugh motive."

B: (mm. <u>14</u> – <u>22</u>) Introduces a new LH figure, which is repeated several times. Loudest section of the piece.

C: (mm. <u>23</u> – <u>30</u>) Switches to $\frac{4}{4}$ time. The melody is based in part on the RH figure from m. 15.

D: (mm. <u>31</u> – <u>38</u>) Returns to $\frac{3}{4}$ time. Uses "laugh motive" in contrary motion.

In m. 37, RH, what does the indication *15ᵐᵃ* tell you to do? <u>play two octaves higher</u>

Articulation Tips

Notice how many slurs end with a *staccato* marking on the last note. There are only a few slurs that do not end with a *staccato* note. Where are they?

Short slurs: <u>mm. 12 and 37</u>

Long slurs: <u>mm. 30–32 and 32–34</u>

What is the dynamic range in these measures?
<u>p to pp</u>

A few notes have been marked with *tenuto* marks. What type of touch is called for when this symbol is present? <u>full</u> In which measures are the *tenuto* notes found? <u>mm. 13 and 23</u>

Moonlight Mood

William L. Gillock (1917–1993)
Student Workbook 7, p. 59

Moonlight Magic

Use three words to describe the light of the moon.

1. <u>silvery</u>

2. <u>shining</u>

3. <u>shimmering</u>

Touch for Special Effects

Whatever you imagine about the moonlight mood, it is obvious by looking at the dynamic marking in m. 1 <u>pp</u> and at the end (m. 18) <u>ppp</u> that delicacy of touch is required to play the piece well.

One chord is slightly louder than *pianissimo*; it is in m. <u>17</u>.

Notice the indications for the damper pedal, and also the note at the beginning to use *soft pedal throughout*. What is another name for the soft pedal? <u>una corda</u>

Technique

Look at m. 8. The end of the long scale passage is marked *freely*. What is the scale? <u>B major</u>

One of the main technical challenges is alternating hands. You have worked on a scale in 3rds with alternating hands. Now look at a completely different pattern in m. 16. How many octaves from B to B will you play? <u>four</u> How many notes are in this "run?" <u>24</u>

How many beats are allowed in the measure for this number of notes? <u>three</u>

Is this the same as the scale in m. 8? <u>no</u>

Theory

Name all four notes played by the RH in this *cadenza*. <u>E sharp, F double sharp, G double sharp, B</u>

Rhythm

Does *Moonlight Mood* have a melody? <u>yes</u> Do you want the melody to stand out clearly? <u>yes</u> How can you use your fingers to make sure that your listeners hear the melody, even though the texture is "mist-like" and very quiet? <u>Voice the top notes by striking the top finger more firmly.</u>

Our Little Garden

Feliks Rybicki (1899–1978)
Student Workbook 7, p. 62

A Musical Picture in Six Sentences

The first two measures of several of the phrases are shown below. Match the letter of each description with the corresponding musical fragment. Identify the measure numbers of the complete four-measure phrase to which each fragment likely belongs. Be careful! One of the fragments shows the *last* two measures of its particular phrase.

A. An introductory phrase: Describe the motive introduced here that recurs throughout the piece. <u>cascading, thoughtful</u>

B. A melody unfolds over a background created out of one specific interval, the <u>6th</u>. In this phrase, this interval travels up and down like the gentle rise and fall of a wave.

C. The texture intensifies as melody becomes dialogue. Observe the melodic fragments going from one hand to the other. This is called <u>imitation</u>.
Which hand leads? <u>RH</u> Which hand follows? <u>LH</u>

D. The original melody returns here. This time the earlier technique of composition continues, creating a feeling of variation and greater motion.

E. The piece dies down at the end of this phrase with a descending arpeggio. Where did a similar gesture already occur in the piece? <u>at the beginning</u>

Expressive Syncopation

Circle the rhythm above that is **syncopated**.

Syncopation can be performed in a variety of ways. It can virtually interrupt the flow, creating sounds that seem to "stick out" between the beats. On the other hand, it can enhance the smoothness and natural flow of sound by giving the impression that the beats are being more tightly woven together. Which of these styles of performance applies to *Our Little Garden*? <u>the second style</u>

Let's look for a few examples of syncopation. Find a pair of measures in which the hands clearly combine the two rhythms illustrated above: mm. 19–20

Which one of the following four syncopated rhythms does not appear in *Our Little Garden*? Mark an ✖ above the rhythm that does not belong. For each of the other rhythms, state one measure where it appears, and indicate the hand in which it appears.

Pentatonic Tune

Béla Bartók (1881–1945)
Student Workbook 7, p. 65

Folk Song Arrangements

What does *scherzando* mean? <u>playful</u>

Setting the Stage

Look at mm. 1–16. How many different notes are used in the first eight measures (not counting the grace note)? <u>two</u> Where does the actual melody begin? m. <u>9</u>

Bartók's music in folk idioms tends to display two broad styles. One style features clear, repetitive rhythms with a strong sense of pulse. The other is freer and more **improvisatory** in nature. In which style category does this piece belong? <u>the first</u>

Pentatony

How many notes do major and minor scales have per octave (not counting the repeated **tonic** at the top)? <u>seven</u>

Look through the LH melody (theme B) of mm. 9–16, and write an ascending scale that contains only the notes Bartók uses. (Start on D.)

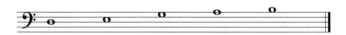

How many notes does this scale have? <u>five</u>

Finding the Form

Now that you have identified these two themes, let's see what Bartók does with them. Here is the beginning of a form chart. Play through the rest of the piece, section by section, and answer the questions for each one.

A   mm. 1–8   (introduction)

B   mm. 9–16   (melody)

A_1 mm. 17–24

Find three things that Bartók does to change the A theme in A_1.

- How are registers (the areas of the keyboard) used differently?
  <u>The theme is played two octaves higher in both hands.</u>

- What has happened to the grace note?
  <u>It has become an eighth note and a new grace note has been added.</u>

- How are notes shared differently between the hands?
  <u>In the last two measures, the RH plays alone instead of the LH.</u>

B_1 mm. 25– <u>32</u>

- How has the accompaniment changed?
  <u>There are no rests; it plays on every beat.</u>

- How has the presentation of the melody changed?
  <u>It is an octave lower.</u>

A_2 mm. <u>33</u> –40

How has the spacing and distribution of notes between the hands changed?
<u>In mm. 33–37, the hands are five octaves apart. In mm. 37–40, the RH repeats the same note pattern (from m. 35), while the LH omits the pattern in mm. 38 and 40, and plays it an octave higher in m. 39.</u>

B_2 mm. 41–52

How does Bartók combine the two themes?
<u>He alternates them.</u>

What role do dynamics play in this combination?
<u>They draw attention to the different themes.</u>

Coda mm. <u>53</u> – <u>56</u>

This section is based on material from the A section.

What significant change does Bartók make in the grace-note motive?
<u>He raises it a 5th.</u>

- How does he use the different registers of the keyboard?
  <u>He moves down four octaves.</u>

Total Articulation

Every note in *Pentatonic Tune* has an articulation mark! Bartók's precise articulation markings help to give the music its *scherzando* quality. It is important to follow them closely.

What marking does Bartók use the most? <u>staccato</u>

What other two signs are used frequently?
<u>tenuto</u>   <u>accents</u>

What sign is used only once? <u>mf</u> Where is it used? <u>m. 56</u>

Prayer of the Matador

Norman dello Joio (b. 1913)

Student Workbook 7, p. 68

Melodic Mode Discovery

Notice that the first note of each measure (mm. 1–7) is sustained. What notation indicates that? <u>double stem</u>

Which two notes of the *ostinato* are treated this way? <u>A and B flat</u> The sound produced is the beginning of a **mode**.

On the staves below, transpose this mode twice, first starting on A, then starting on D. Label these transpositions no. 1 and no. 2. When you transpose, copy the interval distances that appear in the example. As soon as you begin to write out the one beginning on A, you will discover the two "held" notes in the LH you were working on in mm. 1–2.

No. 1

No. 2

Phrygian-influenced Melody and Harmony

The circled notes show the skeleton of which of your transpositions? <u>no. 1</u>

Where does it appear again? <u>m. 11</u> Circle only the "mode notes" on your music.

Look closely at the harmony in m. 19. Play the RH chords. What do you hear?
<u>the Phrygian mode</u>

Melodic Expression

The matador's prayer is felt with strong emotion. He begins to sing gently in m. 5, then quickly bursts into heartfelt song in m. <u>6</u>.

What is the musical term for slight stretching of the tempo? <u>rubato</u>

Bell-Like Chords

Notice the dynamic marking at m. 19. It is <u>f</u>. Notice the articulation marks above the RH chords. They are <u>tenuto</u>.

Lutin
Goblin

Rhené Jaque (1918–2006)

Student Workbook 7, p. 71

Finding the Sections

What form did you discover? <u>A B C D</u>

Tempo

What are the two metronome speeds that Jaque has marked in mm. 1–10?

$\quad$ = 144, $\quad$ = 120

Where else does Jaque use alternating tempos? <u>mm. 31–47</u>

Compare the musical styles in mm. 31–47 with those used in mm. 1–10.

What is different, and what does Jaque do to provide contrast?
<u>The rhythms and melodic shapes are different.</u>

Ostinato

In *Lutin*, Jaque uses a rhythmic **ostinato** to create energy. The *ostinato* pattern contains changing intervals. Draw two measures of the rhythmic *ostinato* below:

What do you think the *ostinato* figure represents in this musical image of a goblin?
<u>mischievous footsteps</u>

Things aren't always what they seem!

Name three or four intervals that you think are dissonant.
<u>2nds, 7ths, diminished 5th/ augmented 4th (tritone)</u>

Name three or four intervals that you think are **consonant**.
<u>perfect 5th, perfect 4th, 3rds, 6ths, octaves</u>

Write an augmented 2nd, a minor 3rd, a major 2nd, and a diminished 3rd—all above G:

Now play these intervals.
You have written four different intervals. How many different sounds did you hear? <u>two</u>

Did all the 3rds sound consonant? <u>no</u>

Did all the 2nds sound dissonant? <u>no</u>

Tritones

Which two intervals are also called **tritones**?
<u>diminished 5th</u> and <u>augmented 4th</u> These intervals have that name because they are made up of three whole tones.

Play a few tritones, and look for some in this piece.

How would you describe the sound, compared to a perfect 4th or a perfect 5th? <u>dissonant</u> Can you find a tritone in m. 6? <u>yes</u> In which hand? <u>LH</u>

A Dramatic Ending

Now play mm. 45–47.
How has Jaque used tritones in these final chords?
<u>She has combined them with other intervals.</u>

What else has she done in these measures to create a dramatic ending?
<u>The dynamics go from f to pp.</u>

Can you hear laughter? <u>yes</u>

Song and Dance

Lajos Papp (b. 1935)
Student Workbook 7, p. 74

Folk Music in Several Parts

Folk music from Eastern Europe often features a slower opening section followed by a faster section. *Song and Dance* follows that pattern. Look at the way this piece ends, however. Is the overall form of the piece **binary** or **ternary**? <u>ternary</u>

How does the title relate to the form? The A sections are the <u>song</u>; the B section is the <u>dance</u>.

Harmony Tells the Story

Write out all the notes of mm. 7 and 8 as a pair of chords in root position:

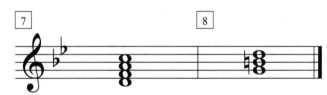

Only *one* alteration is needed for these two chords to create a **perfect (authentic) cadence** (V–I) in G major. What is this change?
<u>The F in m. 7 would need to change to F sharp.</u>

Play both versions and compare their sound. Now, compare the chord in m. 8 with the chord outlined in m. 1:

What is the difference?
<u>m. 8 is major; m. 1 is minor</u>

Reharmonization

Find two examples of two-measure fragments each of which is repeated *once* in reharmonized form. Write out the melodic fragments along with their harmonic backgrounds in the form of root-position chords on the systems below:

Ex. 1

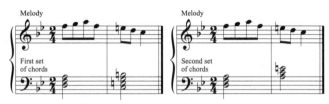

Ex. 2

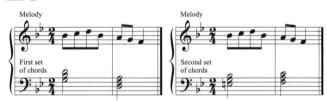

Some Unusual Octave Motion

Sometimes a melody can be repeated with some (or all) of its notes **transposed** up or down an octave. This process is sometimes referred to as octave transposition. There is one two-measure fragment in *Song and Dance* that is repeated *twice*, each time with some type of octave transposition. Each statement is also reharmonized. This passage extends from m. <u>16</u> to m. <u>21</u>.

Katherine

Stephen Chatman (b. 1950)
Student Workbook 7, p. 76

Rhythmic Lilt

The shifting of the rhythmic stress happens when the first eighth note moves directly to the dotted quarter. Which note gets the emphasis?
<u>the dotted quarter note</u>

What is the name for this rhythmic effect?
<u>syncopation</u>

Complete writing in the beats on the above example.

Consider the time signature of the piece: <u>3/4</u> . If you think of *Katherine* as both a song and a dance, what dance style might this represent? <u>waltz</u>

Phrasing the Melody

There are always natural breaks; there is a need to look for them and to *hear* them. On which beat of m. 4 do you hear one of those natural breaks? <u>on the second half of beat 2</u>

The phrase from mm. 4–8 is like a refrain in the ballad; it keeps coming around again. How many times do you see it? <u>six times</u>

Musical Expression

Make a list of all the musical terms you find in this piece. Look them up in the Glossary if necessary, and think of their meaning as you practice.
<u>espressivo poco cresc.; con pedali; poco rit.;
poco accel.; a tempo; ten.; meno mosso; rit. e dim.;
Tempo primo; rit. al fine</u>

Feelin' Good

Brian Bonsor (b. 1926)
Student Workbook 7, p. 79

A Pentatonic Lick

Write the scale of G major on the staff below. Cross out the fourth (subdominant) and seventh (leading) notes. The resulting scale has <u>five</u> (how many?) *different* notes. This is the **G pentatonic scale.**

Pentatonic scales often appear in jazz "licks"—short phrases of fairly rapid notes, usually sounding like a spontaneous flourish. There's a repetitive lick in *Feelin' Good* that is based on the scale you wrote above. Write the lick out here:

Look for a different pentatonic scale that appears partway through the piece. It is heard most clearly at m. <u>20</u>. Write the notes of this scale on the staff below, starting on the **tonic** of the scale.

A Favorite Progression: ii–V–I

As well as pentatonic scales, the ii–V–I harmonic progression is one of the mainstays of jazz. Below is a simple V–I progression in G major:

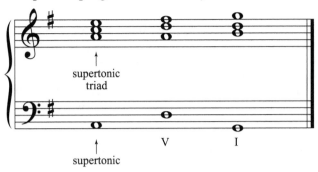

Write the second degree (supertonic) of G major here:

Place two more notes above it, each a 3rd apart. This is the **supertonic (ii) triad.** Now, write the supertonic in the bass staff (on the example containing the perfect cadence above). Place the three notes of the triad in the treble staff. Write them in either root position or an inversion, whichever places the notes as close as possible to those of the V triad that follows. This creates a typical ii–V–I progression, one of the most common idioms of both classical and popular music.

Look for three such progressions in *Feelin' Good*. There are more examples throughout the music, but at least three are easy to spot because of the motion of the bass notes. You will find that many chords have an added 7th, which is very common in jazz.

mm. <u>2</u> – <u>3</u>; key: <u>G major</u>

mm. <u>17</u> – <u>18</u>; key: <u>B flat major</u>

mm. <u>22</u> – <u>24</u>; key: <u>G major</u>

Find the Bridge

The bridge of *Feelin' Good* runs from m. <u>17</u> to m. <u>23</u>. Does this bridge contain any sequences? <u>yes</u>

Find one sequence in the opening A section: mm. <u>6</u> – <u>9</u>

Find one sequence in the closing A section: mm. <u>30</u> – <u>32</u>

‑

Sérénade sur l'eau

Jacques Ibert (1890–1962)
Student Workbook 7, p. 81

Ebb and Flow: Carrying the Phrase

Play the LH alone. As you practice it repeatedly, you should begin to feel the rhythm in your body. This rhythm never varies throughout the piece even when there is an extra "held note" in the bass, mm. 12–14. Is this a **pedal point**? <u>yes</u> On what degree of the tonic scale? <u>dominant</u>

Melody and Accompaniment in One Hand

Notice the Italian in the score above the treble staff: "*il canto sost.*" It means <u>singing and sustained</u>.

Expressing Musical Joy

Notice (and listen) how everything builds to this point with the *crescendo,* beginning in m. 13, running through m. 14, and finally bursting into m. 15. At the beginning of the *crescendo,* the composer starts by reinforcing the melody. How? <u>by adding a voice in a 3rd below the melody</u>

The falling pattern has a joyful sound, cascading in **sequence**. Is this exclusively **chromatic**? <u>no</u> The *rhythm* of the pattern originates in the very first measure of the piece. What was that figure called? <u>barcarole rhythm</u>

Rondo-March, op. 60, no. 1

Dmitri Kabalevsky (1904–1987)
Student Workbook 7, p. 84

A Rondo Form

On the map on p. 85, place the letter A in the appropriate measures to indicate the appearance of the refrain. Label the episodes B and C, respectively. A few questions along the way will direct you toward the distinctive features of each episode.

(Fill in this chart after you have filled in the map.)

	Section A	Section <u>C</u>
Expression markings (explain the meaning of each)	<u>macato – well-marked</u>	<u>dolce – sweetly</u>
Dynamic markings	*f*	*p*
Key	<u>E flat major</u>	<u>E flat minor</u>
Character of melody	<u>march-like</u>	<u>song-like</u>
Character of accompaniment	<u>short, percussive</u>	<u>legato</u>
Use of pedal	<u>none</u>	<u>a lot</u>
Overall mood or atmosphere	<u>rhythmic, bright</u>	<u>lyrical, expressive</u>

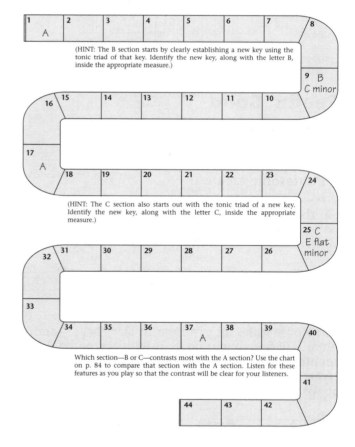

(HINT: The B section starts by clearly establishing a new key using the tonic triad of that key. Identify the new key, along with the letter B, inside the appropriate measure.)

(HINT: The C section also starts out with the tonic triad of a new key. Identify the new key, along with the letter C, inside the appropriate measure.)

Which section—B or C—contrasts most with the A section? Use the chart on p. 84 to compare that section with the A section. Listen for these features as you play so that the contrast will be clear for your listeners.

Student Workbook 8 Answers

Invention No. 13 in A Minor,
BWV 784

Johann Sebastian Bach (1685–1750)
Student Workbook 8, p. 4

Introducing the Subject
You will notice that the subject consists of two parts: a sixteenth-note pattern and an eighth-note pattern:

We can label these two motives "a" and "b." Each motive arises from a broken chord. Play the subject in the example above. Then play it in solid (blocked) chords.

How many chords are represented by motive "a"? two

How many are represented by motive "b"? two

Broken Chord Pattern Hunt
For each of the following excerpts, identify the measure, whether the excerpt derives from motive "a" or motive "b," and the type (from the numbers 1, 2, 3, and 4 above).

	Measure	Motive	Type
	3	a	2
	3	b	1
	2	b	1
	6	a	3
	10	a	1, 2, 3
	7	b	3
	5	a	1, 4
	12	b	3, 4

Now, identify the four places in the music where motive "a" is played by both hands at the same time. m. 11 m. 12 m. 13 m. 19

Measure 19 is the beginning of a long extension of motive "a" in the RH. How long does it continue? To m. 21

Is there an extension of motive "b" as well? yes Where, and for how long? mm. 20–21

The long climb toward the ending begins with motive "a" and creates another extension. Does the direction of the long climb imply a slight *crescendo* in the sound? yes

Imitation and Sequence
The imitation jumps off the page at first glance. On which beat of m. 1 does the subject enter in the LH? 3 How many beats behind the RH subject is it? 2

If you consider the entire subject, consisting of motives "a" and "b" together, is the first imitation *exact*? no What is different? motive "b" falls in the LH, m. 2

On the first page, the imitation is closer in mm. 5–6 . What is the distance of imitation (in beats)? 1

Sequences are piled on top of each other, just like the imitation that begins before the subject is over. Bach uses sequences to pass through several keys on his way to important **cadences**.
Where does the first sequential passage begin? m. 3

Name the cadence and key in m. 6. perfect cadence in C major

Where does the second sequential passage begin? m. 9

Name the cadence and key in m. 13. perfect cadence in E minor

Practicing outside the Box
3. Block both sections of the subject in each hand. How many chords can you make out of the RH in m. 1? 4

Suite No. 1 in D Major
Eighth Movement: Gigue

Johann Ludwig Krebs (1713–1780)
Student Workbook 8, p. 7

How to Build a Dance Movement

Krebs builds clear phrases and rhythms by using simple, recognizable musical elements. Below are five descriptive phrases; place the letter name of each with the musical building block it describes.

A: descending broken chord figure
B: rising figures featuring expanding intervals
C: rising and falling broken 6ths
D: broken chords rolling down and up
E: sets of broken triads

Placing the appropriate letters on your score will give you a visual "map" of how Krebs uses each of these building blocks to create his piece. By the time you answer the following questions, you will know the music even better.

Observe the circled notes in the LH of mm. 1–2 shown above. Label each D (dominant) or T (tonic). How does m. 2 seem to answer m. 1? _m. 1 moves from Tonic to Dominant; m. 2 moves from Dominant to Tonic_

Toward which key does the music move in mm. 5–8? _A major_

What note indicates this modulation? _G sharp_

Which scale degree of the new key is this note? _leading note_

Measures 9–12 "sit" on the tonic /(dominant) of the new key.

In mm. 17–18, building block _A_ is repeated in a (rising)/ falling **sequence**.

In mm. 19–21, the music moves to another new key. Look for a telltale leading note (_D sharp_) and a broken chord near the end of the phrase that gives away the key, which is _E minor_.

The return of building block _A_ in m. 23 and building block _B_ in m. 27 tells you that the form of this piece is: ☑ **ternary**

During mm. 23–32, the music does *not* move toward the new key you identified in the first half of *Gigue*. What does it do instead?

It remains in the home key (even though some accidentals occur).

Little Prelude in D Major,
BWV 925

Johann Sebastian Bach (1685–1750)
Student Workbook 8, p. 10

Subject in Imitation

The imitation in m. 2 starts on a different scale degree from the subject. Which degree? _Dominant_ Is this, then, a new key? _no_ Rhythmically, how does the imitation differ from the opening?

The imitation replaces the rest on beat 1 with a note. However, this first sixteenth note is the end of the tenor countersubject. The imitation still begins on the second sixteenth note, the lower A.

Is this based on the pattern "a" or pattern "b" of the subject? _b_

This melody is turned into a **sequence**, eventually ending at m. _8_.

Sequences

In practicing the first RH group in m. 8, anchor your thumb on the last tied sixteenth note and play the chord attached to it by feel, *without looking*. It is good practice to play each hand this way. Pay close attention to the fingering in the last RH group in m. 9. Is this standard triad fingering? _no_

For the LH in these measures, measure the distance of the octave leap with your hand and fingers, then continue to play the LH separately with your eyes closed. Each part is a sequence in itself, and both parts played together also create a sequence.

Where does the pattern end? _m. 10_

What happens in the LH here?
imitation of pattern "a"

The RH has a different sequence pattern (descending) and it continues toward a **perfect (authentic) cadence** in the tonic key at mm. 12–13.

When the sixteenth notes appear together in both hands, pay special attention—the hands move in *both* parallel and contrary motion!

Does the sound build with this effect? _yes_
The next perfect cadence occurs in mm. _14–15_.

Tonal Center or Modulation?

There are several accidentals in this piece. Do they indicate **modulation**? _no_

The first obvious pattern change comes at the "improvised sequence" section mentioned earlier. Now look at the measure immediately preceding it (end of m. 7).

Do you see a perfect cadence over the bar line? _yes_

In what key? _D major_

Now look for the long tied note where the texture seems thicker (with more voices): m. _15_

Do you see a perfect cadence leading into m. 15?
yes

In what key? _D major_

Is this is the beginning of the final section? _yes_

Accompaniment in Two Voices

How many voices do you see in this excerpt? _two_ In the RH in m. 2? _two_

Listen to the countersubject in m. 1 as if it were being sung by tenor and bass voices. Listen to the countersubject in m. 2 as if it were sung by _soprano_ and _alto_ .

Coda

The final section (mentioned earlier) gathers more voices together (how many? _four_) and seems to convey a type of grandeur that is typical of one of Bach's preludes in the *Well-Tempered Clavier*. One device that gives that impression is the long tied note in the bass. The note D is the (degree of the scale) _tonic_ and the tied effect, including the drop to the lower octave, creates a _pedal point_ .

Each of the voices has its own distinct character, which makes this a challenging section to play. Again, practice with both hands for the treble staff (soprano and alto) and for the bass staff (tenor and bass). Carefully observe the fingering when you play all parts together. Discuss with your teacher the passages you want to bring out. Do you see and hear imitation in these measures with four voices? _yes_

Suite No. 7 in G Minor, HWV 432
Fifth Movement: Gigue

George Frideric Handel (1685–1759)
Student Workbook 8, p. 14

Can you name a Baroque dance other than the *gigue*? _allemande, courante, sarabande, gavotte, minuet/menuet, bourrée_

Find That Jig Rhythm

There are many varieties of this dance, all of which have one thing in common—a recurring long–short rhythm. In what form can you observe this rhythmic "signature" in *Gigue in G Minor*? Circle one of the following patterns:

Below is a sketch of the structure of a typical measure of $\frac{12}{8}$ time:

Where indicated by the arrow, write a full measure of the rhythmic pattern you circled above. Line up your notes carefully against the correct pulses of the $\frac{12}{8}$ rhythm.

Comparing Gigues

Find the other *Gigue* in your *Piano Repertoire 8*, and identify it on the example below. Two measures from each of these two pieces appear below. How many voices (or layers) are there in each of the examples?

1. Title _Gigue in D major_ Composer _Krebs_
   Number of voices _two_

2. _Gigue in G Minor_ (Handel)
   Number of voices _four_

Dancing with Broken Chords

Part of the appeal of Handel's music lies in its sturdy, robust construction. For instance, many of the broken-chord figures that you practice as part of your technique are used in this _Gigue_. Let's revisit a few of these patterns by matching each description below to its correct musical example.

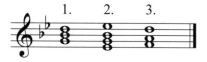

Triad in first inversion _3_

Triad in root position _1_

Four-note chord in root position _2_

Find the pair of measures in which these three types of chords appear consecutively in the LH, in broken form: mm. _9_ – _10_.

In what _order_ does each type of chord appear?

1. _triad in root position_
2. _triad in first inversion_
3. _four-note chord_

Now you are ready for something a little trickier. Write out each of the chords indicated below on the staff provided.

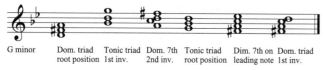

| G minor | Dom. triad root position | Tonic triad 1st inv. | Dom. 7th 2nd inv. | Tonic triad root position | Dim. 7th on leading note | Dom. triad 1st inv. |

As in the previous example, there is a two-measure stretch in which all of these chords appear consecutively. You may have to look hard, as the chords are distributed between the two hands, and most of their notes are played in broken, not blocked form. The consecutive chords are in mm. _16_ – _17_.

Fantasia in D Minor, TWV 33:2

Georg Philipp Telemann (1681–1767)
Student Workbook 8, p. 17

A Fantasia

Look through the score of Telemann's _Fantasia in D Minor_.

What markings divide this work into two main sections? _fermata, Fine, and end bar line_

Which section has a more contrapuntal texture with patterns of repetition such as imitation and sequence? _the Presto section_

Which section has a contrasting texture and a somewhat freer, more improvisatory and expressive melodic style? _the Adagio section_

The end of the _Adagio_ section is marked _D.C. Presto al Fine._

What Italian words does _D.C._ abbreviate? _da capo_

What does the complete marking tell you to do?
Go back to the beginning of the Presto section and play to the Fine.

Taking the _D.C._ into account, what is the overall form of this fantasia?
☑ **ternary**

First Section: _Presto_
Contrasting Texture, Integrated Form

What is the relationship between the voices in mm. 1–4? _parallel motion_

What is the relationship between the voices in mm. 5–8? _contrary motion_

Let's see how these two textures are combined by Telemann to create contrast and interest as the _Fantasia_ unfolds (mm. 1–37). Use **U** for unison texture and **I** for imitative textures and indicate the key of each segment.

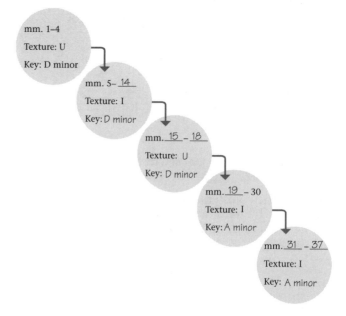

Where is the first sequence in the *Presto* section?
<u>mm. 6–9</u>

Where is there an upside-down version of this
sequence? <u>mm. 20–23</u>

Find a sequence in which the two voices toss a
motive back and forth as the music changes key.
mm. <u>mm. 38–41</u>

Articulation

Compare the sound of the beginning (mm. 1–4)
and end (mm. 76–78) of the *Presto* section.
<u>These two segments are forte, unison, and mm. 3 and
77 have identical notes. Both segments end with a
strong unison sound.</u>

Second Section: *Adagio*
Harmony

Name the 7th chord in mm. 79–80. <u>diminished 7th</u>
How would you describe the sound of this chord?
<u>suspenseful, dissonant</u>

Does it emphasize the tonic of the key? <u>no</u>

To what chord does this 7th chord resolve? <u>D major</u>
Where is this pattern repeated? <u>mm. 83–85</u>

On his way to the final cadence, Telemann visits a
number of different keys. Here is a list of the keys.
Write the appropriate measure numbers after each
one.

A minor: mm. <u>85</u> – <u>86</u> or <u>93</u> – <u>94</u>

G minor: mm. <u>81</u> – <u>82</u> or <u>88</u> – <u>89</u>

D minor: mm. <u>91</u> – <u>92</u>

Circle of descending dominant 7ths: A–D–G–C:
mm. <u>87</u> – <u>90</u>

Sonata in D Major, op. 12, no. 3
First Movement

Samuel Arnold (1740–1802)
Student Workbook 8, p. 20

Sonata Form, English style

This graceful and charming first movement is
clearly in **sonata form**. Identify the three main
sections:

Exposition: mm. <u>1–28</u>

Development: mm. <u>29–41</u>

Recapitulation: mm. <u>42–68</u>

Exposition

Theme 1 is made up of three motives, almost as if
Arnold was improvising at the piano and wanted to
elaborate further. The first theme begins in the <u>tonic</u>
key.

How many different note values do you see in
mm. 1–4? <u>five</u> How many types of ornaments?
<u>two</u>

Name three types of articulation that you would
use to play Theme 1a.
<u>detached</u>   <u>legato</u>   <u>lifts (from slurs)</u>

How would you describe the character of the
melody in 1a?
<u>optimistic, happy, youthful</u>

What is the idea in 1b that links it to 1a?
<u>stepwise sixteenth notes</u>

Describe the pattern in 1b. <u>rising and falling five-
finger pattern</u>

Do mm. 5–8 create a **sequence**? <u>yes</u>

How is the sequence used? <u>back and forth between
the hands</u>

What chords are outlined by the sequence pattern
in mm. 5–8? <u>D major, G major, E major, A major</u>

The motive in Theme 1c spells out the scale of
<u>A major</u>.

Even before he reaches the second theme, Arnold
has begun to *modulate*!

What is the RH articulation in mm. 9–12? <u>two-note
slurs, staccato</u>

What is the name and key of the cadence in
mm. 11–12?   <u>perfect cadence in A major</u>

Describe what happens in mm. 12–15.
<u>Theme 1c is repeated as a bridge to Theme 2.</u>

In sonata form, theme 2 is usually in the key of the
dominant. At m. 16, what device is used to
emphasize the key? <u>dominant pedal point in the LH</u>

Does the RH have a real melody? <u>no</u>

What is the musical material in the RH? <u>scale
passages</u>

How would you describe its character? <u>bright, showy</u>

How does it contrast with theme 1a? (Remember the dynamics.)
<u>Dynamics are f, whereas in Theme 1a they were p;</u>
<u>Theme 1a is more melodic and graceful.</u>

After the cadence in mm. 23–24, and to end the exposition, there is a flourish of descending 3rds:

This is called a *codetta*. How would you describe the pattern?
<u>descending A major scales in 3rds</u>

Does it relate to themes 1 or 2? <u>Theme 1c (bridge)</u>

Development
The short development makes use of every motive in the exposition! Play mm. 28–31. What do you hear? <u>Theme 1a</u>

Is this a **transposition** of 1a? <u>yes</u> Is it an *exact* transposition, note for note? <u>yes</u>

On your score, label all the examples of the different motives from the exposition. How is m. 38 different from m. 9? <u>It rises in 3rds instead of falling by step.</u>

Recapitulation
Do all the motives in theme 1 return? <u>no</u> Which one is left out? <u>1c</u>

In what two ways is 1b varied?

1. <u>Alberti bass instead of imitation in the LH</u>

2. <u>Cross-hands leap of two octaves</u>

Which two measures are entirely different from anything in the exposition? <u>mm. 52–53</u> Or *are they*? Where have you seen that ornament before? <u>m. 6</u>

Coda
In a piece with a *coda*, the movement basically comes to a close earlier, with a perfect cadence in the tonic key. Can you find that place before the *coda*? <u>mm. 61–62</u>

At m. 62, the *coda* begins. How is it like the *codetta*, mm. 24–28? <u>It is a descending scale pattern in 3rds.</u>
How is it different? <u>It is in D major instead of A major; it includes an appoggiatura.</u>

The three-measure ending including the final chords makes a statement by itself.
Where is the musical material taken from? <u>Theme 1b</u>

What is the harmony behind the decoration?
<u>perfect cadences in D major</u>

How would you describe the mood of the ending?
<u>bright, playful</u>

Sonata in G Major, op. 49, no. 2
First Movement

Ludwig van Beethoven (1770–1827)
Student Workbook 8, p. 23

First Movement: *Allegro ma non troppo*
Drama in Music
Beethoven uses momentum to create drama. How do you think the tempo and the triplet figures contribute to the dramatic character of this movement?
<u>The Allegro tempo and the triplet figures give the</u>
<u>impression that the music is in constant motion.</u>

Register Changes
Register changes will usually catch the attention of a listener. In this movement, register changes have a dramatic effect. A change of register on the piano usually changes the character of the sound as well. Where is the first register change in this movement? <u>m. 5</u>
How does it affect the character of the sound?
<u>It sounds more delicate.</u>

There are several more register changes in mm. 36–52. Write the measure numbers here.
<u>mm. 45 and 47; mm. 49 and 50</u>

Dramatic Character
The opening phrase of the first theme is from mm. <u>1</u> to <u>14</u>. The statement is then repeated and extended.

How would you describe the character of the first theme? Is it outgoing, joyful, or confident? What words would you use? <u>cheerful, upbeat, optimistic</u>

The second theme is from mm. <u>21</u> to <u>35</u>. How would you describe the character of the second theme? <u>easygoing, subdued, lyrical</u>

Is the character of one theme more colorful than the other? <u>The first theme is more heavily ornamented.</u>

Composers often use dynamics or articulation to color the musical character.
List other ways a composer might indicate the character of a theme.
<u>note values, textures, accompaniment styles, register</u>
<u>and tempo changes, ornamentation</u>

Beethoven's Architecture
Fill in the following sonata-form chart to help you see the structure, and thus decide on your personal interpretation of this music.

Exposition: mm. 1 – 52

theme 1:   mm. 1 – 14   Key: G major
Character: cheerful, confident

bridge: mm. 15 – 19   Key: G major
Character: driven, lively

theme 2:   mm. 20 – 35   Key: D major
Character: peaceful, mellow

closing theme: mm. 36 – 48   Key: D major
Character: powerful

codetta: mm. 49 – 52   Key: D major
Character: driven, lively

Where else is material from the bridge used?
in the codetta

Development: mm. 53 – 66
Name the last chord of the exposition. D major

Name the first chord of the development. D minor

What is the opening key of the development
section? A minor

Which elements of the two main themes are
present?
the rhythm from the opening measure of theme 1; the
quarter-note rhythm and repeated-note figure of
theme 2

What other key does the music pass through?
E minor

The preparation for the recapitulation begins with
the **sequence** in mm. 63–65, where one key
resolves into the next.

Name the chord in m. 63. B major

What is this chord in the key of E minor? Dominant

What chord is implied in m. 66? D7, dominant 7th
of G major

Recapitulation: mm. 67 – 74
Insert the measure numbers and the keys to which
each section **modulates.**

theme 1:   mm. 67 – 74   Key: G major
closing theme: mm. 75 – 81   Key: D major
bridge: mm. 82 – 87   Key: G major
theme 2:   mm. 87 – 102   Key: G major
closing theme: mm. 103 – 116   Key: G major
coda: mm. 116 – 122   Key: G major

What is the surprising twist in mm. 73 and 74?
The theme modulates to C major.

What type of cadence ends the movement?
perfect cadence

Both the *coda* and the *codetta* contain a **pedal
point**: the chords change, but the bass note remains
the same.

What chord progression is used in mm. 49–52?
I – V⁷ – I in D major

What chord progression is used in mm. 116–122?
I – V⁷ – I in G major

Sonatina in E flat Major,
op. 20, no. 6

First Movement

Jan Ladislav Dussek (1760–1812)
Student Workbook 8, p. 26

Exposition

First Theme Group
The exposition is usually built out of two themes,
or groups of themes. In the case of this movement,
the themes are very short, almost like a motive.
Here is the beginning of the first theme, called
motive "a":

Describe what Dussek does with this motive during
the first several measures:
He repeats it in rising fragments.

Does the writing create calm or excitement?
excitement

After a short contrasting passage, motive "a" returns
at m. 11.

Which type of **cadence** concludes the section ending
just *before* the measure you identified?
☑ **Imperfect (half) cadence** (bass and harmony
moving from tonic to dominant)

Let's return to the contrasting passage that occurred
before the return of motive "a." Let's call it motive
"b":

mm. 5 – 10

Bridge to Second Theme Group

Observe what happens following the return of motive "a" that you spotted earlier. Does the music stay in E flat major or does it **modulate** to a new key?
It modulates to a new key.

Where are motives "a" and "b" used in this **bridge** passage?
Motive _a_ from mm. _11_ – _14_
Motive _b_ from mm. _15_ – _18_

This passage takes the listener from the *first* to the *second* group of themes. To do this, it leaves the home key (E flat major) and travels to a new key.

Second Theme Group

At what measure is the new key made absolutely clear? m. _19_

Dussek uses basic musical patterns to show the new key. Identify two of these patterns. _scales_ and _broken chords_

These patterns combine to create motive "c," the main motive of the second group of themes. Which of the motives of the first group returns during the second group? Motive _b_ at mm. _29_ – _32_. Describe how Dussek alters this motive in these measures.
The scale rises instead of falls; the hands cross at m. 29.

Development

How long is the development section? (HINT: It starts after the double bar and ends when the music of the opening returns in the home key.)
mm. _37_ – _53_

Development sections do what their title suggests—they explore new ground, often by traveling to new (and sometimes remote) keys. Name *two* keys that this development section travels through. (A key is most easily found by the presence of the notes of its tonic triad, and also of the leading note of the key.)

Key: _F minor_ notes of the triad: _F, A flat, C_
leading note: _E_
Key: _G major_ notes of the triad: _G, B, D_
leading note: _F sharp_

Now, observe the LH in the four measures leading to the return of motive "a." What note is emphasized throughout? _B flat_ This is the _dominant_ (scale degree) of the home key; its function is a _dominant_ **preparation** (once again, fill in the scale degree) that creates a sense of expectation prior to the recapitulation.

What expressive marking does Dussek add to heighten the feeling of waiting for something to happen?

Symbol 𝄐 meaning: _pause_

What is the meaning and the effect of *smorz.* (*smorzando*)? _dying away_

Recapitulation

This final section, as its name suggests, revisits the events of the exposition. However, instead of

modulating to a new key for the second group, it _remains in the same key_.

There are other changes as well. What has happened to the bridge passage this time?
It has been omitted.

How is the very end of the recapitulation different from the ending of the exposition?
Motive "a" returns a final time.

Do you feel that this helps create a more or a less effective ending? _more effective_

Sonatina in A Major, op. 59, no. 1
Second Movement

Friedrich Kuhlau (1786–1832)
Student Workbook 8, p. 29

Kuhlau's Form

You can begin your exploration of Kuhlau's exciting piece by identifying the three large sections:

A   mm. _1_ – _71_
B   mm. _72_ – _111_
A₁   mm. _112_ – _187_

Key changes help establish each section. What simple but effective key change sets the middle section apart from the sections around it?
A major to A minor

The dominant in this piece is _E major_.
Where does the second theme begin? m. _60_
In this movement, the transition that sets up this new theme is quite short. It begins at m. _53_.

Simple Themes and Brilliant Music

It is interesting to see how a composer achieves so much effect with such simple material. Let's start with the opening motive (motive "a").

How would you describe its sound?
☑ short, plucky sounds

Compare mm. 3–4 to mm. 1–2. How are they related? They contain the same figure transposed down a 3rd.

This composition technique is called _sequence_; short motives are often extended into longer statements this way.

Kuhlau uses this motive in new ways as the movement unfolds. He **transposes** a portion of it an octave (higher)/ lower at mm. 11–12.

He offers a **variation** of it in the rolling broken chords starting at m. 34. This new version is transposed an octave (higher)/ lower at mm. 45–48.

Choose the adjective that suits it best ☑ military

As in the case of motive "a," this short motive is immediately answered in the music. Is the answer a **sequence**, or is Kuhlau instead creating contrast? contrast

Describe four ways in which the answering phrase creates contrast.
1. dynamics – mf – p
2. register change
3. LH has 3rds instead of octaves
4. RH eighth notes change (become more distinctly melodic)

Where does this motive appear in the LH only? mm. 25–29
How does Kuhlau create a strong sense of forward propulsion in the ensuing passage?
 rising figures and increasing dynamic level

The development section of a sonata-form movement is usually based on one or more motives or themes from the exposition. What does Kuhlau do in this piece? He presents entirely new material in the B section.

The Return of A

Going measure by measure, compare the first-theme area in the A section (mm. 1–59) to the first-theme area in the A₁ section (mm. 112–162).

Are there any changes to the opening themes and motives? no

What about the transition?
 It is omitted in the A₁ section.

What purpose does this change serve? In the tonic key, the second theme can follow the first theme without a transition.

Now compare the second themes in the the two A sections. Are they the same or different? different: in the A₁ section, the second theme is extended and leads to a cadence

Finally, compare the end of each A section. What do you notice?
 The end of the A section is not forceful and leads into the B section with trill-like sixteenth notes; the A₁ section ends dramatically with forte cadences.

Sonata in G Major, Hob. XVI:39
First Movement
Franz Joseph Haydn (1732–1809)
Student Workbook 8, p. 32

Decorating the Beats

- Division into smaller groups of two or four: One eighth note can be divided into four thirty-second notes.

- Division into smaller groups of three: One eighth note can be divided into *one* of the following sets (triplets or sextuplets). Circle the correct one.

Find two places where such triplets appear in this movement.
mm. 38–39; 45–47

- Division into dotted rhythms: One eighth note can be divided into *one* of the following dotted rhythms. Circle the correct one.

Find several places where this dotted rhythm appears in this movement.
mm. 1, 9–11, 14–15, 23, 29, 30, 33, 52–74, 76, 80, 94, 99, 101–103

The Variation Idea
mm. 1–2:

mm. 37 – 38

Compare the two examples shown above. Which hand plays identical music in both? <u>LH</u> In the other hand's part, circle those notes that occur in both versions. The *last* such note is circled as an example. As you can observe, the original version still exists in the variation, even though slightly hidden from view.

There are many other decorated passages to discover. Below are three musical fragments as they first appear in the movement. The other three fragments are variations that appear later. Match each fragment to its variation, and supply measure numbers for each of the fragments.

Fragment A: <u>35</u> – <u>36</u>

Fragment B: <u>9</u> – <u>10</u>

Fragment C: <u>13</u> – <u>14</u>

Variation of fragment <u>C</u>: <u>49</u> – <u>50</u>

Variation of fragment <u>B</u>: <u>88</u> – <u>89</u>

Variation of fragment <u>A</u>: <u>39</u> – <u>40</u>

Find the Form

Now let's figure out how Haydn has put all the pieces together. Fill in the following chart. For each section, determine the key. Also look for recurrences of the opening theme (labeled Theme 1). (HINT: Theme 1 always returns in varied form.)

mm. 1–16: Theme 1
Key: <u>G major</u>

mm. 17–32: Theme 1, or new material? <u>new</u>
Key: <u>G major</u>

mm. 33–52: Theme 1, or new material? <u>Theme 1</u>
Key: <u>G major</u>

mm. 53–75: Theme 1, or new material? <u>new</u>
Key: <u>E minor</u>

mm. 76–95: Theme 1, or new material? <u>Theme 1</u>
Key: <u>G major</u>

mm. 96–105: This is a closing section, the *coda*.
Key: <u>G major</u>

Which one of the following letter schemes best represents the overall form?
☑ A B A₁ C A₂ *Coda*

Prelude in B Minor, op. 28, no. 6

Frédéric Chopin (1810–1849)
Student Workbook 8, p. 35

Character

If you were to orchestrate this prelude, what instrument would you choose to play the LH melody? <u>cello</u>

What instrument might play the RH melodic figure in mm. 7–8? <u>violin</u>

Melodies

Chopin uses two main melodic motives. The first, a rising and falling arpeggio figure that dominates the LH part, appears at the opening:

Name the broken chord at the beginning. <u>B minor</u>

How many times is this motive stated? <u>five times</u>

What does Chopin use to lengthen or vary this motive in mm. 5–8? <u>a partial scale (B minor)</u>

Where does the LH play just the opening fragment? <u>m. 13</u>

In what key? <u>C major</u>

The second motive first appears in the RH in mm. 7–8:

How does it differ in shape and direction from the first motive?
<u>The melodic contours are reversed.</u>

Where is it repeated and extended in the LH? m. <u>15</u>

Harmony

How would you describe this constantly recurring pitch as you hear the melody?
<u>insistent, haunting—like a bell tolling</u>

What is the opening accompaniment chord?
<u>B minor</u>

For how many measures does Chopin repeat this chord before changing the harmony? <u>four measures</u>

Conversely, in other measures, the harmony is constantly shifting as Chopin changes one or two notes from chord to chord. Look at mm. 6–8 for example. Compare to mm. 1–5. Would you describe these measures as **consonant** or **dissonant**?
<u>dissonant</u>

Phrasing and *Rubato*

In the first eight measures, how would you describe the shape of the melodic motives? <u>rolling</u>

Where does the phrase want to move ahead?
<u>mm. 5–7</u>

Where does it want to linger? <u>mm. 13–14</u>

Where does the melody transfer in the RH?
<u>mm. 7–8</u>

Nocturne, op. 88, no. 3

Heinrich Hofmann (1842–1902)
Student Workbook 8, p. 38

Weaving a Texture

In each of the following examples, indicate whether voices are moving in **parallel** or **contrary motion**. In each example, circle those notes that create the motion you have identified.

mm. 1–4: <u>parallel</u> motion

mm. 1–4: <u>contrary</u> motion

mm. 1–4: <u>contrary</u> motion

mm. 1–4: <u>contrary</u> motion; <u>parallel</u> motion

In the cases of parallel motion, what are the two intervals that occur between the voices moving parallel to each other? <u>3rds</u> and <u>6ths</u>

What relationship exists between these two categories of intervals?
<u>They are inversions of each other.</u>

Where is the Music Going?

At what point does a melodic phrase appear that seems distinctly different from A? m. <u>17</u> (You will know that this is the new phrase you are looking for because it appears more than once, just like A.)

Now look for repetitions—with slight variations, of course—of these ideas. Overall, which of the following letter schemes best describes the form of the piece?
☑ A A₁ B B₁ *Coda*

Painting with Pedal

Expressive high points in the music may call for deeper pedaling—two such places might be mm. <u>14</u> and <u>35</u>.

Andante sostenuto, op. 72, no. 2

Felix Mendelssohn (1809–1847)
Student Workbook 8, p. 41

Melody and Acccompaniment

In music, each key has its own particular color and character.
What is the key of this piece? <u>E flat major</u>

Many people associate this key with particularly beautiful singing lines. Does the melody begin in m. 1, or is this an accompaniment introduction?
<u>an accompaniment introduction</u>

What mood do you believe is set in mm. 1–4?
<u>peaceful, calm, serene</u>

The melody of *Andante sostenuto* unfolds in a graciously flowing *cantabile* manner, like a song, carried by the RH over the murmuring LH accompaniment. Here are five steps to help you hear and establish the balance between melody and accompaniment. Start with the first phrase, mm. 4–8.

1. Play the RH melody alone and try to sing through each fingertip. Does each phrase sound like a voice or a *legato* instrument? <u>yes – either</u>

2. Play the LH lower notes alone, omitting the thumb notes. Can you hear a bass melodic line? <u>yes</u>

3. Play the melody as written, along with only the lower LH notes. What is the interval between your hands? <u>a 10th</u>

Harmony

Andante sostenuto begins with a short introduction and ends with a brief epilogue.

What are the measure numbers of these two passages?

mm. <u>1–4</u>   mm. <u>39–42</u>

Does Mendelssohn use the same material for both? <u>yes</u>

Mendelssohn uses fairly basic harmony. Name the two chords in the introduction, and label them in your score. <u>E flat major</u> and <u>dominant 7th of E flat major</u>

Brief **modulations** often occur in **sequences**. Find two sequences between m. 14 and m. 18. Name the **cadences** and keys for each figure.

1. Cadence: <u>perfect</u> Key: <u>B flat major</u>
2. Cadence: <u>perfect</u> Key: <u>A flat major</u>

Matching Phrases

Mendelssohn uses matching phrases to move the melody forward. One phrase is like a question, and the next is like an answer. Here are four excerpts from the music. Each one is an "answering" phrase. Find this phrase in your music, and play it along with the measures that precede it. Then add the measure numbers for the whole excerpt, and write the melody of the questioning phrase in the empty staff.

Excerpt A: mm. <u>14–18</u>

The question phrase introduces the leading note of the key of <u>B flat major</u>.

How is this key related to E flat major? <u>Dominant</u>

This answering phrase introduces the subdominant of the key of <u>E flat major</u>.

Excerpt B: mm. <u>18–20</u>

The musical flow relaxes here.
Is this a falling or a rising sequence? <u>falling</u>

Excerpt C: mm. <u>22–26</u>

The answering phrase is a slight variation of the questioning phrase.

Excerpt D: mm. <u>26–32</u>

This phrase paves the way for the climax of the piece—a climbing melody over a tonic chord (mm. 33–34).

Is this a first or a second inversion chord? <u>second inversion</u>

Where do you see the same chord in the same inversion, just before the final cadence? m. <u>38</u>

An Important Event, op. 15, no. 6

Robert Schumann (1810–1856)
Student Workbook 8, p. 44

A Brilliant Tone Color
How many octaves does the first chord span? <u>three</u>

In which inversions are the RH chords written? <u>first and second</u>

What are the softest and loudest dynamic markings in the music? <u>mf – ff</u>

What does this suggest to you?

<u>The important event should be heard loud and clear.</u>

How can you help these fingers to voice the top notes of the chords?

<u>by accenting the top notes and by keeping the lower notes lighter</u>

Rhythm and Accents
Schumann was deliberate about his accents as well as his bar lines.

Do the accents follow a regular pattern? <u>no</u>

Are they always on the same note value? <u>no</u>

Playing Octaves

Does the LH play octaves all the way through? <u>yes</u>
How do the LH octaves affect the character of the music and the sound of the harmony?
<u>They give the music a sense of strength and</u>
<u>importance. They also give harmonic stability, often</u>
<u>doubling the root of the chord.</u>

Cadences

This piece is a theory teacher's dream because of its clear **cadences**.
Name the four cadences in mm. 1–8.

<u>perfect in E major (m. 2)</u>
<u>perfect in A major (m. 4)</u>
<u>perfect in E major (m. 6)</u>
<u>perfect in A major (m. 8)</u>

Label these cadences in your score, and look through the rest of the music for more. There are two brief **modulations** in the middle section, ending with a cadence in mm. 15–16.
What is the sequence of keys in mm. 9–16?
<u>D major, G major, D major</u>

What is the cadence mm. 15–16?
<u>perfect cadence in D major</u>

Performing with Flair!

Where are the two long *diminuendos* in the music?
<u>mm. 6–7</u> and <u>22–23</u>

How will you shape them: will you treat them both the same? If not, how will you make the second one different?
<u>Make the second diminuendo end at a softer dynamic</u>
<u>to indicate the end of the piece.</u>

There are no special markings in the last measures. Do you think a slight *ritardando* would be acceptable, or would it stall the rhythmic momentum?
<u>A ritardardo would stall the rhythmic momentum.</u>

Prelude, op. 43, no. 1

Reinhold Glière (1875–1956)
Student Workbook 8, p. 47

Sensing the Harmonic Rhythm

Observe the writing in Gliere's *Prelude*. At first glance, does its harmonic rhythm appear steady and predictable, or irregular and unpredictable?
<u>steady and predictable</u>

How does this contribute to the overall character of the music?
<u>It creates a calm, natural flow.</u>

Which of the following expresses the harmonic rhythm of this piece?

Complex Harmony—Making It Simple

Now, as each new harmony occurs, write it in the form of a triad in root position on the staff below. Identify the triad you have written.

Do the same for mm. 8–10.

In the first musical excerpt above, look for a "hidden" melody at the top of the texture. Does this melody line move up or down by step? <u>down</u>
Circle all of the notes that form this melody.

A Subtle Change of Touch

Obviously, this music calls for a *legato* style of performance. There is, however, one spot where the score clearly indicates a change of touch): m. <u>46</u>

The markings in this measure suggest <u>separation</u>.

If you play this passage with pedal, the result can be described as **portato** touch. *Portato* is halfway between <u>staccato</u> and <u>legato</u>. How might Gliere's writing here make the ending more effective?
<u>It contrasts with the legato writing in the rest of the</u>
<u>piece and prepares the listener for the silence in m. 48</u>
<u>preceding the final chord.</u>

Chanson triste
A *Sad Song*

Vasili Sergeievich Kalinnikov (1866–1901)
Student Workbook 8, p. 50

Three Plus Two Equals Five

Explore the special musical feeling created by this meter by looking for details such as:

1. Descending pairs of stepwise eighth notes.
Find several measures between m. 1 and m. 8 where these occur.
m. 2 LH   m. 3 RH   m. 6 LH   m. 7 RH

In which part of the measure do these paired notes appear? beats 4 and 5

As you become familiar with this music, consider the effect of such details on the phrasing.
Do you feel that these falling gestures create moments of relaxation or of increased intensity? relaxation

2. Rhythmic grouping in the LH.
Play the LH part all the way through, listening particularly to the rhythm.
Do dotted half notes always fall on the same beat of the measure? If so, which beat? yes – beat 1

Do groups of four eighth notes always fall on the same beats of the measure? If so, which beats?
yes – beats 4 and 5

Write the basic rhythmic pattern as described above:

In this LH rhythm, can you hear a pattern of strong and weaker beats? yes

Where do you find the strong beat of the measure? on beat 1

Does the second part of the measure contain an equally strong beat, or a weaker beat? a weaker beat

A Modal Melody

Chanson triste is in the key of G minor. In this key, you expect to find the accidentals F sharp for the harmonic form of the scale, or E natural and F sharp for the ascending melodic form. In mm. 1–8, the accidental F sharp appears in some measures but not in others. In those measures where the leading tone is not raised, the music has a **modal** sound.

Which form of the minor scale has no accidentals?
natural or melodic descending

Name a mode that has the same sound as this scale.
Dorian

You have already discovered the close connection between rhythmic pacing and melodic direction in this piece. Notice the grace-note figures, which generally fall on beats 1 or 4.
What do the grace-note figures add to the rhythmic movement? They draw attention to beats 1 and 4.

What do they add to the melodic curve?
They add decoration.

In m. 7, the grace notes anticipate beat 4 by one beat.
How does this affect the design of the phrase? It upsets the established pattern.

Another example to consider is at the approach to the climax, mm. 15–16.

How do the grace notes affect the pacing of the phrase here?

they create a rhythmic and melodic agitation that gives the impression of prolonging the approach to the climax

Looking for Musical Sections

Is the opening section, which is in the key of G minor, repeated anywhere near the end of the piece? yes Where? m. 17

Identify the section that establishes a different key center?
mm. 9–14 key of E flat major

Consider where this section lies in the music, relative to the others, and choose one of the following letter-schemes to illustrate the form:

☑ ABA

The name given to such a form is ternary.

Play the two opening measures of each of sections A and B, observing the expression markings. Although the rhythmic styles are fairly similar, do you feel a change of mood in going from one to the other? Describe the feelings each of these creates:

A: far away, melancholy, pensive

B: a bit more optimistic, confident, stoic

The B section is marked *poco più mosso*. List two ways in which this marking creates contrast with the A section.

1. The A section is marked Andante.

2. At the end of the A section, there is a ritandardo.

Poetic Tone Picture, op. 3, no. 1

Edvard Grieg (1843–1907)
Student Workbook 8, p. 53

Three Characteristics of Norwegian Folk Music

Look at mm. 7–9. Within these measure, there is an illustration of all three characteristics.

In mm. 7–8, which version of the Grieg formula is shown? _2_

Name the combination of intervals: _major_ 2nd and _minor_ 3rd.

In m. 9, which version of the formula is shown? _1_

Name the combination of intervals: _minor_ 2nd and _major_ 3rd.

Which notes show evidence of the Dorian mode? _the RH notes of mm. 7–8_

Where do you see an accented note in the RH (the *springar* rhythm)? _the D on beat 2 of mm. 7–8_

Harmonic Color in the Picture

What is the key of the piece? _E major_

What is the chord in m. 1? _B major_

What is the relationship between this chord and the key of the piece?
This chord is the dominant of E minor.

Because the piece does not begin on the tonic, there is a kind of instability to the effect.

Identify the following chord blocked from m. 3.
diminished 7th of E minor

Listen to the bass note, A, that sets up the chord. In which inversion is it? _second_

Where does the harmony finally reach the tonic chord? _m. 6_

Listen to the LH as you practice mm. 1–6. The lower notes (stems down) form the harmonic support to the texture above; play them with some weight. Notice the accents in mm. 1–2. What is the pattern and direction of these lower notes?
descending scale fragment

Block and play the broken chord in m. 15.

Is this sound a surprise? _yes_ The F sharp, the second note or supertonic of the E minor scale, is lowered to F natural.

Melodic Design

The melody, like a bird, often flies upward. Particularly in the first line, the melody enters in m. 3, perches on a precarious note (an *appoggiatura*) that resolves downward to a chord note, then swoops and dips slightly to land on the high _mediant_ (degree of the scale) of the tonic chord.

Measures 15–18 emphatically show a rising melody combined with broken octaves. These are the most powerful measures in the piece. When you practice the section, try playing the broken chords *downward*.

Is the sound as powerful? _no_

In the second section, mm. _19–42_ , the melodic fragments show variations of m. 4.

Drama in the Picture

Incorporating *rubato* is a personal decision; you can experiment with the flexibility implied in the music until you are satisfied with the picture. The following words may help. What are their meanings?

poco accelerando _gradually increase tempo a little_

ritardando _gradually decrease tempo_

Tempo 1 _return to the first tempo_

con fuoco _with fire (force, speed)_

agitato _agitated_

How are mm. 55–58 different from mm. 15–18?
They are marked ff instead of f.

Milonga del ángel

Astor Piazzolla (1921–1992)
Student Workbook 8, p. 56

Rhythmic Style

Here are four syncopated rhythms from *Milonga del ángel*:

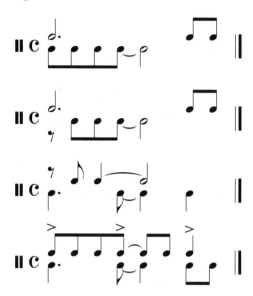

What do all four rhythms have in common?
Beat 3 is tied over from the previous beat.

Play the RH melody alone from mm. 1–8. What do you notice?
The first measure is repeated three times and m. 5 is repeated twice.

How do these notes sound when the changing LH harmonies are sounded against them?
They make a dramatic difference to the sound.

In mm. 10, 26, and 27, there are sixteenth-note figures that need to blend smoothly into the melody line. What do they remind you of?
mordents

What do the subtle chords of mm. 17–20 remind you of in a dance band?
percussion or the strumming of chords on a guitar

Create Your Own Dance Band

Now look through the music for rhythms that involve triplets. Copy each different one here, and indicate the rhythmic value of the triplet figure.

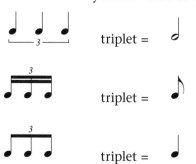

A Contrasting Section

What is the key of *Milonga del ángel*? _B minor_

The middle section of this dance features a thicker chordal texture and richly **dissonant** harmonies. Where does this section begin? _m. 33_

Piazzolla uses specific intervals and repeated patterns to create a rich and intense musical statement. Here is the chord formed by the first RH and LH notes in m. 33:

Extract a triad in root position from these notes, and write it in close position beside the chord. In the third measure, write the two remaining notes above the bass note, and name the intervals formed between the bass note and each of these notes.

These intervals—especially the larger one—give an edge and sparkle to the harmony. To prove it, play m. 33 replacing all the C naturals with B, and then play it as written. Which version has more spice?
the orginial

There are two patterns in mm. 33–44. The first one involves the LH rhythm.
Can you see a repeating rhythm here? _yes_

How long is it, and how many times is it repeated?
It is two measures long and is repeated twice.

Now look at mm. 39–44. Find a sequence in this passage.

How long is the pattern? _two measures_

Does it involve both hands? _yes_

What is the interval between repetitions? _minor 3rd_

Is this a falling or a rising **sequence**? _rising_

Pink and **Crimson**

Robert Starer (1924–2001)
Student Workbook 8, p. 59

Pink—Cool Jazz

This opening phrase seems to evolve from one small motive in a spontaneous, expressive manner akin to **improvisation**.

What does Starer do with the rhythm of m. 1 in m. 2? <u>He compresses three beats into two.</u>

The double notes in the LH part expand up to the first beat of m. 3, then contract. Write the name of each LH interval on the example above.

Shades of Pink

The theme of mm. 1–4 is repeated a number of times through the piece.

Where is the theme repeated? <u>mm. 10–13, 14–17, 23–28</u>

What is the relation of the key in mm. 10–13 to that of mm. 1–4? <u>one 3rd higher</u>

Do you feel the new key has a "brighter" sound? <u>yes</u>

Rather than present straight repetitions of his melody, Starer repeats the triplet motive in m. 13 (**transposed** down <u>an octave</u> from m. 11) as a link between two statements.

What is surprising about the key introduced by the statement in mm. 14–17?
<u>The key abruptly returns to B flat major.</u>

Is there any clue in the music that might suggest the shade of pink Starer has in mind at this point?
<u>dynamics; crescendo to f</u>

Expressive Dissonance

The notes on the first beat of m. 1 (C, A, and G) create a dissonance. However, the G is an *appoggiatura*, and the musical tension is relaxed when it **resolves**.

To which note does this *appoggiatura* resolve? <u>F</u>

Where are the other expressive *appoggiaturas* in the LH part? <u>mm. 2, 10, 11, 13, 14, 15, 23, and 24</u>

Slow Jazz Rhythms

Play mm. 1–4 again, and this time, pay particular attention to the rhythm.
How does the change from $\frac{3}{4}$ to $\frac{2}{4}$ enhance the forward motion of the phrase?
<u>It increases the frequencey of the strong pulse.</u>

Crimson—The Whole is Greater than its Parts

Crimson owes much of its effect to the skilful combination of simple but effective musical building blocks. The following are five excerpts from the music. Find each one, add the measure numbers to the excerpt, and play it. Then match each excerpt to the description that best fits it, and answer the questions.

Excerpt A
mm. <u>45–46</u>

Excerpt B
mm. <u>1–2</u>

Excerpt C
mm. <u>3–4</u>

Excerpt D
mm. <u>25–26</u>

Excerpt E
mm. <u>36–37</u>

Excerpt <u>A</u> : a final touch of humor—a simple **cadence** after all the excitement
What kind of cadence does Starer use? <u>perfect</u>

Excerpt <u>B or D</u> : a melody in which the notes are all the same interval apart.
What is the interval? <u>3rd</u>

Excerpt <u>C</u> and Excerpt <u>D</u> : two examples of broken triads
Identify the triads as major, minor, diminished, or augmented.
Excerpt <u>C</u> : <u>minor and diminished</u>
Excerpt <u>D</u> : <u>augmented and major</u>

Excerpt <u>E</u> : two driving *ostinato* figures—one in each hand.

These figures clarify the subdivision of the $\frac{7}{8}$ rhythm into a pattern of <u>4</u> plus <u>3</u> .

Why do you think this piece is called *Crimson*?
<u>The ryhthms, time signature, and dynamics are hot and full of life.</u>

Comparing Colors

Starer's pair of pieces presents the perfect opportunity to showcase strong musical contrast. Place each term from the following mix under its appropriate title in the two columns below.

Pink	*Crimson*
long, sustained sounds	violent dynamic contrasts
dreaming and sentimental	short sounds
changing meter	unchanging meter
fluid, flexible rhythms	sharp, jagged rhythimc outlines
gentle dynamic changes	insistent and impetuous

Early Morning Exercises,
op. 3 / 86, no. 2

Dmitri Kabalevsky (1904–1987)
Student Workbook 8, p. 63

Humor in Music

Early Morning Exercises is divided easily into sections, and Kabalevsky gives good early-warning signs as to where each one begins.

How many different sections are there? _three_

What is the length of each section _eight measures_ and what are the two warning signs?
double bar lines   _new key signature_

How many times does the first section return (in a slightly varied form)? _two_

First Section

Dissonance

There are many interesting features of the piece. Of course, if you play the RH alone for the entire piece, you will not hear any dissonance at all. Kabalevsky adds surprising clashes in the LH. You can see and hear the first one almost right away in m. _4_. Name the notes and interval.

Notes: _E_ and _E flat_   Interval: _minor 2nd_

Is this the only example in the first section? _yes_

What musical material does Kabalevsky use as a **bridge** into the second section? _C major scale_

Second Section

What is the key of this section? _A flat major_
Here Kabalevsky varies the rhythm of the melody, beginning his jaunt through the piece to a more "swinging" style. He also varies the LH accompaniment. Instead of single notes in the bass, he introduces _broken octaves_.

The articulation contributes to the humorous effect. Describe the pattern of the LH articulation.

two measures alternating slurs and staccato, one measure all staccato, then three measures alternating

Where do you hear the first dissonance? _m. 10_

Now look at the following excerpts from this section.

Here are the boxed notes written as intervals in close position. You will find that only one of these intervals sounds as written!

	1.	2.	3.
Written as:	2nd	2nd	2nd
Sounds like:	3rd	2nd	3rd

First Section Revisited

Kabalevsky produces slight changes each time the first section returns.

Can you spot the changes in mm. 17–24? _yes_

What trick does he use in mm. 17–19?
He replaces a note with a rest.

What trick does he use in mm. 22–23?
chromatic arpeggiation

The effect is sly and cheeky as he adds more and more humor to the piece. Notice the LH in m. 24. Where else do you see this fancy chordal effect?
_m. 40_

Third Section

What is the key? _E major_

What is the connection between the key of the second section and the key of the third section?
A flat major (four flats) and E major (four sharps): they are equidistant from C major

Now everyone exercising has warmed up and is starting to dance! How would you describe the rhythm pattern in the RH? _syncopation_

Notice the leaping LH common in ragtime music. What is the distance of the first LH interval jump in m. 25? <u>two octaves</u>

The bottom note then begins to close the gap by moving in a scale-like pattern. To what scale degree does it go? <u>the dominant</u>

What articulation makes it sound funny? <u>portato and staccato</u>

Look at the ascending scale in 3rds mm. 31–32. What are the dynamics? <u>crescendo to ff</u>

First Section Returns! (The Final Episode)

Naturally, Kabalevsky gives his finale a slight twist. The familiar melody in the RH is decorated by using the **chromatic** "slide" effect from m. 22 and incorporating the design from the LH of m. 31. Can you identify the trick? <u>slow melodic trill</u>

In the final flourish of the last measure, there is no pedal indicated as there is in m. 24. Would you be tempted to use it here to add resonance to your sound at the end? <u>yes</u> Could you do it and still have the rolled chords come off with a *staccato*? <u>yes</u>

Petites litanies de Jésus
Petites litanies de Jesus

Gabriel Grovlez (1879–1944)
Student Workbook 8, p. 66

Texture

Polyphonic texture features two or more independent melodic lines played simultaneously. **Homophonic** texture features one main melodic line supported by a chord-based accompaniment.

Which of these textures prevails in *Little Litanies*? <u>homophonic</u>

How does this contribute to the musical effect? <u>It gives a choir-like quality.</u>

Keys and Modes

Little Litanies moves through several keys and **modes** as it unfolds. Find some of these by answering the questions below. Then match each scale (or mode) to the musical fragment that belongs with it.

Scale of <u>A flat major</u> matches fragment no. <u>1</u>

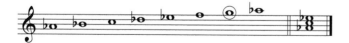

Scale of F natural minor matches fragment no. <u>3</u> (HINT: It is the relative minor of <u>A flat</u> major, and therefore has the same accidentals.)

Write the scale and its tonic triad here:

G Dorian mode matches fragment no. <u>2</u> Two notes create this mode, the lowered <u>third</u> degree and the lowered <u>seventh</u> degree.

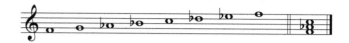

Call and Response

Locate all the responses and compare their melodic direction and dynamic markings.

Response	Melodic Direction	Dynamics
mm. <u>5–6</u>	<u>downward</u>	<u>diminuendo</u>
mm. <u>12–13</u>	<u>upward</u>	<u>p</u>
mm. <u>19–20</u>	<u>upward</u>	<u>crescendo</u>
mm. <u>27–28</u>	<u>up–down–up</u>	<u>pp</u>
mm. <u>33–34</u>	<u>downward</u>	<u>diminuendo</u>

What makes the fourth response sound so different from the others? <u>pp subito; una corda; chords have no 3rds; direction changes</u>

What texture is always present in the responses? <u>homorhythmic</u>

Now look at the invocations, or calls that precede each response. They are made up of two or more short phrases. Which of these sections does *not* begin with an ascending triplet upbeat figure? mm. <u>21–26</u> Which section in the piece serves as the dramatic high point of the piece? mm. <u>21–26</u>

What features or markings contribute to this effect? <u>plus accentué; thicker texture; more rhythmic activity; tenuto ff marks; B flat major chord with LH grace note</u>

Compare mm. 1–6 and mm. 29–34. What do you notice? <u>They are identical.</u>

Interpretation

Several French terms are used in the score. Define them here, and think how they contribute to the overall beauty of this piece. Be sure to observe these terms when you play.
naïf, tendre et fervent <u>naïve (simple), tender, and sincere</u>
un peu plus fort <u>a bit more strong</u>
plus accentué <u>more accented</u>

What does the comma in m. 11 tell you to do? <u>take a breath</u>

Roda-roda!

Octavio Pinto (1890–1950)
Student Workbook 8, p. 69

Parts of the Game

The double bar lines divide the music—and presumably the game—into three sections. Label the first section A in your score.
Is the A material repeated in the third section? _yes_
Are the two A sections exactly the same? _no_ If not, label the third section A₁ in your score.

Name three ways in which the B section provides contrast.
1. _It is in a different key (A major)._
2. _ornamentation_
3. _The melody is played by both hands in mm. 13–14._

Is this piece in binary, rounded binary, or ternary form? _ternary_

What clues does the articulation give you? _the long legato phrase_
What does *pp subito* mean? _suddenly very soft_
What is the interval distance between your hands? _four octaves_
The motion of these two melodic lines can be described as _parallel_ motion.

Playing a Game Song

What articulation markings do you find in the A and A₁ sections?
accents, slurs, staccato

How does the articulation of the B section contrast with that of the A sections?
There are longer legato phrases.

In mm. 1–2 and 3–4, the LH plays four consecutive triads and a 7th chord. Play these figures, and listen to the sound.

Why do you think Pinto included the 7th chord?
To decorate the perfect cadence that follows.

What term describes the movement of the voices in the triads? _stepwise_

Does the other consecutive triad figure (mm. 5–8) in the A section also move in a stepwise direction? _yes_

Compare the rest of the LH part of the A section and the A₁ section. Which triad figure does Pinto change, and what is the difference?
In mm. 28 and 29, he adds 7ths to all the triads.

In the B section, how does the texture differ from to section A?
There are no three- or four-note chords.

Does the texture of Section B remain the same or are there contrasts?
It is similar throughout the B section.

Also in the B section, there is a more complex example of **parallel motion**. Play the slurred figure in mm. 11–12.

Play the notes on each beat as solid (blocked) chords. The notes form _7th_ chords in _root_ position.

There are two similar figures in the B section. mm. _15_ and _17_

Where does Pinto use solid (blocked) consecutive 7th chords? _mm. 28–29_

What's going on above the chords? _octaves in the RH_

The End of the Game

Now take a closer look at the A₁ section.
Find the parallel octaves filled in with 5ths. What does this figure replace in the A section?
a single melodic line, playing the same notes as the octave figure

What effect does Pinto achieve by varying them in this way? _It prepares for the ending._

What other difference can you find between these two passages?
The single-note figure in mm. 6–7 is slurred, but somewhat stronger than f. The "filled-in" figure in mm. 25–26 is accented, and only f.

Where does Pinto use broken octaves? _mm. 28–29_
What do they replace in the A section? _pairs of repeated notes_

Besides changing the notes, how does Pinto add excitement in the last three measures?
He adds an accelerando, accents to the last two notes in the RH, and a sf and staccato dot to the final LH note.

Student Workbook 8

Celebration Series Perspectives Answer Book

O Moon

Alexina Louie (b. 1949)
Student Workbook 8, p. 72

Exploring the Title

Could the "O" be a visual representation of the moon? <u>yes</u>

Is someone invoking the moon through this music? <u>yes</u>

Grace-Note Phrases

According to Louie's instructions, the grace-note phrases in the third line of the music are played rapidly, or as fast as possible. Since these figures are divided between the hands, it is fairly easy to play them evenly and quickly.
What type of scale do these phrases form?
<u>whole-tone scale</u>

Cluster Chords

Play the chords in this example, then find them in the music.

Now play the RH chords alone. Do you recognize any of these triads or 7th chords? Write the names above the chords you can identify.

Now play the LH alone.

How do the LH chords 1. and 2. compare?
<u>They are the same, inverted.</u>

How do chords 2. and 3. compare?
<u>2 is a semitone lower than 3</u>

Do chords 3. and 2. have the same relationship as 5. and 4.? <u>yes</u>

Can you describe the sound you hear? <u>The sound builds up.</u>

These clusters gather notes one note at a time, like a rolling ball of snow. Circle the series of descending notes, then play them.

Where have you seen and heard this scale before?
<u>the grace notes in the third system</u>

What type of scale is it? <u>a whole-tone scale</u>

What happens to this scale in the last cluster chord? <u>It is to be held for a pause.</u>

Find the Tritones and the Major 7ths

The intervals of a **tritone** and a major 7th have a strong effect on the sound colors of this piece.

What is a tritone?
<u>an augmented 4th or diminished 5th — an interval equivalent to the distance of three whole tones</u>

Play both intervals and listen to the sound. How would you describe them?
tritone: <u>unsettling</u>
major 7th: <u>jarring</u>

In m. 2, the four pairs of grace notes span the interval of a <u>major 7th</u>.
The distance from the first grace note to the main note is a <u>tritone</u>.

Sneaky

Stephen Chatman (b. 1950)
Student Workbook 8, p. 75

Cool Jazzy Rhythm

Chatman puts together a picture of sneakiness using musical techniques (or devices) that people associate with its meaning. One of those techniques is rhythm. What is the time signature? $\frac{6}{8}$

Melody with Special Effects

How many different types of articulation marks do you see? <u>four</u>

List them here: <u>slurs, staccatos, tenutos, accents</u>

Harmony

Large chords occur in only two places: mm. <u>3–4</u> and m. <u>51</u>.

Name the first two chords, and the key.
1. <u>diminished 7th</u>
2. <u>dominant 7th</u>
Key: <u>B flat major</u>

Sneaky Dynamics

The beginning is bold. How do you know that?
<u>It is marked f.</u>

In terms of dynamics, the opening is challenging. Why?
<u>You only have two measures in which to reduce the dynamic level from f to pp.</u>

After you know the notes well, practice mm. 1–4 again and again to listen to the sound. You have a very small amount of space in which to shape the line. Are you going to build a *crescendo* and then play a *diminuendo*? <u>yes</u>

Evening at the Village

Béla Bartók (1881–1945)
Student Workbook 8, p. 78

Two Contrasting Styles

Draw lines to match each feature listed in the right column with the appropriate heading in the left column.

- playful or dance-like character
- flexible pulse
- fast tempo
- emphasis on melody
- storytelling or song-like character
- sustained notes
- many short notes
- steady pulse
- slow tempo
- emphasis on rhythm

1. *Lento, rubato*

2. *Vivo, non rubato*

Arch Form

The alternation between *lento, rubato* and *vivo, non rubato* sections creates an arch form. Fill in the measure numbers for each section, and add a small number (A$_1$, A$_2$, etc) to indicate a section that is similar but not identical:

A   mm. _1_ – _9_
B   mm. _10_ – _20_
A _1_   mm. _21_ – _29_
B _1_   mm. _30_ – _41_
A _2_   mm. _42_ – _55_

Telling the Story

A

Notice the frequent use of 3rds, an expressive interval frequently used in folk songs. Three of the phrases end with the interval of a 3rd and are marked with special markings. Name each marking and describe how you might color that note.
1. _tenuto – with a small rit._
2. _accent – with a small pause_

The first two phrases begin similarly, with a marking over the first note.

What special musical quality is given to this note as the phrase opens?
It is played unaccompanied, mf, with an accent, and espressivo.

Lastly, play the lowest LH notes in the first section. What does this pattern form?
E minor scale (natural)

The pattern descends right to the end of the section. How does this affect the mood of the section? _It feels unfinished._

B

In the first *vivo* section, there seems to be a change of energy!

What do you think is happening?
Perhaps the characters are dancing or whispering excitedly.

What do you see in the notation that suggests your idea? _staccato articulation, soft dynamics, scherzando marking_

At the end of this section, what is the meaning of the whole measure rest?
Perhaps the characters are catching their breath or returning to a more serious attitude.

A$_1$
The second *lento* section (mm. 21–29) is not quite the same as the first.

How do the changes in the harmony affect the sound? _It sounds more optimistic._

How has Bartók changed the rhythm? How has that affected the sense of movement?
It feels more spirited, excited.

A$_2$
Does this section contain the most intense dynamic levels? _yes_

In this section, how does the presentation of the melody differ from the first *lento* section?
In this section, the melody is played in octaves by both hands.

How does the accompaniment differ? What does this represent in your story?
In the A2 section, both hands play syncopated chords, one octave apart as the accopaniment, between each statement of the melody.

A Traditional Scale

Play the melodies of both the *lento* and the *vivo* sections, and listen particularly to the notes that Bartók has chosen.

Do these two melodies have a similar sound? _no_

Build a scale from the notes of the melody of the *lento* section.

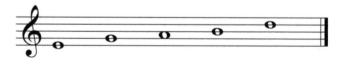

How many notes are there in the scale? _five_
What term would you use to describe this scale? _pentatonic_

Is the melody of the *vivo* sections based on the same scale? _yes_

A Syncopated Rhythm

Bartók uses **syncopated** rhythms in both sections. Look for rhythms in which notes are played between the beats and held through the next beat. Write one syncopated rhythm from each section of the piece.

The Little Shepherd

Claude Debussy (1862–1918)
Student Workbook 8, p. 81

Beauty of Sound

There are many possibilities for experimenting with varieties of color. Debussy has indicated expressive shaping with *crescendos* and *diminuendos*, and even added extra instructions: *più p* (m. _16_) and *un poco più forte* (m. _19_) for example.

Pedal or Finger *Legato*?

The entire first line can be played using only the fingers, moving smoothly from key to key. In the dotted rhythm section (mm. 5, 6, 7, etc.), try an experiment using no pedal at all. You will soon notice that the RH is easy to play smoothly. Why? _The phrase lies under the fingers._

Harmony

The key of the piece is _A major_ and the important **cadences** at the ends of sections reflect this key. Name the type of cadence and the key in the following measures.

1. Cadence at mm. 9–11: _Perfect_
   Key: _A major_
2. Cadence at mm. 16–18: _Perfect_
   Key: _E major_
3. Cadence at mm. 29–31: _Perfect_
   Key: _A major_

Do all the cadences show the same pattern? _yes_

Jazz Exercises Nos. 2 and 3

Oscar Peterson (1925–2007)
Student Workbook 8, p. 84

Jazz Exercise No. 2
Simple Cadences

Look for **cadences**, keeping in mind that the harmonic motion within a cadence is most easily observed in the bass. Identify the cadences suggested by each of the following phrase endings, and supply a measure number for each.

Imperfect (m. _4_)   _Perfect_ (m. _8_)

Imperfect (m. _12_)   _Perfect_ (m. _16_)

From what you observed above, describe the overall pattern of cadences and phrases.
The cadences occur regularly, altering imperfect and perfect cadences. This occurs every four measures, resulting in phrases of equal length.

Jazzy Figuration

Find a section that clearly contrasts with the opening section:
mm. _17_ – _25_ . A section such as this is often referred to in popular songs as the **bridge**. Observe the following figure from the bridge passage.

m. _18_

Which intervals occur without exception *within* consecutive pairs of notes? _semitones_ Circle the second note of each pair. What basic musical pattern is created, and in what key, by the notes you have circled? _arpeggio of E minor_

Now look at m. 17. The notes of the first three beats create a dominant 7th chord. Write this chord in root position:

This is in fact the **dominant 7th** chord of the key you identified in the previous paragraph. What cadence is suggested by the combination of dominant 7th and the harmony within the pattern in the following measure? <u>perfect</u>

How does Peterson anticipate the harmony of the second measure?
<u>The notes of the E minor triad are played at the end</u>
<u>of m. 1.</u>

Would you describe this effect as being *on* or *off* the beat? <u>off</u>

Jazz Exercise No. 3
Sequence Hunt

This piece features several **sequences**, the musical fragments that recur at different pitch levels. Here's a "sequence puzzle."

- Find the fragments below that have the same pattern at different pitches. Connect them with a line.
- Find each fragment in the Peterson score. Write the measure number above the fragment.
- Mark each fragment with a number (1, 2, 3) to show *where* it occurs within its sequence.

Extending the Triad

The triads on which traditional harmony is based can be expanded by adding notes in rising 3rds above the three notes of the triad. This creates 7ths, 9ths, and even 11ths or 13ths above the original root. On the staff below, write a triad using each note of the C scale in turn as a root.

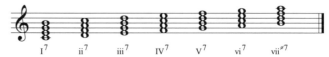

Now add a 3rd above each triad, creating a 7th above each root. Use the notes of C major, without adding any accidentals. Label the chords I⁷, ii⁷, etc. Play this seventh chord scale and listen to the sound.

Find Some Basic Harmonic Progressions

Two of the most basic harmonic progressions in jazz appear repeatedly throughout this composition.

These two progressions are written below, along with three musical fragments from the piece that each contain one of these progressions. Draw a line from each excerpt to the progression that matches it; identify a key for each excerpt, based on the progression you chose.

II–V–I   II⁷–III⁷–IV⁷

Key: G minor
a.

Key: B flat major
b.

Key: E flat major
c.

Etude Allegro

Yoshinao Nakada (1923–2000)
Student Workbook 8, p. 88

First Section

Because you will be practicing slowly at first, it's important right away to figure out what is going on. What is the musical material made of? How would you describe the pattern in each hand in m. 1?

RH
 sixteenth notes moving back and forth by 2nds in the top voice

LH staccato 3rds moving back and forth

The entire first section runs to m. 22 and is made up of a number of technical tricks, many of which can be practiced in other ways and in other keys.

The crisp *staccatos* in the LH require wrist lifts, higher in slow practice than in fast. Could you describe the LH motion as also back and forth? yes

Middle Section

How does Nakada approach the change of key in m. 23? with a ritardando, Vⁿ of C, and a surprise resolution to A flat major

The middle section (in the key of A flat major) is a lovely contrast with the two fast outer sections. What is the LH pattern called? Alberti bass

By blocking the chords implied, you will hear some beautiful harmony. Identify the blocked versions of the following chords:

Key: A flat major | E flat 7 | F minor | D minor | C minor

How many **modulations** do you hear? four
To what keys? C minor; C major; A minor; C major

Nakada breaks his LH pattern at the end of the middle section. Notice the LH in mm. 45–46. Is he getting ready for the return to the back and forth pattern? yes

Return of the First Section: (Final Section)

The final section repeats the first section. Is it exact? yes, at first

Until where? m. 61

Then Nakada "spins out" the broken-chord material and changes the LH to create an elaborate extension. This extension functions as a *coda* and contains the climax of the piece.

How would you describe the pattern at m. 69? alternating triads between the hands

At m. 70? C major scale (descending), alternating between the hands

What is the dynamic marking at m. 69? ff

How does Nakada create a flourish at the end? He uses a glissando.

How much of the keyboard is covered during this special-effect flourish? three octaves

Mysterious Summer's Night

Larysa Kuzmenko (b. 1956)
Student Workbook 8, p. 91

Musical Breathing

Although the time signature of the music is 4/4, you may find it helpful to count an easy pulse of two beats to the measure. How will this slower meter affect the motion of the music? It makes it feel as though there is a rise and fall in each measure.

Harmonic Ebb and Flow

Play the RH of mm. 5–7, then look at its upper

notes.

If you write the notes in this passage in scale order, what type of scale would you have?
 a chromatic scale

Where does Kuzmenko use similar sets of notes with actual scale motion? mm. 14–15

She uses 7th chords with altered notes or additional notes. Play m. 10.
Name the notes of the 7th chord in the first half of that measure. C E G B flat

In that measure, Kuzmenko further obscures the identity of the 7th chord with a **cross-relation**. Which note appears in both natural and flatted forms? E

A Larger Structure

Many of the gestures seem to fall into groups of four measures. Write and name the final chords in each of the following measures:

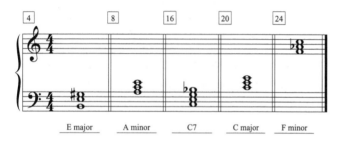

| E major | A minor | C7 | C major | F minor |

Mysterious Summer's Night falls into three sections:
A   mm. 1–8
B   mm. 9–16
A₁ mm. 17–24

What is the key of the A section? A minor

How would you describe the character of this section? mysterious, foggy, confused

Does the B section present a contrasting character? yes

How would you describe it?
 more angry, expressive, forceful

What markings does Kuzmenko use to enhance the contrasting character? f, molto espressivo

The B section is highly chromatic but seems to suggest C as the dominant of F minor. The section ends with a cadence in mm. 16–17:

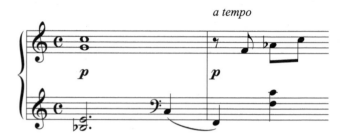

Name the type of cadence and the two chords.
 perfect cadence   C7, F minor

What is the key of the A₁ section? F minor

The Pedal

How many times will you change the pedal in m. 14?
 three times